Karina Hubert is a life coach, yoga teacher and highly intuitive, insightful clairvoyant and tarot reader, working with her spirit guides. She uses her psychic abilities in a practical way, combined with much warmth, empathy, understanding and a totally non-judgemental attitude.

The world of tarot has been around her since her childhood like a world of fairy tales. Wherever she went, she always had a deck of tarot with her, which she worked with, and another one she studied… furthermore, life always brought somebody in her way who needed help and of course, cards turned up, too. Even now there are people who send her letters, weeks, months later, regularly writing as follows: 'I did not believe it would happen what you told me. My life had been so different, I could not even imagine a variation you came up with. Now I know every word you said was true.'

She had created this tarot deck and has written this tarot book because she wanted to pass on some of the knowledge she gathered throughout the decades. She wanted that, if you find yourself in trouble and you have no one to turn to with your problems, you have something to reach for, calm down and find yourself. You can even see romantic and hopeless love affairs and fates that interwove and come apart to enable both parties to experience their own love stories.

The present love initiation tarot has been created because everyone desires true love. To reach this euphoric feeling we have to know that love alone is not enough for a sincere and deep relationship. Acceptance is very important, and so is the understanding of the partner's personality and that we let them live even those plans and dreams we do not necessarily agree with, but we can stand beside them. If we really love somebody, then we grant them the freedom to be who they want to be and to be where they want to be. If we really love somebody, we let them to be a part of our lives by their own will.

To Dora, Dominique and Julien

Karina Hubert

Le Grand Tarot de l'Amour

Love and Secret

Austin Macauley Publishers™
London • Cambridge • New York • Sharjah

A CIP catalogue record for this title is available from the British Library.

ISBN 9781528941594 (Paperback)
ISBN 9781528983440 (ePub e-book)

www.austinmacauley.com

First Published 2022
Austin Macauley Publishers Ltd®
1 Canada Square
Canary Wharf
London
E14 5AA

I humbly express my gratitude and thanks, with all my heart to:

My husband, Julien for his love, patience, honest insights and mainly because he always believes in me, he is capable of anything for me, and for being there for me. He is my other half who fills each day with magic and with whom everything is possible.

My little son, Dominique, with whom I can relive the joys of childhood, who constantly inspires me, and through whom I am able to get more deeply into the sometimes challenging, difficult destiny of women of old times when I look at him at nights amid writing and researching.

My daughter, Dora, who as a teenager teaches me patience, understanding and releasing, and through whom I can relieve how it feels, at the age of 16, to believe in the lifelong love that you found in high school. It is an amazing and at the same time wonderful contrast how differently I regard relationship issues nearly at the age of 40.

My mother-in-law for her love, creativity, support and wise advice.

Marie Jean and Claude Martin, who have tirelessly supported and believed in me ever since I moved to France.

My friends, Marie and Miguel, for their clever insights, impeccable taste, enthusiasm and friendship.

My place of residence, Nernier, which as a little pearl of Lake Geneva, each day fills me with energy and fascinates me with its new wonders, new residents – who constantly inspire me. This small magical village is my own fairy-tale Narnia.

Finally, I greet all my readers with love. Thank you for joining me on this journey of self-knowledge/discovery. For indeed, each of us are always on the road, searching the path where we can make our lives happier and more meaningful. Now I am going to accompany you through this wonderful road. Along the way, everything will change, everything will fit in and then you will realise that it is not the GOAL that is important, but to be on the road, to travel. To get to know our little, inner world. There will be moments of greater pain, but afterwards there will be a lot of joy and miracles… even if you are sceptical. Let us do this together!

Preface

Welcome, dear readers!

My intention with this tarosophic love book is that the messages, warnings and advice of the ancient age would reach you, so you can discover the wisdom of love's eternal cycle for yourself, that is the royal path of love (TAR – path, road, royal – RO, SOPHIA – wisdom). However, since everything is connected with everything, you may receive indications and responses regarding other areas of life as well. I am discussing the historical origins of the cards a bit later, but I definitely think it is important to emphasise now, that tarot is not a deck of fortune-telling cards in the ordinary sense of the word, but much more than that. Although it is indisputable that in initiated hands it gives answer to almost every question. During our life, we often experience situations that the cards represent with different symbols, images and symbol systems. The sequence of cards presents the progress, which we all need to go through, so the card is nothing more than the eternal cycle of existence itself, which will be circular and whole through the repeated letter 't' in the word. (Tarot – 'Existence')

Our ancestors invented numerous packets of cards for educational purposes. With them, they taught law, logic skills, geography, mythology, and, no matter how amazing it sounds, the Bible too. Also King Louis XIV himself acquired his historical knowledge through similar cards at the initiative of Cardinal Mazarin. In France, until the end of the nineteenth century, there was a special deck of cards available, which taught historical knowledge to children. Five years ago, when I was pregnant, I was doing some research for an article about King Louis XIV when I came across some very interesting documents about these educational cards and the correlations of tarot cards. I was bewildered by the author's style and by what he described. My interest steeped in adoration for the ancient symbolism inherent in tarot has become limitless, as I more and more strongly felt the need to create a real love tarot card. Partly for divination purposes, but with a deeper meaning. Supplemented with great love stories and history, insisting, by all means, on historical facts.

It was a real challenge for me, because for obvious reasons I did not understand how this could be just the right period for a task of this magnitude. But the idea did not let me rest, even in my dreams I kept seeing the figures of the cards and was writing the text for each of them. Because I listen intensely to my instincts and my inner indications, I was not thinking for long, I just simply jumped right into it. A few weeks later, I developed the great arcana system of love, the last card of which was managed to be finished the day before my son's birth. Then I certainly received two gifts at once: a beautiful child and a joyful task that involved a great deal of concentration as well. I had no doubts, I was not nervous either, because I had no idea what kind of responsibility this required. I would not have guessed that from that day on, I have to watch my every spoken or written word with great responsibility.

Maybe it has just recently started to become apparent to me that besides my family, my every single thought, word and deed was perpetually revolving around Tarot, tying its publication to an invisible deadline. I cannot thank my family enough for staying always beside me understandingly. There is no adequate word to describe how grateful I am for my husband, who supports me with his constant love and presence, for my daughter, who always ensures that joy and pleasure is present in our lives and of course for my little son, whose loving arrival forged us into a real family, and initiated such a creative process in me, the end of which I still cannot see. All the love of my heart, besides my family, belongs to my mother-in-law, who to this day stands beside me like a mother instead of my mother, encouraging me and inspiring me. Without them, I could not have gone through with the work.

I created my tarot deck because I felt drawn to share my knowledge of tarot card reading and inspire you to use the tarot cards for personal growth and connecting with the Divine. I've been reading for more than 20 years, and have been reading and teaching professionally for ten years or so. I picked up my first tarot deck at age 16 and 15 years later, I had some excellent professor and tarot master; and I also studied tarot with wonderful tarot readers in France before I created my own tarot deck.

In 1983, when I was 8-year-old, I was pronounced dead for about 10 minutes before coming back to life.

I fell into a swimming pool while on a family vacation. Not knowing how to swim at that time, I began to drown. I was to be overcome by a feeling of calm and peacefulness; as I slipped under for what was likely to be the last time in this world. I knew that I was leaving this world and all that I have been a part of for what seem to be something new and better. I knew I was going to die, I was in good hands. I wasn't hot or cold, hungry or tired – just a peaceful neutral kind of thing. I knew there was light that got larger. Either I was moving towards it, or it was moving towards me, then I had seen millions upon millions of stars of all shapes, sizes, and colours. As I approached there, it seemed like I was joining a universal consciousness; a being made up of the thoughts, emotions, and experience of everyone and everything that had ever lived. It was the most beautiful thing I had ever seen. From this point forwards I had a choice to make of me. How should I continue on this path. This death experience taught me that I still have a choice about how to spend my life and how to help people.

I hope you and your team accept my opinion. Please let me know. Thank you so much!

Introduction

A few centuries ago, we lived in a world in which the word was still important, there were ceremonies, everything had its rightful order. It was not our Facebook profile that defined us, nor the number of people who liked our pictures. It was not the number nor the value of the gifts under the tree that mattered, but the fact that we could be together. We paid attention to our loved ones, it was not a problem to find time for a chat, for playing games or for a tale. And in that inconceivable era, people knew exactly what they do and why. And also from where to where they were heading. Of course, that was not a perfect world either, but spiritually it was much easier to proceed, it was filled with signposts, which designated the direction. People knew that life was a constant change, and that there was a time and order for everything. They lived in eras, according to the seasons, just like nature. The epochs were separated by holidays and ceremonies, so it would be clear for everyone: something is over and something else begins. They could prepare themselves in spirit, and things did not 'fall' on their heads like bolt from the blue, as it happens today, in the life of 'civilised people'. Furthermore, and most importantly: they did not adhere convulsively to things that they knew. Life tales played a huge role in all this. Those are symbolic preceptor stories through which people could experience certain life stages of existence, even as a child getting ready for adulthood, marriage and parenthood. Filtering through these stories, they could experience male and female social roles, or even the changes that come inevitable with age, or moreover birth and death.

Secrets were passed on from parents to children, which made them initiates. They knew life as it is and they did not want to force anything out of it. They were capable to give and accept. They knew that everything happens for a reason, each occurrence has something to show them, even if at the moment it is difficult to live with it. But the change, which led to today's world was inevitable. The development of technology made other values come first. The world has accelerated, life itself has accelerated.

In the above-mentioned old ages, people were aware that progress is inevitable, change will 'blow' a new world toward posterity. They knew that ancient principles would be incurred in oblivion for a while, and that there would be less people 'walking' on mystic paths. Therefore, a small group of old masters decided to keep the sciences of magical and analogical thinking secret, until the right time comes (to be revealed), until then they just passed on the secret within their secret circle. This is how the transmission of the knowledge of tarot also ever happened.

Tarot is not just a card game, but also an ancient, timeless wisdom. Its cards indicate life situations, turns of fate steeped in symbolism. Just as long ago, it is still very helpful if everyone gets to know the 'life' stories related to the cards, because our ancestors lived and understood each stage of their lives through these educational stories, they were getting prepared for adulthood, marriage and parenthood even as a child. Filtering through these stories, they could experience the male and female social roles, or even the changes that come inevitable with age, or moreover birth and death. This book carries the message of this old world in itself. It is for those path seekers and road enthusiasts who no longer seek the causes and responses outside, but inside. Those who are already beginning to understand that we attract certain people and events to ourselves.

In that ancient world, women's free will was limited and they were not allowed to prevail. Their duty was to obey their husbands and fathers, who took for granted that women had no thoughts, but turbulent and unpredictable emotions, and therefore it seemed best to discipline them already in the convent, instead of providing them education. Since marriages were concluded on basis of ranks and parental choices, members of royal houses were quite sure that they would not marry out of love, more precisely, not they were getting married, but their estates, names or their countries. However, there were always exceptions. Love bloomed, rulers abdicated, some women became official mistresses, no matter how powerful the impact of the church was. For the sake of exceptional women, laws were made, monarchs changed their lifestyle and their attitude toward women. Defying all habits and expectations, some women decided to stand up for themselves. Some of them took on their special skills and aptitudes publicly, but most of them kept these secret until the end of their lives. Many people paid a terrible price because they were training themselves, were searching for masters and took part in meetings where everyone studied the universal truths including the '*as above, so below*' principle (Tabula Smaragdina). The cautious ones, however, knew very well, that the world in which they live, would not tolerate inexplicable things, and that the church was condemning those women who were clever. Because the old world was also afraid of knowledge, though it was yearning for it. Therefore, women following the mystical path concealed the indwelling light, studied and carried out their spiritual work in secret.

Card divination was a common practice in the Middle Ages, almost every family kept one deck of cards, even though starting from the 1450s onwards, they could have been accused of witchcraft for that. People tirelessly researched the laws of fate, the relationship between the position of the planets, the rebirth of the soul. They were sure that everything is connected, they planted medicinal herbs next to culinary herbs in secret, according to the phases of the Moon, and some of them claimed to know the influence of the Moon on the sex of the unborn child. That is exactly why I attached one or two more interesting love and life stories next to the interpretation of the cards. These historical rambles show that others had doubts and weaknesses also, but they always had a new opportunity or a new situation in which they could prove their worth, their commitment and in the meantime, they were asking questions, struggling and evolving as well. I did not always choose the most well-known personalities and in case of famous people, legendary monarchs, I also tried to describe what can only be found in a few places. For all my life, I have been interested in 'life' stories, women's place in society, and their fight for power, therefore I have been studying the works of renowned historians for many years. During my readings I came across many interesting figures who lived an extraordinary life. Many times, I felt I was right there with them, in that era, in that particular situation they experienced. It is a shame that teachers deal with more interesting historical stories, situations, only for a few lessons, outside the required curriculum, because after an enjoyable lesson, history would be a lot closer and interesting to everyone. Our children would understand how lucky they are, in some ways, because they did not have to go through the loss of parents, the loss of their love in senseless wars, they have no need to fight in order to learn and get an education. At the same time, they are at a considerable disadvantage too, because, unlike earlier, no one teaches them honour, standing up for themselves, sticking together as a family from an early age.

If you keep this card in your hand today, it is time for the messages of old times to address you. Do not expect accurate information about what will happen to you, but rather turn to it with confidence, because, by recognising and taking the circumstances into account, it will help you to learn to decide autonomously and thus take your own destiny in your hands and 'mould' it according to your will. Devote time for the cards and let your intuition guide you. Choose the one that best appeals to you and close your eyes, the answers will arrive shortly. Do not forget that there is a reason for everything, nothing is coincidental. Not even the fact that you are holding this book in your hands right now. All I ask from you is to read the messages and the related stories to the cards with your heart, because this is the only way to drive you closer to the greatest mystery: yourself. It can help you to unravel the human being.

Hubert Karina
Nernier, France.
14th March 2014.

A special tarot in the MIRROR OF LOVE, which teaches, advises and leads you through some paths of love in history

Foreword

The time has come for me to create a new deck of tarot cards. This tarot with historical figures of Hungary and the three important nations following it, will help you to understand the mysterious world of tarot better and gain a bit deeper self-recognition. Or take the deck out without fear if you are in a period when the heartening words and advice of a wise master would serve you right.

The world of tarot has been around me since my childhood like a world of fairy tales. Every book I read at that time was connected to it somehow, and now, from the distance of 25 years, I know they led me to the path I walk upon. What started to be but a game, later turned to be very serious and made me aware of the fact that it is an age-old, mystic art.

My family is engaged in parapsychology and we had some serious debates over using the cards instead of my clairvoyance skills to help people. There were times when I acted accordingly, but the cards found their way to me and I felt that I would lose a part of myself if I barred them out of my life definitively. I decided to tread my own path and I broke up with the attitude of my family, who see the cards as the Devil's Bible.

Wherever I went, I always had a deck of tarot with me, which I worked with, and another one I studied... furthermore, life always brought somebody in my way who needed help and of course, cards turned up too. Even now, there are people who send me letters weeks, months later, regularly writing as follows: 'I did not believe it would happen what you told me. My life had been so different, I could not even imagine a variation you came up with. Now I know every word you said was true.'

Tarot is not barely a tool of fortune-telling for me, but also a system of initiation which brings us self-recognition; we can use the very depth of our creativity; we can understand the messages of our passed-away beloved ones; we can receive signs in connection with our health and well-being.

If you use these cards, just rely on your intuitions and read the short description belonging to the card. Be aware that tarot will always find you when the time is right to open doors to this wonderful world. Now I am offering you the keys to unlock these doors.

What is Tarot?

Tarot is a deck of cards symbolising a wonderful spiritual world, which has always been thought to be magical by the initiates. They used it for mystical purpose, asked it for advice and trustingly waited for its spiritual messages. Several legends are attached to the cards as a result of its mysterious symbolism. Tarot is not simply a tool for fortune-telling, but also a kind of initiation and intensive meditation. It improves intuition and also helps us contact our spiritual leaders. If we are careful and open, it can show us the present phases of our lives and grants intuitive assistance to understand our relationships. It includes ancient wisdom; its symbols carry ancient knowledge originating from the depth of our souls and anyone can receive their own message if they are 'tuned up' to it, thus they get to the very heart of Tarot.

Why have I compiled love Tarot?

Everybody has a different concept and opinion about love and feels differently while experiencing it. For some, love equals to complete self-devotion; for others, short-term relations with no obligations mean love.

I know this feeling is different for everyone; for a long time, it was only a desire of mine to experience it intensively. Most of the time it was only the feeling I wanted, so every man entering my life carried the promise of true love. It took a long time to understand that every love is special love in a different way. We can learn something from every love affair. We can almost 'die' of a break and as a result of our wavering states of excitement and 'jealousy scenes', we can easily end up in really awful situations. Still, every man who gifted me with his love, enriched my life with a lot of teaching until I was able to attract the man who was really the true love of my life. Not only in the sloppy and careless sense of the word.

Before that I had talked a lot about what a real woman was like, but I became a real woman on his side. A real woman, who is not jealous but solicitudinous. Who is not doubtful but confident. Who is able to touch and to appreciate a touch. A real woman who can wait, not just expect. Who seduces with her eyes and smile, with her personality. A real woman who finally outgrew the narrow-minded, false idea that she has to compete with other women.

The world is in change and so are the forms of love relationships, but there is one thing which is certainly eternal: this feeling is one of the most important sources of energy and happiness for human beings. However, relationships today are rather complex, the parties try to find the real one based on different expectations and conceptions, and when they feel that something does not work, they quickly quit the relationship instead of working on it. This can cause serious traumas on both sides, not to mention the complete transformation of family patterns. No one else but we can change this.

I have created this tarot deck because I wanted to pass on some of the knowledge I gathered throughout the decades. I wanted that, if you find yourself in trouble and you have no one to turn to with your problems, you have something to reach for, calm down and find yourself. You can even see romantic and hopeless love affairs and fates that interwove and come apart to enable both parties to experience their own love stories.

The present love initiation tarot has been created because everyone desires true love. To reach this euphoric feeling, we have to know that love alone is not enough for a sincere and deep relationship. Acceptance is very important, and so is the understanding of the partner's personality and that we let them live even those plans and dreams we do not necessarily agree with, but we can stand beside them. If we really love somebody, then we grant them the freedom to be who they want to be and to be where they want to be. If we really love somebody, we let them to be a part of our lives by their own will.

The Structure of Tarot

In earlier times, tarot was regarded as a mystery, privilege of the high-born and of exclusive communities. Interpreters of cards in our times make efforts to grant people the power of self-recognition and an opportunity to change themselves and their lives. This way one might confront his hidden motivations and desires, or the subconscious patterns of his behaviour.

The night-side of tarot resides in the fact that the number of interpretations is almost infinite. Some claim that the majority of the cards of the Major Arcana denotes that we have no power over the given situation, while the majority of the Minor Arcana suggests that fate is in our own hands. Probably tarot cards were originally designed for playing, but the main aim besides this was teaching.

Love Tarot, similarly to the old basic cards of Venice and Marseilles, includes twenty-two cards. The meaning of twenty-two in numerology is 'everything', 'wholeness' and the whole 'world'. According to the Hebrew alphabet, it is the complete knowledge of 'God', 'All Wisdom and truth'. According to various thinkers and old tarot masters, everything that takes place is part of the language of God, and Hebrew letters are the aspects of God, the parts of divinity and the units of energy. If we could identify Hebrew letters with the 22 cards of tarot with complete certainty, this approach would also be true for Tarot. This is the reason why the books of authors thinking alongside numerology are usually divided into 22 chapters, as their major goal is to throw light upon ancient mysteries.

The tarot deck includes 56 minor arcana symbolised with four suits; in love tarot four nations are connected to them:

- SWORDS (spades – element of Air) – HUNGARIAN
- CUPS (hearts – element of Water) – FRENCH
- WANDS (clubs – element of Fire) – GERMAN
- COINS (diamonds – element of Earth) – ENGLISH

Courtly cards belong to each suit:

- KING
- QUEEN
- PRINCE
- PRINCESS

Numerological cards are also included, ranging from ace to ten.

Two additional cards are also included namely:

- INTUITION
- REASON

Major Arcana

I. The Magician

At the bottom of the card: Count Saint Germain and Adam

On the first card of Tarot, we meet a Magician with special abilities. He is an insider and owner of powers which make him the ruler of three worlds. He is the 'beginning', 'creation' and 'creative power'.

Meaning: Now is the time for action, a period is approaching on you when your personal attractiveness is increased thus you have to believe in your abilities and your charm.

II. The High Priestess

At the bottom of the card: Saint Elizabeth and Eve/Lilith

She is the opposite of the Magician, generally passive and reserved. The High Priestess sits still while the Magician stands. She wears a tiara on her head and holds an open book in her hands with the inscriptions of alpha and omega, referring to the mysterious power of the knowledge of the beginning and the end.

Meaning: From now, you have to focus on your inner self towards the recognition of the pictures of the unconscious and the soul. Keep a diary of your dreams, soon you are going to need a deeper understanding of them. Prepare for the more intensive presence of your intuitions, look into the depth. Listen to your inner voice, 'he' knows the answer.

III. The Empress

At the bottom of the card: Queen Elizabeth and the Queen of Sheba.

The Empress impersonates 'the real woman with the beauty of the woman'. She is the symbol of fertility, expecting a child. She is a beautiful and proud woman surrounded with riches and wealth.

Meaning: This card promises full renewing and fulfilment. Your emotional life is renewed and leads you to completeness.

IV. The Emperor

At the bottom of the card: Franz Joseph and King Solomon

He is the husband of the empress. He is the external and visible possessor of power, however, in love Tarot, he is a mature man ready for being a father and aware of his responsibility.

Meaning: You have arrived at a certain period when you have to settle your life so far, and you have to create security for yourself in order to reach harmony. You are able to give good pieces of advice and also to take them, you have to improve your capacity to lead.

V. The High Priest

At the bottom of the card: János Vitéz and Péter Pázmány

Generally, this is the twin brother of the Emperor and his opposite. God manifests itself in the Emperor – through deeds, and in the High Priest – through teachings. The Emperor has earthly, while the High Priest spiritual power.

Meaning: You are doing a lot of things that others accept. But now you have to learn to adapt to new situations too. A new tutor is entering your life, and you also have to pass on the knowledge.

VI. The Lovers

At the bottom of the card: Sissi and Gyula Andrássy/ Siegfried and Brünhild from the opera cycle by Wagner

This card is the unambiguous symbol of love and decision in love tarot. In the card a woman stands in the middle lured by two men in two directions.

Meaning: Many things can gain happiness for people: beauty, wealth, power, fame or knowledge. However, you know that they are really enjoyable only if you have somebody to share them. You are a social being, the greatest joy and sorrow are equally brought to you by your relationships. The card in this case refers to the ambiguity and the decision you have to face. You have to come to a decision to turn your life in a good direction. A new love might come across, your feelings towards your partner might change or simply you fall in love with something which is about to start in your life.

VII. The Chariot

At the bottom of the card: János Hunyadi and Nimrod.

The card symbolises victory. A man wearing a crown drives a richly ornamented war chariot, similarly to the entry of the victorious Roman generals celebrating their glory in a triumph, though in the card it is night and a woman also sits on the chariot, for every ruler and man has to have a woman behind/beside for the sake of balance. It signifies that the strength of a man is not granted by money or power but an outstanding woman, who is not only able to look up to her love, but is also able to love and respect him with admiration and can stand by him in times of hard decisions. She can console him, encourage him, and while loving the man from the very bottom of her heart she even lets him fight so that he could be true to his principles.

Meaning: Your courage is going to reap its reward, you are under spiritual, divine protection; the card means success and victory, your hard work has a result. Care for the one who supports and stands by you, because you could not have been able to achieve this all.

VIII. Strength

At the bottom of the card: Countess Antónia Zichy-Batthyány and Maria Magdalena.

There is an amazon in the card with the air of power, besides a lion sitting majestically and accepting the power of the beautiful woman. They are linked with the sign of infinity; the energy of Kundalini is manifested in the snake.

Meaning: You need strength and courage to face your fears. Learn to accept your instincts and desires, transform the powers radiating from them into a creative force.

IX. The Hermit

At the bottom of the card: Géza Gárdonyi and Christian Rosenkreuz

The Hermit is the card of introversion, the observance of ourselves, retirement from the world, self-restraint, purity, and the focusing on spirituality.

Meaning: You are soon going to meet someone, who can add a lot to your life in order to be able to find/recover the master inside as a person seeking for the right path. This is the card of self-recognition.

X. The Wheel Of Fortune

At the bottom of the card: István Széchenyi and Alexander the Great

There is a mandala also known as the Wheel of Fortune in the card indicating the free will of man. Goddess Fortuna stands in front of the wheel, and there are also three women depicted on the wheel: they symbolise memory, intelligence and the ability of reading the future, as these are the characteristics necessary for understanding the past, the present and the future.

Meaning: You will be fortunate, let it be anything you desire; it seems that you are going to succeed in everything and there is nothing that could stop you. The laws of fortune are at your service.

XI. Justice

At the bottom of the card: King Mátyás Corvinus and Bishop János Vitéz

Justice is a classic virtue, thus the card depicts a pretty, but earnest woman, who holds a sword and scales in her hands. This picture symbolises the weighing of the Soul, too, thus the card is also related to karma.

Meaning: It is you who frames your life; nothing happens independently of you. Your beliefs, misbeliefs, ideas and choices influence everything. You have to realise that responsibility is attached to the control of your words, ideas and attention, as the power surrounding and coming to life within you is enormous and intelligent.

XII. The Hanged Man

At the bottom of the card: Count Gyula Andrássy and Judas

There is a young man in this card hanging upside down, hung by his left leg. In former packs, this card was often referred to as the Thief or the Traitor, as many identify the hanged man with Judas, the forefather of traitors, whereas the purses of money and the coins falling out of his pocket are usually identified with the thirty pieces of silver.

Meaning: You are accepting that the events which happen in your life really have to take place, and you are ready to make sacrifice for them. At the moment, you are highly depending on your past and the person you wanted to belong to so much. You have to perform an exercise for releasing in order to let new energies stream into your life; you can ascend to a totally different level with the help of these energies.

XIII. The Unnamed Card (Anonymous Arcane, Death, The Reaper)

At the bottom of the card: Count Lajos Batthyány and Pilate

This is the card with the most ill-fated number; the creators of former tarot cards did not even name it fearing that this act might invite the Reaper into their lives. I do not name it either; the space for text remained blank. However, this card is not the symbol of death alone; it also stands for transformation and change. Instead of the conventional skeleton, this card depicts Hades, The God of the dead. He does not seem to be perilous, still, he is respectful and earnest. He is a reserved creature being superior to everything, nestled in a male body; all his acts, deeds and motivations are dreadfully logical.

Meaning: The transformation process – showing you that it is time to move forward – is bringing you the power of renewal. You have to put an end to the old in order to clear the way for the new.

XIV. Temperance

At the bottom of the card: Ferenc Deák and Saint Stephen of Hungary

This is the card of the classic virtue of self-restraint and self-control, as well as the card of Time. The Magician and the High Priestess are depicted in the card as spiritual Teachers; the High Priestess holds the silver (femininity), the Magician the golden (masculinity) pitcher; the disciples, the followers can be seen in the background, smaller than the main characters, and water connects the two energies as the symbol of eternity and forwards Knowledge by streaming towards them.

Meaning: Your transformational process – that started not so long ago – is still ongoing, but you have calmed down and become more patient. It is highly important to remain persevering and assiduous – this will yield the desired fruit. The fulfilment, the union you have been waiting for is really close.

XV. The Devil

At the bottom of the card: Haynau and Bloody Mary

This is the card of temptation, negative force, passion, habit, dependence and financial success. This is the reason why the card is dominated by a handsome, attractive, well-dressed man; his eyes are expressively suggestive, thus indicating the negative pole. Temptation never arrives in a devilish form (which is particularly true for love)… still, it can be dangerous and able to ensnare you.

Meaning: Everybody has some monomania, passion or craze. Yours are coming into the forefront event more significantly now. You are almost becoming obsessed by sensuality; your sexual energies are not under your control. You might attract relationships into your life that will not be able to work in the long run.

XVI. The Tower

At the bottom of the card: Erzsébet Báthory and Nimrod, as well as his wife, Semiramis.

The card shows destruction, but it can have various interpretations. The reason behind is that the card also means external intervention, generally an intervention of God or the Spiritual World if we have been receiving warning signals for a long time, but do nothing at all.

Meaning: A sudden change is going to happen in your life. It is also possible that you are going to get a clearer view of a situation. The message of the Tower is always revealed with the help of the cards around it.

XVII. The Star

At the bottom of the card: Saint László King of Hungary and King David.

This card is the symbol of harmony and creative forces. A young, naked woman pours water to the ground from a pitcher; this symbolises the source of inspiration received from above. Although the woman is naked, she does not excite the feeling of lechery, but that of purity instead.

Meaning: This card promises fortune, high expectations and success. Your relationship is going to shape up just as you wish; you can reach your goals now and enjoy life free from care.

XVIII. The Moon

At the bottom of the card: Flóra Sass and Virgin Mary

The Moon is the planet of the night; it symbolises beauty and light in the dark infinity. The Moon is also a symbol of the feminine principle, devotion, fertility, as well as the cyclic character and changeability of nature. In this very card the Moon Goddess appears in a windblown veil with a crescent-shaped coronet, sitting on horseback and holding a torch, while shedding light on the mortal.

Meaning: The card is the symbol of the three levels of human life. Water symbolises the unconscious mind and the murky past, Earth stands for the material universe and the conscious mind, whereas the Moon lighting in the sky is the allegorical representation of the superior world of the soul. This card tells you about unforeseen events, or sudden changes you have never thought of before. You are more sensitive now, so control your emotional outbreaks consciously; do not make too much of tiny little things. Pay attention to your dreams, your intuition, and keep a diary of your dreams and intuitions if you can. Later you will be surprised! Moving, a change in your workplace or in your feelings are all-possible.

XIX. The Sun

At the bottom of the card: Saint Stephen, King of Hungary and Saint Francis of Assisi

The Sun is the active, masculine principle symbolising fire and consciousness. The Sun provides light, heat and life on the Earth. There is The Sun in the card; its rays are shines at young lovers.

Meaning: Whatever you begin to do, you are going to be successful now; you are making progress towards you goals deliberately and consciously. The card predicts good relationships and successful marriage. Enjoy this satisfactory and happy period of your life! A situation can be offered to you that is worth thinking about, and you might also have the opportunity to go on a fantastic journey.

XX. Judgement

At the bottom of the card: Álmos, chief of the Hungarians and Jesus

Archangel Michael can be seen with his huge wings, blowing his trumpet. There is a halo around his head. There is a man under him, opposite us (right side) and a woman with her hands lifted for prayer; but we can only see half of their bodies, as a child rises from the water and looks at them while turning his back on us.

Meaning: This card forecasts new recognitions and your need to change your lifestyle. Now you can become more conscious; simply concentrate on your mental-spiritual-physical equilibrium. Also pay more attention to your health! This is the card of rebirth and children.

XXI. The World

At the bottom of the card: Adam and Eve

The World Tree appears in this card. The World Tree refers to life and death, everlasting development and growth, as well as continuous revival. The meditating, contemplative Adam sits under it with the beautiful, expectant Eve dancing in front of him; her nakedness is hidden by a single veil on which the symbol of the World Tree also appears. She dances, this symbolises joy, harmony and the order of the Universe.

This is the universal dance of the Woman who is going to give birth to a child shortly; this child will become the new born baby of the Fool card. This is how the internal evolutional and initiatory process of tarot starts again.

Meaning: You are going to achieve all your wishes and goals; real perfection is near. You have already learnt the lessons so far, and if something does not work in your life the way you want, it has a single reason: you do not use the appropriate method for reaching your goals, or this goal is not what you really wish to fight for.

You are able to give and accept gifts alike. You are ready for happiness and making others happy. A new life cycle is coming; the current phase has just ended. Draw strength from your experiences.

You are free and ready for another 'journey', as you know one of the greatest secrets of self-fulfilment: all you need is time and a little bit of introversion if you want to achieve something good.

XXII. The Fool

At the bottom of the card: Béla IV of Hungary and Nehemiah

This is one of the most mysterious cards of tarot – the one of the beginning and the end. There is a young boy in the card who leaves home to try his luck; his green gown is on his shoulder, the inevitable satchel is next to him, and he holds a stick is his hand; this stick resembles the stick of the Magician, but it is still rudimentary, as the boy has to learn a lot until he can catch up with the Magician.

Meaning: Life is calling you for a new adventure, and it is only up to you how you take on it. A new situation is awaiting; it can be a new job, a new relationship, or founding a new family.

If you are still pondering over whether to undertake something or not, this card suggests that in reality you have already decided; be optimistic ad enthusiastic; you are starting off with a clean slate, this is the time for a new start. You are ready for that.

How to use Tarot cards

Tarot is thc mirror of our life, existence, the print of our thoughts, feelings and emotions, that shows the most accurate picture of our 'whole' being. It provides help in finding our destiny, waking our spiritual memories, in shedding some light on our personal life-plan and exploring our spiritual plans. It is like a GPS, which navigates us safely through the unknown roads of our lives. In order to entrust ourselves to this particular map, the most important thing is to know how to use it. If we get to know it well, the tarot's magical cards will help in taking decisions in all areas of life and love, since rationality is often a bad counsellor in times of crisis, while the subconscious probably knows the right way. The tarot brings this knowledge to the surface, from within us.

Find your own card!

Nowadays you can choose from a wide range of tarot cards, the point is that the card should 'speak' to you and address you. For me it is important that the interpretation of tarot has changed more and more into a psychological analysis of personality and thus the goal has become finding self-knowledge and personal mission. This is why I have created my own cards and use these instead. Sometimes I work with complementary cards also, I have several favourites actually. At the same time, you should know that 'shuffling' the card decks should be made carefully, because the symbol systems are never the same, even if they may seem to be very similar.

In order for my students to realise this, once a month we select a different deck of cards together and we review it, to see the differences between the symbol systems. It is highly important for them to become aware (and you too), of how different cards give different answers regarding the particular person's developmental stage, current life situation, of course in the light of the raised issue and life matter.

Thus we observe the same (learned) spread several times with the same cards. Although we know that the interpretation varies, sometimes the difference is quite shocking for us too. They are all tarot cards, still they are not replaceable, neither the cards nor the meanings can be changed with one another. **For every symbol system is complete only by itself, they should not and cannot be mixed with each other.** Thank you, for taking the honour of using my card.

Cleansing the Tarot Cards

From now on, every card sheet will give you some sort of guidance, instructions. Your sole job is to apply the advice to your own situation, thereby helping yourself to reveal the source of your problems, to untangle the entangled emotional threads. Before you get started, it is important to cleanse, initiate and charge your card with your energies. Precisely for this reason, if you have the possibility, buy a new deck of cards, which does not carry the imprints, energies of the previous owner.

- After you have unwrapped the cards, place them on a tray and put it out in the midday sun, for half an hour.
- Hold the cards in your hand, the cards shaping a fan and move them over the candle flame nine times, three times with the pictures facing the flame; three times the backside of the cards facing the flame and three times just keep them over the flame for half a minute. Of course, meanwhile, visualise or say to yourself three times:
- The cards are perfectly clean.
- Hold the deck of cards in one hand loosely, while letting them fall, over and over again, onto your other palm and in the meantime blow on them repeatedly, while say three times the above sentence in thought.

If we are talking about a used deck, then I suggest to apply all three methods, one after the other.

Initiation of the Card

When using the cards, intuition plays an important role, therefore I ask you to deal with them in a calm environment, in an absorbed, deepened state, do not take them out if you are upset.

Furthermore, you will need an app. 40 x 40 cm kerchief, a candle, incense, a little holy water, if you do not have holy water – spring water will do just fine, and one of your favourite minerals, which can be a simple stone as well. If this is done, spread out the kerchief and light the candle as well as the incense and initiate the tarot card before the first use. This is extremely important, allow time for this!

The initiation of the tarot card is based on the system of the four elements, Earth, Air, Fire and Water which, beyond the completeness of life, symbolise also the qualities of perception, thoughts, intuitions and feelings.

- Put the tarot deck inside a circle, which may be a circle drawn on paper clockwise or even a necklace as well. This circle includes and amplifies energies.
- Pull the cards over a plate of salt so they would recharge with the energy and protective power of Earth. During this ritual, think of magical, ancient steady stones and circles, high jagged cliffs, mountain ranges, vast sandy plains.
- Place the deck above a lit rosemary or pine-scented incense to take over the power and purity of thoughts, or above sandalwood fragrance for spiritual and healing energies. Thus you confer the cards sharp perception, searching intuition belonging to the element of Air.
- In order to enhance the Fire element and its creativity, light a gold, yellow or red candle and hold it over the cards. (For instance, I just move the cards back and forth, one by one, over the flame)
- Finally, drag the cards over a bowl of water in which rose petals are floating, rose or lavender oil will also do just fine, for the harmony of the deeper feelings and susceptibility of those people for who you will spread the cards.
- Let the circle and the cards within untouched for a full day, then grab the deck and wrap it in dark silk and then put it in a box.

Protection

Avoid divination and the analysis of the soul when you are exhausted and moody, because your readings must be entirely harmonious and positive. Since you dig deep into the depths of the soul, you become very susceptible to mood changes and to every energy. Therefore, it is essential to create a spiritual medium, in which you can work and which you have to close, when you are done.

If you use the card in public place, then first with your mind's eyes draw a circle clockwise starting from north and visualise how it draws you into the golden light. If you have finished reading the cards/fortune-telling, close this circle as well counter clockwise, again starting from north and in the meantime imagine a dark crystal, a smoky quartz or an obsidian that eliminates the golden light and your soul is cleansed again.

If you read the cards for someone else, draw special protective circle around that person so if the negative feelings of anger or sadness would overcome them, these would dissolve once the reading is done.

For greater protection, wherever you spread the cards, you can put crystals in the corners of the room, even at the four corners of the table where you work or on the floor right in front of you. Thus you create a spiritual/mental energy field, which is free of all negativity, both intended and involuntary. (The following precious stones belong to protective crystals: agate, amethyst, green and red chalcedony, garnet, black and red jasper, lapis lazuli, tiger's eye, topaz and turquoise)

If you read the cards for someone else, drag a crystal pendulum or an amethyst over the card in counter-clockwise direction, to keep away any negative feelings. After that, wash the pendulum and the amethyst in running water, then put them to rest in black silk for a while. Do not give the cards into the hands of children until they turn 15.

If you only read for yourself, make this a special event in your life, and schedule it in a time when you can work quietly and undisturbed. Perhaps take a scented bath before and wear comfortable, warm clothes. It is always worth lighting a candle and placing crystals near you.

However, do not forget the most important thing! The magical power is within you and it does not require any special circumstances other than you intensely focusing on your soul.

Meditate on the Cards of Tarot!

A divination or prediction cannot tell up-coming, specific events. The level of reality where someone will be in the future, that is the degree of awareness someone will be able to face a problem is unpredictable. The prognosis can speak only about the nature of the experiential plan of a particular stage of life.

However, if you deal with your dreams gladly, telling others about it with enthusiasm, analyse them, twist and turn them or even keep a dream diary, then meditation may be the solution and this self-developing technique can come very close to you. (If you have not meditated yet.)

You certainly know that the ancient science of dream interpretation is nowadays the borderline between psychology and esotery, as several psychologists are using different types of meditation. The interpretation of meditation, similarly to dream interpretation, is actually a decoding, the explanation of the seen inner images.

Many people accept that in our dreams, meditations we communicate with higher powers, when they express their will for us through dream images. I believe that the images seen in our dreams and meditation are some sort of symbolical messages, which the subconscious convey to us. I find meditation on a chosen tarot card fantastic, a wonderful opportunity for self-improvement. If you decide to give it a try, I would prefer you had a small diary for it. I like to write down my dreams and meditations as well, because writing itself gives me energy to fulfil my goals. In the beginning it may seem weird, if you have not kept any diaries yet, but later you will find it very useful. It will be interesting to replay every life event in the light of your dreams and meditations. Soon, beside the books presenting the Minor Arcana, the book containing the tarot meditation will be published, but until then feel free to dive in, trust yourself and rely on your intuition!

Cartomancy and Meditation

- Decide which method of cartomancy you will use.
- Decide whether you want to receive answer to a specific question from the cards or just want to explore the path of self-knowledge through them.

- Light a candle and incense, quiet down and you may even do a few simple breathing exercises.
- After cleansing, hold the card in your hand and think about that certain question or about the area of your life, where you want to make a change.
- Shuffle the cards and then pick the cards according to the selected method and put it down in front of you.
- First, look carefully at the cards and allow your intuition to work, then look up in the book the description, task, meditation belonging to that specific card and read the story belonging to that given card as well.
- Close your eyes and let your subconscious whisper to you, how this card relates to your current life situation. First, deal with the most obvious interpretation, and if it does not fit the question raised or with your situation, associate creatively, until you realise what the drawn card refers to in your case.
- If even after these, further questions arise in you, you can shuffle the cards again, look inward and pick again.

Meditation

Meditation is a practice, which helps you to get to know yourself better, discover yourself. Through meditation you get to know your inner self, who you really are. Meditation is good not only for eliminating the unnecessary stress. Beside the fact that it calms your mind down, it has a lot of favourable effects, which are very important in your everyday life. If you decide to meditate over the tarot cards at home, then by all means you should know some basic rules.

- There are numerous methods for meditation. The easiest and most common way is to sit down nice and comfortable, keep the spine straight and vertical. (You can even sit in a chair.) Concentrate on the drawn card until it suddenly becomes blurry and the internal images begin to flow toward you. This is similar to the guided visualisation. The guided visualisation helps you to enter a deeper meditative state and it is also good, when reached that meditative state, to achieve the predetermined goals. Now if you focus on the card, you will be able to calm your mind step-by-step and let the subconscious images in. In case you feel that you got stuck in a circle of thoughts, think back firmly on the card you have been concentrating on. It is perfectly normal if people start to itch in such cases, to feel uncomfortable. Do not start to think about it, rather just observe the itch and 'let it go'. If you meditate regularly, you will be calmer, more peaceful, more composed.

- Meditation is good and useful anytime. Most people pick a card in the early morning, meditate on it and carry the collected energy with them for the whole day. This is the easiest way to learn the meaning of the trumps: so each morning feel free to pick a daily card! However, do not forget: meditation has a better effect on you before meals, than immediately after a meal.
- When you try it out for the first time, you may feel that you cannot endure it for more than 15-20 minutes. It does not matter, because every beginning is hard and in case of meditation too, only practice and regularity can help to prolong the duration.
- Meditative music can help to create the right atmosphere, it helps if it is difficult to 'just' get started and meditate. You can use music to suppress the surrounding noise, the neighbours.
- During meditation, seek the answers to your questions within yourself. Find a quiet corner and do not do anything, just relax. The rest will come by itself, or not, but sooner or later you will experience for yourself, people always get to know the world through their own experiences. Sitting or lying down – it is your choice (whatever seems more sympathetic to you) and leave the rest to nature!

Shuffling the Cards

Just a few more additions before the spreads (spread types), which I consider to be extremely important.

Most of the authors ask you to focus on your question during the shuffling of the cards. I however, will ask you to try to empty your mind instead, to keep it clear. Why? You may possible have heard about psycho kinesis. If not, no problem, I will explain to you what it is about. Psycho kinesis is nothing more than the immediate action of the mind in a situation. This occurs, for example, when someone with the help of their will can influence which side of the thrown dice would be upward. However, few people know that this psychokinetic ability is used more often instinctively, involuntarily. Thus the psychokinetic effect may occur after shuffling, during the spreading of the cards. This means that the cards involuntarily produce the answers that you would like to receive. This, however, will not take you forward.

Beside the psychological capability, there is another factor to which I would like to draw your attention: I have written this book so that you would not need anyone else to interpret the cards for you. I want you to read the personalised instructions from them. Why? Because even a newbie fortune-teller notices how much a person requesting the divination, tells of themselves before picking the cards. He/she learns about your plans, desires, hopes, problems and current life situations. This is not a problem if a complex therapy is taking place, however it may be hazardous in cartomancy. The intuition of the card interpreter develops very rapidly and thus they quickly learn how to interrogate you without you noticing it. This will result in the fact that you yourself will imply the divination and you already are likely to consider the circumstances coming out from the cards to be true and probable. Because knowing certain facts about you, your past, your present and your future, makes it easy to insert them into a broadly interpretable observation, which, however, can be applied to a lot of other people.

Guess who has become aware of this first? Gypsies! Already in the nineteenth century, ethnographers found records, in which Gypsy teachers enumerate examples of divination that can be definitely told to anyone:

"Soon you meet someone who will have a great influence on your life."

"Soon you meet someone who will fall madly in love with you."

"In the course of your life you had a very difficult debate with one of your relatives."

"Your boyfriend treated you badly."

"You have been in jeopardy several times, some of them were life-threatening."

According to Gypsies, you have to act out these statements very effectively, then you will succeed in winning every client's trust. As a result of making a living from teaching and card interpretation, it is not surprising that some of the Gypsies learned to read in the minds of customers at an incredibly high level and gave them advice which deemed fit to the person.

With reference to this subject, I need to write about the power of self-fulfilling prophecies also. These predictions have such a powerful impact on the questioner's mind, that the person will involuntarily make them come true later.

For instance, if someone tells you that difficulties and disputes are expected in your family life, and you had fears in this regard anyway, it is not hard to guess that your approach is about to change and all hell will break loose. Divinations related to death are more dangerous, we can meet plenty of self-fulfilling prophecies related to this as well. The lesson is that caution is indispensable, whether the card provides information on death or financial situation. Because we cannot help it, take such predictions more seriously, deal with them more carefully as such a simple prediction can arise serious problems. Precisely for this reason, pay extra attention that your children under 15 years of age cannot touch Tarot.

These are my warnings for you. Of course, I am not saying you should not interpret the cards for others or should not let them read the cards for you. But I considered mentioning them to be my duty, because tarot is not just a game. Just like meditation, tarot and every other divination method are based on the principle that everything that happens is part of an interconnected plan. Therefore, the randomly spread sequence of cards are part of this pattern too, and may help in understanding the further details of your life plan, such as human relationships, your past, present and future. Beyond the superficial meanings, there are hidden and perhaps never suspected relations, which make the prediction possible. The best is when you get in harmony with yourself and with the Universe, because then you will receive more reliable answers. Remember, tarot cards serve as a guide for your current life situation, they do not make decisions for you, they do not live your life for you. Instead, they help you to reach a deeper self-knowledge and to see more clearly.

Spread Types and Readings

The cards can be laid out based on different methods. You can find lots of spread types on the internet, thus here I will point out only the ones I consider important, which are less known, and the ones I definitely recommend to my students. You may begin with the simplest method of spreading, until you get to know the love tarot symbol system, then you can gradually skip to the more complicated ones. The easiest way to learn the tarot is to pick a daily card from the whole deck each day, then meditate on it whether in the morning or in the evening (then you will understand why this card came to you precisely on that day.) This daily card-picking includes a special helper: while you are learning the cards better, you are getting closer and closer to yourself as well.

In case you want to try out something else immediately, besides the daily method, begin like this: from the deck choose the face card (with an image on it from Major Arcana), which most appeals to you. This represents you. If you read the cards for someone else, then obviously pick the card for them or let them choose for themselves. We will refer to this card as the Significator. If you decide to follow the proposals of old masters, remember that you can use the High Priest to indicate men, and the High Priestess to indicate women. Personally, I think it is better if you choose the card that 'speaks' to you. Always follow the method that you prefer, the one that is the simplest for you. I personally use the Significator card recommended by ancient masters only when I look for specific answers: for instance, in case of legal affairs I choose Justice as a Significator card, and in case of forbidden love, the Moon.

Once you have found your Significator card, take it out from the deck and put it on the table face up, then shuffle the other cards. (Advanced tarot readers can leave the Significator card in the deck and mix with the other cards, however I suggest applying this only when you already 'feel' the card, do not force it until then!). Once you have shuffled the cards, split the deck into two piles, turn over the smaller pile then put the card deck together and shuffle it again. You do this so that some cards would surely come out in reversed position and that these cards would not be the same. (The reversed cards are the ones which appear upside down. You will find their meanings on each card, I detail their meaning on the Minor Arcana cards as well. Until then it is enough for you to remember that reversed cards always indicate regression; i.e. suggest that you need to return to an earlier life stage if you want to solve your problems. They also strongly indicate that you do not want to face something, you deny something or run away from something, perhaps you are you looking for excuses to avoid a conflict.)

In the next step take apart and re-shuffle the deck of cards, do this at least three times in a row before you lay out the cards. The question often arises as to who should shuffle. Many people believe that the querent should shuffle, while others swear that both the querent and the card reader should shuffle, however the best is when the person who does the card interpretation shuffles the cards. You have the right to choose in this case too. I always ask the querent to shuffle, then if the answer is not clear I shuffle again and pick a card again. The point is that no matter who shuffles the cards, the querent should focus – but not too hard – on the raised question. In general, one should split the deck into two small piles with the left hand, but I think it is more important which hand you pick out the card with. If you use your left hand, then you expect an answer from intuition, if you pick with your right hand, you are curious about the rational response.

The Most Simple Beginner Method

Take two cards from the top of the deck and place them face down next to the Significator card. (I find it more useful if you turn the cards only when you have already pulled out all of them, because then your thoughts will not wander around the already seen cards.) The first card indicates the current state of the querent, the second card represents the name of the person connected with him/her or refers to the situation in question.

The three-card method is similar to this: pick three cards and put them under the Significator card. The first one shows something from the querent's past, the second one shows something about their current situation and the third one refers to the future, it indicates an event that is going to occur soon. These simple methods are not suitable to provide broader and more comprehensive responses, because the same spread can be interpreted differently from different points of view. The cards are not enough and thus you will have to move on and learn the more complex methods of spreading.

The Five-Card Method

This method is suitable only to answer simpler, less important questions. After the shuffle and splitting the deck in two, ask the querent to choose a number between one and twenty-two. If for example he/she chooses seven, then pull the seventh card from the top out of the deck and put it on the table. Shuffle again and ask the querent to choose another number... until you have placed all five cards under the Significator card. The first card refers to the positive things, the second one to the negative factors, the third card shows you how to bring the two in accordance, balance the two. The fourth card shows which strategy should be followed, the fifth card indicates the possible results.

The seven-card method, the so-called Arc or Horseshoe method

Here you do not need the Significator card, through this spread type you can receive an answer to a specific question. After shuffling and splitting the deck, put back together the cards and take the first seven cards off the top, then spread them out on the table to form an upright arc, from right to left. (Bottom right will be the first card, therefore the cards must be read from right to left!)

- Past
- Present
- Non conscious factors
- Negative impacts, obstacles
- The approach of people in your community
- You have to do this
- Possible outcome

Celtic Cross

This spread type is also known as the Great Cross and almost everyone uses it. According to Waite, this method should be used to answer specific questions, so he renamed it into ancient Celtic method. Select the Significator card in the usual way and put it on the table. Shuffle the cards, split the deck in half and then re-shuffle. Start to put down the cards which you have taken from the top of the deck, on the table. Put the first card on the Significator card, this is the so-called cover card, which refers to the surrounding atmosphere of the querent's question.

Place the second card (card number two) across the first card. This card crosses the querent, thus it shows the obstacles which the querent has to face. The third card (card number three) is to be placed above the Significator card, it crowns the previous cards, i.e. it shows the querent's plans and objectives, as well as, the expected/occurring best results. The fourth card (card number four) is to be laid under the Significator card, it is the base card, it refers to the foundation and background of the current situation, shows the querent's attitude. The fifth card shall be placed on the left side of the Significator card, it will be behind it so to speak, therefore this card refers to the recent past and its possible effects. The sixth card will be on the right side of the Significator card, it will be in front of the situation, so this card shows the near future. Lay out four more cards to the right of the Significator card in a vertical column, so that the seventh card would be in the bottom and the tenth on the top. The seventh card is the one that reveals more about the current situation and attitude of the querent. The eighth provides more information about the influence coming from the querent's environment. The ninth card symbolises the hopes and fears of the querent. The tenth card is the most important one, because it shows you the final result, every possibilities, factors and influence shown by the rest of the cards are summed up in this. If the tenth card is a face card from the Major Arcana, the result depends mainly on the person that the card represents (you can deduce symbolically who that person is.) In this case, you can get more information by laying out another Celtic Cross, but be careful to use the face card as the Significator. Pay attention! The cards laid out in this case will not refer to the querent but to this other person, interpret them accordingly.

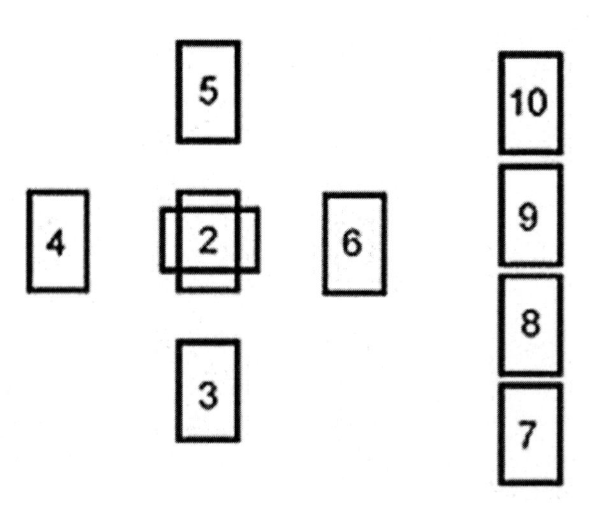

The Clock or the Zodiac Spread

Put twelve cards around the Significator card, as if they indicated the clock dial. According to the first method, the first card indicates the events of the month ahead of you, the second card the following month and so on, until the end of the year. If you do not use a Significator card, then after the twelve cards are laid out, put a thirteenth card in the middle of the 'clock', this has to be interpreted as a general indicator of the year ahead.

In a second method, the twelve cards of the clock can be interpreted as the twelve houses of the Zodiac as well, in this case the first card represents the first house. If you know your own horoscope, and happen to be familiar with astrology, you may combine the cards with your own radix to get more refined results. The houses:

- The querent him/herself, i.e. personality and character
- Money, material goods, movables and spiritual wealth
- Mental agility, communication, self-expression, smaller journeys and movement accidents.
- Childhood, parental relationship (mostly father), home, occultism
- Love and sex, children, gambling, entertainment, student-teacher relation, secondary education
- Health, work, workplace, distant relatives, father-in-law, pets, duties
- Marriage, spouse, partner, business partner, business relationship, outside world, smaller litigations, public, acting in public, grandparent, exams
- Accident, surgery, death, heritage, physical sex, deadly love
- Religious and philosophical views, serious litigations, politics, brother-in-law, sister-in-law
- Career, exquisite social status, fame, boss, ambition, mother, motherhood (as a profession)
- Friends and social life, desires, hopes, ambitions, patrons, old age or platonic love
- Enemies, seçrets, limitations, occultism, army, convent, prison, overseas, mother-in-law

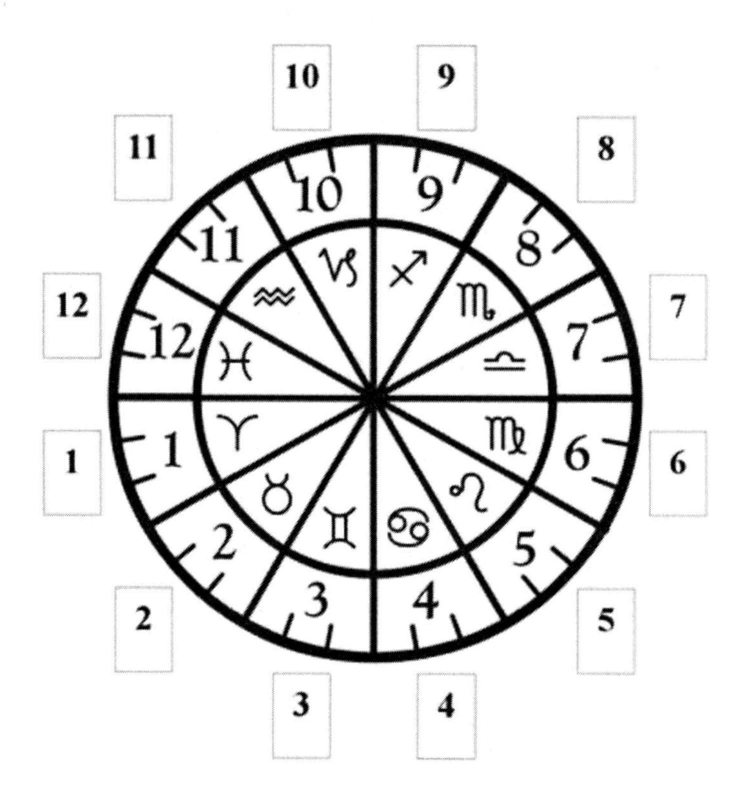

Annual Task

You already know very well that the tarot card is perhaps the most important instrument in developing self-knowledge and in mapping out the future. If you would like its help to get predictions year after year, I will show you a simple, relatively quickly done spread, which you can use every year from now on.

Although people want to evade the effects of constant uncertainty, they struggle to do so or cannot do it at all. "What will be my fate, what does the next year hold for us?" many people are interested in this, but only a few people know it in advance, as it requires to live a life and possess such knowledge, which only a few do among working people. This is a spread, which helps you to clarify the main task of the next year. This is not the same as the annual card interpretation, however, it points out the most important thing to do and what kind of help you will get (from heaven) in order to achieve that. This helps you to see clearly what awaits you. Before you start, make a brief reckoning. In order to do this, think about the following three questions, more than that, take a pen and paper, it is best to write down the answers:

- What was the best thing that happened to you in 2014?
- What was the worst thing that happened to you in 2014?
- What will/should you do, or perhaps do differently in 2015?

These are very important questions. They help you to begin the new year prepared and also to look differently at this current year. For the last question, you may ask for help from the tarot cards.

Simple love divination

This is quite a common spread method, but very useable. With this, you can answer questions (though not in one word), e.g. does X, Y love me?

From the laid-out tarot cards, you have to pick out 4 in sequence. Spread them like this:

- 2.
- 4.

Interpretation

- The current state of the relationship
- How does the querent relate to the relationship (how does she/he experiences it)
- How does the partner relate to the relationship and to the querent
- What should the querent do to improve the relationship

The karmic relationship spread

If you suspect that you have a karmic connection with someone, with this spread you can check it out. Lay out 8 cards in the following manner:

--------1--------7--------5---6--------

------3---4------8----------2----------

Each card answers a question:

- How did you meet this person in your previous life?
- How was your relationship?
- What kind of feelings did you have towards him/her?
- What kind of feelings did he/she had towards you?

- What kind of karmic repayment do you have regarding him/her?
- What is your present task with him/her?
- What do you have to avoid, if you do not want to accumulate any further karmic burdens regarding him/her?
- What kind of positive effects can you expect in the future from this relationship?

Karmic wheel (Wheel of Fortune) spread type (One of my favourites)

Imagine that the Significator card located in the middle of a compass. After shuffling, take the first three cards off the top of the deck, and put them down in the northern point of the table, while saying it aloud: "Three above you." Place the next three cards at the southern point of table and say aloud: "Three below you." Continue this until you lay out nine triple cards.

- North: 'Three above you'
- South: 'Three below you'
- West: 'Three behind you'
- East: 'Three in front of you'
- Northwest 'Three for your house and your home'
- Northeast: 'Three for your hopes and fears.'
- Southwest : 'Three for the unexpected'
- Southeast: 'Three for the expected.'
- Put this under the second pile and say: "Three for which is certainly going to happen."

The first card pile symbolises the querent or the general atmosphere surrounding the issue. The second pile refers to things under the querent's control. The third and the fourth pile illustrate the past and the future respectively, and the meaning of the rest is quite obvious according to the above. After this you do not have to do anything but turn the cards over and read them. If something remains unanswered, then pick another one from the original deck and study the whole thing all over or you can also meditate on it.

The Tree of Life Spread

Choose the Significator card, but leave it in the deck. After shuffling, take ten cards off the top of the deck and lay them out according to the kabala Tree of Life model. Start with the Kether and finish it with the Malkuth. Continue laying out the cards, until in each point there will be seven cards. Put aside the remaining 10 cards.

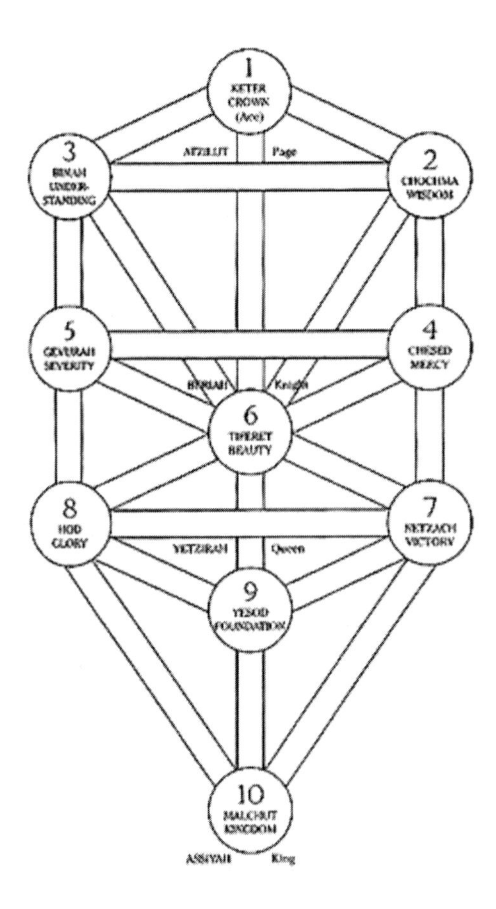

The meaning of the cards in the different points of the tree is the following:

- Spirituality in your life
- Initiative and responsibility
- Sorrow, fears and boundaries
- Finance, constructive things
- Enemies, destructive things
- Reputation, conscious mind, mental agility

- Love, affection
- Business, communication, arts
- Health, unconscious mind
- Home and family

Take your time and examine each little seven-card stack carefully. The pile in which you find your own Significator card is highly important, thus pay extra attention to it. It may indicate problems or tasks that require improvement, development in the given area.

Opening the Key

This type of spread was recommended by Mathers and Crowley as well, I often use it too. Several versions are known, so do not be surprised if you encounter another one later on. It is a complicated spread system, I would not recommend it for beginners. It requires a perfect knowledge of the cards and the related symbol systems, experienced use of the cards, so do not get started if you are not completely ready for it. These complicated spread methods contain relatively few pre-defined instructions, based on them every experienced card reader will develop their own system further. In these spreads the card readers rely on the conscious intellectual processes, based on these they combine the interpretations into meaningful responses.

If you already know the cards and their related symbol systems, first choose a Significator card, but leave it in the deck. Shuffle the deck and split it in the usual way, then lay down the cards in two piles, to the left. Split in half both piles again and put the cards down to the left from the previous two. Therefore, you will have four little piles. From right to left, these represent the following:

Wands: things related to work and business
Swords: losses, quarrels and problems
Cups: love, marriage, happiness
Coins: money and material goods

After this, find your Significator card. In whichever pile you find it, that stack indicates the nature of your question or problem. If it is not working, stop and do not try again for at least 3-4 hours, if the matter is very serious, wait at least a day.

If it works, spread the pile containing your Significator card out in a circle, face up, make sure that the Significator card is on top of the circle, but be careful not to change the order of the cards. Now you have to choose various cards from the circle, starting from the Significator card. First, see in which direction the Significator card looks and start to count in that direction. (If the Significator card is precisely in front of you, always start to the left).

In case of Kings, Queens, and Princes, count four.

In case of Princesses count seven, for Aces count eleven and in case of smaller cards count the value of the card.

In case of the Fool, the Hanged Man and the Judgment Day, count three.

Proceed with the counting until you arrive back at a card again. Then stop and read the existing cards from right to left and interpret them to the existing problem. If you still have not received a proper answer to your question, then shuffle these cards again and put the rest of the cards as well in the deck. Shuffle the entire deck again and split it apart in twelve piles, which correspond with the known astrological houses. Find again the deck that contains your Significator card, again it will be essential in terms of your question. Spread them out and start to count as described above and stop when you get to the same card second time. Read and interpret it.

If this is not enough either, then shuffle the whole deck again and lay out the Tree of Life. The pile containing the Significator provides the answer again, and again you have to count then interpret.

This method has a more complicated version too, in this case you have to pair up the cards and only then interpret them. When you reach the same card for the second time, and look back and see which cards you have touched, you have to take into consideration where that specific card is in the initial spread. Is it between two cards of the same colour or between opposite cards? These also provide information to a more experienced card interpreter.

This spread type has a more sophisticated part too: after you have reviewed, interpreted all this, starting with the cards next to the Significator (remember, the Significator was on the top of the circle) begin to pair up the cards, so you quasi put them down next to each other (one from the left side of the circle and one from the right) and then you will have to read these cards together as well.

Le grand jeu

This cannot be left out from the book, although this is a more complex spread method as well. At first it is very difficult, but if you know the cards and keep practicing, soon you will feel the cards. There are several versions of this method too. Pick out the Significator card from the deck, then shuffle and split apart the deck in the usual way. Place sixty-six cards in the following manner:

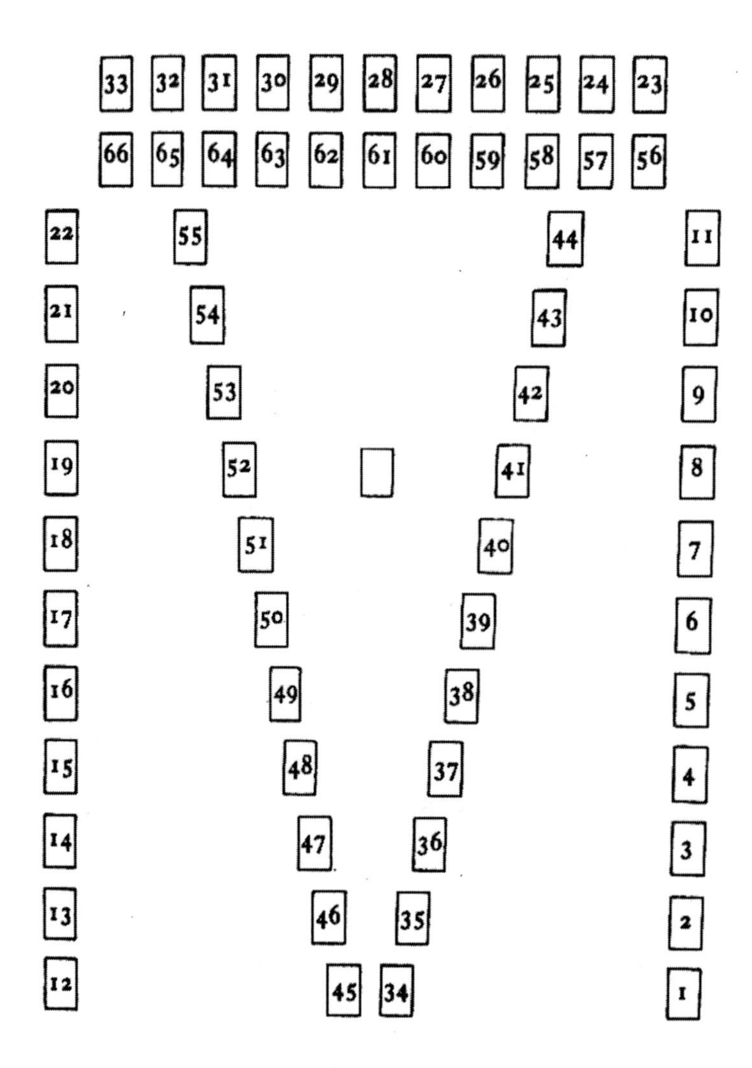

The cards in the top two rows indicate the present. The cards from one to 11 and from 34 to 44 show the past. The rest of the cards indicate the future. Once you have studied it all, read the cards in pairs too, meaning the 1st card with the 34th, the second one with the 35th and so on....

After this, gather the cards so that at the bottom of the deck there would be the 66th card, put the 2nd card onto it and so on, until the 33rd card, which will end up on the top of the deck. Then spread the cards again in a circle, the Significator being the starting point. The 33rd card should be on the right of the Significator, the 66th card should be the last card of the circle, to the left of the Significator. (If the Significator card is right in front of you like 'face to face', you can place the cards in counter clockwise direction).

Now comes the pair reading in the following way: first the Significator with the 66th card, then match the cards from right and from left (obviously the Significator is on the top of the circle, therefore you move downwards, from left and from right – pairing the 'to be interpreted' cards from opposite directions). Continue until only one card is left. This card holds a surprise: whether it is wise advice, a remonstrance or a warning.

The combinations of the cards – an important addition for advanced readers

Some 'minor things' may have great importance in the tarot as well, thus I consider these pieces of information to be highly essential. Let us take a look at them quickly.

If in a certain spread (layout) most of the cards are face cards, this refers to human relationships and encounters, this indicates social or business meetings. The following list of card-combinations come from Mathers, I have evolved a lot through his teachings:

Four Aces: good sign, great forces are working
Three Aces: money and success
Four Kings: meeting important people
Three Kings: elevated social status, high position, honours, award
Four Queens: lots of disputes
Three Queens: female deceit
Four Princes: speed, haste
Three Princes: unexpected news, encounters
Four Princesses: new plans, new ideas
Three Princesses: company of young men

Four Tens: responsibility and fear
Three Tens: commercial affairs
Four Nines: responsibility
Three Nines: letters and messages
Four Eights: expected news
Three Eights: lots of travelling
Four Sevens: amorous disappointments
Three Sevens: contracts, alliances
Four Sixes: happiness
Three Sixes: profit
Four Fives: regularity
Three Fives: disputes, conflicts
Four Fours: peace, tranquillity
Three Fours: hard work
Four Threes: decision, determination
Three Threes: deceit
Four Twos: conversations
Three Twos: reorganisations, lifestyle changes

Furthermore, it is also important: the meaning of the card is strengthened if it is located between two identical coloured cards, and weakened, if it is surrounded by opposite coloured cards. The opposites: Wands-Cups (Fire-Water) and Swords-Coins (Air-Earth).

For instance, if the Queen of Cups lands between two other cards of Cups, then it carries an even more positive message, but if it falls between two Wands cards, then the intensity of its meaning weakens. If two opposite coloured cards end up next to each other, they tend to neutralise each other's meaning.

The Magical Road of The Major Arcana

The MAJOR ARCANA follows the path of the INDIVIDUAL/ HERO from birth all the way to resurrection, through 22 stations (i.e. initiations), until a new return. This is the tarot's magical initiatory journey, that can be found in almost every culture of the world. The Cards of the Major Arcana draw the attention on inevitable, crucial road junctions (on situations not influenced by us), decisions and opportunities.

0-22 Man is born into the material world being unconscious, instinctive, symbolised by the **Fool** card.

- His Celestial father is the **Magician**, from whom he brings along the ability of creation.
- The meaning of his life, his true fate is kept secret by his celestial mother, in the guise of the **High Priestess**.
- At the time of his birth, his earthly mother the **Empress** and
- earthly father, the **Emperor** take care of him, like a small child is taken care of by solicitous parents
- When the time for learning has come, the **High Priest** will be his teacher, master.
- As his experience and knowledge grows, he becomes more and more separated from the parental house, and he himself takes the decisions, about which the **Lovers** card informs.
- He takes everything he received from his heavenly or earthly father and mother to start on the road, which is shown by the **Chariot** card.
- He gets to know his own innate strength, ego, which is represented by the **Strength** card.
- The knowledge and experience acquired on the way makes the hero wiser and wiser, which is depicted by the **Hermit** card.
- He experiences the variability of life, the twists and turns of once above – once below; of which the **Wheel of Fortune** speaks.
- Meanwhile, all his deeds and decisions are put on a scale, which the card of **Justice** shows.
- Slowly he learns to see the world from a different perspective, which is highlighted best by the **Hanged Man** card.
- His earthly roads end with the card of **Death, the Unnamed card**
- He gives account, in another dimension, for the acquired decisions and knowledge, which appear in the form of the **Temperance** card.
- He descends to Hell, the **Devil** card, in order to get rid of his ties.
- He flies up to Heaven to meet his own perfect being, his spirit, according to the **Star** card.
- He wavers between the two places, in order to escape the dangers of temptation, the **Tower**,
- from where a dark and difficult road, the **Moon,** leads him further

- towards the Light, through the card of **Sun**.
- At the end of his journey he has to give account again, according to the **Judgment** card
- and if he is found worthy, the Universe will be his reward by the **World** card, so he would set off again
- on the Great Journey, through the card of the **Fool**.

'It's never too late to be who you might have been.'
(George Eliot)

THE MAGICIAN

THE COMTE DE SAINT GERMAIN and ADAM

The Interpretation of the Picture

'The root of visible things is in the invisible.' On the first page of my tarot we find a Magician with exceptional qualities and abilities. He is an insider of such powers that make him a ruler over three worlds. He himself is the Beginning, the Creation and the Creative Force. The possessor of Power. A child matured into a man. His face is young and with his penetrating gaze we have the impression that he can almost look right into us, because the light emanates directly from his third eye. He wears a hat that seems to have the shape of the number eight which is the sign of infinity, i.e. the symbol of infinity of the cosmos, the cycle of things and the symbol of eternal life. The Magician's hand gestures are very important: with one hand he raises his wand towards heaven, with the other pointing to the ground, it is the symbol of 'as above, so below' magical principle. Confidence and determination characterise him; he himself is the youth that prepares to conquer the world. However, who can also act egoistic and if he chooses so can also misuse his power. This card is the card of willpower and initiation. Something new begins therefore adaptability and wisdom are very important. If the Magician appears upside down in a display, it indicates something unpleasant.

Number: I.
Letter: A
Main elements: Water, Fire, Air, Earth

Important Symbols Appear on the Card

A Cup: this symbolises the element of Water, it reflects the world of emotions
A Coin: this symbolises the element of Earth, indicates material things
A Sword: this symbolises the element of Air, refers to the world of spirit and thoughts
A Wand: this symbolises the element of Fire, it reflects life energy and sexual force

Furthermore, it is essential to notice that he holds up a wand with a serpent motif (the symbol of Hermes) with this pointing directly toward God's energy coming from above. In addition, the black and white chequered floor is important, which indicates that he is familiar with both positive and negative worlds. The serpent devouring its own tail, on the tablecloth, is an old Gnostic and alchemical symbol. This is the **Ouroboros**, which is the symbol of time, continuity, cyclicality and the unification of opposites.

Astrology: Sun, Venus, Mars, Jupiter, Saturn, Pisces, Aries, Leo, Taurus

Meditation: the Creative Force Meditation (CFM)

The possible meanings of the card in a display, if you picked this

Archetype: the Creator

Negative pole: Self-Destructive

Psychological Interpretation: the completion of the self, healthy confidence

Spiritual Interpretation: individual living in high spiritual consciousness

General Interpretation

It is time to act, now comes the time when your personal attractiveness increases and therefore you have to believe in your abilities and in your own seduction power. You must strive for balance and if you can achieve that inside you as well as outside, you will be irresistible and everybody will respond with love to the confidence emanating from you. You are able to create your own reality and the answers to your questions will appear shortly.

Interpretation of the Reversed Card

You are not capable to control your powers, everything is falling apart. You are watching your situation from a wrong point of view, and you have not realised yet what you are really capable of. Turn inward, calm down and find those forces within you, that you previously used incorrectly or have not used at all. Listen to your intuitions, because progress will start only when you achieve balance on all the three levels in your life (physical, mental and spiritual). Once you achieve this you can make your dreams and ideas come true.

Love Interpretation

First of all, if you are single, be prepared for a new period in your life that is about to begin, because the One meant for you is approaching. You have changed a lot recently and maybe you were about to give up the search. Finding true love is certainly not easy. However, now you are ready for it. On the other hand, in case you already have a partner it is high time to add new colours to your relationship. It would be definitely useful for both of you. Together you are now able to make a change. However, do not force anything. Instead, pay attention to yourself, to your sweetheart and concentrate on what your relationship has been lacking recently. The last period has pushed both of you into the routine a little. In order to make the magic reappear between you and strengthen the attraction, you should start something new together.

Material Interpretation

You have certain skills which you have not used yet. It is high time to bring forth those skills, because right now the entire Universe is supporting you in everything. Consequently, you may even find new sources of money. If you are already involved in something, it is possible that you only need to change your strategy and be right on the way to success.

Work

In case you are looking for a new job, or just want to test yourself in other fields you can go for it. The Magician's card shows that you are standing under strong protection and you may succeed in everything, if you work out the details properly. In addition, it is the best time to invest your money wisely or start a new business.

The Question of Study

This card indicates that a person may come into your life, from whom you can learn a lot, and who inspires you as well. Moreover, if you 'walk' on a spiritual path, you may encounter a new master too, because you are ready. It is an adequate period to invest more time in learning, maybe take on a new course.

Health Interpretation

If so far you have been sick, the card indicates that now you may find the most suitable therapy. The response for both physical and psychological problems is lying within us, the issue is not the disease itself. Look for connections, you will be surprised how easily everything can be solved, especially things you have experienced as difficulties. Last but not least, the card shows a good doctor, and in case of mental illness a good psychologist.

Family Interpretation

The Magician always refers to creation, in this case the adjacent cards will show whether you should expect for example the arrival of a new member of the family, a marriage or perhaps moving.
Task: The creation itself. You should start something new, try something different.

The Message of the Card

Now you are able to shape your life, the way you really want. A joyful, beautiful period is ahead of you, you are now capable to inspire others to stand by you and by your plans. If you take on some new studies, you will have the feeling that it is going so easily, as if you had always known this new area. You will solve your tasks easily, you will make good decisions and your initiative skills will be limitless. Trust yourself, you are capable to do everything and you can achieve anything.

Emotions

Sense of initiative, decision making, confidence, learning, exams, success

Stage of life:

Creation in any area of your life

About Saint Germain

As the son of Rákóczi, I deservedly put Saint Germain, a Hungarian (as well), on the Magician card. This exceptional man lived and worked as a real Magician.

To begin with, the Count was outstandingly educated and his great talent for languages was almost supernatural. He spoke German, English, Italian,

Portuguese, Spanish, French, Greek, Latin, Sanskrit, Arabic and Chinese, so fluently, that the inhabitants of those countries thought that life had brought a fellow countryman in their way. He was an excellent chemist and alchemist, who loved music and also sang beautifully, nonetheless he had a reputation of being a very good conversationalist. Even Madame de Pompadour was impressed by his incredible memory and by his stories, 'memories' dating back two thousand years, which he performed as if he himself had been a part of them. He knew the secrets of monarchs very well, often even better than the local secret services. Furthermore, he made good use of both hands i.e. used both hemispheres of the brain equally. This was proved by the fact that he wrote with both hands simultaneously: with one hand he was writing a love letter and mystic documents with the other one. According to his friends, thanks to his extraordinary telepathic sense, the Count sensed if he was needed somewhere and appeared there, just out of the blue, without even using the door. He was an excellent diplomat and patron, and his immeasurable riches were recorded everywhere. Around him mystery emerged, it was rumoured that he possessed the elixir of youth. Having black hair, slightly brown skin and with his continuous youthfulness (almost always looked 40 years old) ladies were constantly questioning him about the elixir. He never revealed his secret and always referred only to his diets, which, despite the luxurious royal dinners, consisted always of the usual oat flour, oatmeal served with chicken. His eyes were glittering magnetically day and night.

Most significantly, the source of his occult knowledge has been completely unknown, but one thing is certain, that he not only knew the theory of the most profound philosophy, but he also transferred it into practice. More than that, he was perfectly familiar with the principles of Eastern Esoterism, constantly practicing meditation and concentration. In conclusion, it is important to know, that Count Saint Germain created a famous and unrivalled manuscript, the *La Très Sainte Trinosophie*, which, for all students of Freemasonry and the occult sciences, is the most important work to be studied. This is one of the most valuable manuscripts that has ever summarised the Hermetic sciences

About Adam

According to the story of the Old Testament, Adam is the first man created by God in his own image, out of the dust of the earth. He himself is the first Magician. God placed Adam in the Garden of Eden and made him Master of the animal world. From his rib, God created Eve, the first woman, who became Adam's wife. Adam and Eve, in the Garden of Eden, transgressed God's command, according to which they had been forbidden to eat the apple offered by the serpent, consequently they were cast out of Paradise. In the Egyptian initiation system also a crawling serpent appears, which symbolises the tempter who entices man to even deeper physical ties. The twelve levels of initiation, however, are illustrated with a straightened snake. As this symbol reveals the Mistress of the Tree of Knowledge and Recognition.

In conclusion, according to Genesis, God created Adam in His own image. So, this means that man is the miniature image of God, and down here he is the ruler of things.

'Women can see even without looking there.'
(Jókai Mór)

The High Priestess

Saint Elisabeth and Eve/Lilith

She is the Magician's antagonist, generally passive and reclusive. The High Priestess sits calmly while the Magician stands. On her head she wears a tiara, in her hand she holds an open book or a scroll on which the alpha and omega symbols are written, referring to the mysterious power of recognition of the beginning and the end. In her other hand she holds the papal keys of Heaven and Hell (gold/silver, Sun key, Moon key). Behind her two columns stand, these are the two large, dark, bronze pillars of Jachin and Boaz, which used to stand in the porch of the temple in Jerusalem, and at the entrance of the Egyptian Hall of Justice (Hall of Ma'at). According to the Egyptians, after death the soul is weighed in the Hall of Justice. These columns are parallel to the tree of knowledge of good and evil. Similar to the Magician, the High Priestess' divine feminine side also includes the possibility of evil, bleakness, hatred and death. The High Priestess' expression is serious and inscrutable that alludes to mystery, her whole appearance radiates power. She is the one who makes just decisions calmly. This card is the symbol of Virtue, Prudence and Discernment.

Number: II.
Letter: B
Main element: Water
Astrology: Moon, Saturn, Taurus, Cancer
Meditation: internal intuition development
The possible meanings of the card in a display, if you picked this:
Archetype: the Virgin
Negative pole: The Whore
Psychological Interpretation: Balance, deep inner wisdom
Spiritual Interpretation: the culmination of a woman's intuition

General Interpretation

You have to direct your attention inward, toward the understanding of the images of the unconscious and soul. Keep a dream diary, soon you will need a deeper understanding of your dreams. If you work in the therapeutic or esoteric field, you can have even more powerful spiritual experiences and with patient sympathetic attitude you can help a lot of people who turn to you, now the healing activities are coming into prominence. Now you do not have to transmit and receive energy in the usual way, but in a slightly modified way, intensely focusing on your intuitions. You must carefully observe the deeper meanings of things as well, that are hidden below 'the surface'. Listen to your instincts, deep inside yourself you already know the answers to your questions. Do not analyse too much, do not let your emotions take over, momentarily only your internal instincts can help you to see clearly.

Interpretation of the Reversed Card

You are confused. The information that is reaching you is not coming from clean sources. Momentarily you are quite weak to just rely on your instincts, because you are quite thrown out of balance. First of all, reveal your inner female strength, it helps restore the order within you, i.e. Harmony. Beware, now things are not what they seem. Until you reconcile with yourself, do not make decisions, because the outcome will be completely different from what you expect.

Love Interpretation

This period does not favour major decisions, you should rather recede into the background to observe and wait. The cards next to this one can help you decide whether a third person has entered in your relationship or you are just in a rough patch. At the moment, in both cases, it is wise to wait out patiently until the truth comes out. If you have met someone recently, do not reveal your cards just yet, because there is a big chance for you to become a toy. If you can still continue to behave mysteriously, then a deep mutual trust may develop between you and the right person. However, take one step at a time. Pay attention to your dreams and your inner intuition, you may obtain some valuable insights.

Material Interpretation

The High Priestess urges on precaution, do not engage in anything abruptly. You should not have permanent plans and expectations. Let things follow their own course, and time will bring the expected solution.

Work

For the moment do not change jobs, and don not want to start a private business either. Wait! Do not disclose your plans to anybody, because they may turn out exactly the opposite! If you are patient, opportunities themselves will come to you.

The Question of Study

Read a lot like the High Priestess! Let books unfold a world which you had thought to be mysterious. Your intuition will evolve and you may be richer with unforgettable experiences. The exams can be successful, but do not cheat because you will get caught immediately. The High Priestess knows and respects the law.

Health Interpretation

Recovery is near. A new therapy and a new healer can help you.

Family Interpretation

If you wish to have children, this is the right time for conception. However, this also has to be treated with discretion, do not let everybody know. On the other hand, if you do not plan to have a baby, you should be very careful, because now you can remain pregnant easily.
Task: You have to trust yourself and your intuition. You can gain deep spiritual experiences, if you let your inner voice guide you. Only this way you can find the right places and people.

The Message of the Card

This card alludes to precaution and patience in every aspects of your life. For this you do not have to become passive, you just need to follow your inner intuition. In case you have any new ideas, write them down, but do not start the implementation right then. Rather, listen to your dreams, your thoughts, your subsequent periods will be very meaningful and productive.

Emotions: expectancy, reception, precaution
Stage of life: introspection, fertility, conception

Personalities illustrated on the card: St Elizabeth of the House of Árpád and Eve/Lilith

Saint Elizabeth of the House of Árpád (1207-1231)

She was a younger contemporary of Saint Francis.

She was the daughter of King Andrew II and Gertrude of Meran. By the time Elizabeth was four years old, she had already been engaged to the prospective Count of Thuringia, Louis, who later got fond of her very quickly. But her mother-in-law did not like Elizabeth's habits, she considered her religious practices exaggerated, so she did everything to make her life difficult. Her marriage with Louis proved to be harmonious and happy and her husband accepted the fact, that he possessed her heart together with God. It was because Elizabeth was able to create a perfect harmony between her love for God and the love for her husband. In 1227, Louis launched a crusade but on the way, he became ill and died. At that point, Elizabeth's world collapsed, she lost the man she deeply loved. This tragedy gave her the opportunity to follow the desire of her heart: the Franciscan poverty, therefore she left the castle along with her children. She went to a Franciscan monk, Conrad, in Marburg, whom she asked to guide her soul. Conrad lived in absolute poverty and asceticism, and being a very strict spiritual leader, he often whipped Elizabeth, compelling her to renounce on everything that was dear to her. She entrusted her children in the care of educators, because she admitted that she could not take care of them and serve God at the same time and wearing the grey habit Franciscan Order, she kept serving as a nurse in Marburg. Numerous legends are connected to Elizabeth and mostly she is portrayed with roses in her apron and basket. The origin of this lies in the story, according to which, after the death of Elizabeth's husband, she continued to care for the poor. On one occasion, while she was carrying bread for those in need, she met her brother-in-law, Henry. To the question as to what was she carrying in her basket, Elizabeth answered: roses, as she was afraid that she might be prohibited doing further charity. When she showed the content of her basket, instead of bread there were fragrant roses – as God did not want this holy woman to lie. Elizabeth's very deep intuitions were famous as well, she foretold the date of her death three days earlier. At her grave, several miraculous healings have taken place, to this day people who wish to be cured visit the place. Pope Gregory IX canonised her in 1235.

The reason St Elizabeth appears on the High Priestess card, is because although she was a Franciscan and gave up the earthly possessions, all her life she helped with advice and food for the poor and everyone who turned to her, while she was always listening to her inner voice. Last but not least at her grave even to this day miraculous healings occur.

Eve/Lilith

She is Adam's mate, the companion whom God created at the request of Adam. God cast a dream on Adam and while he was asleep, He took out Adam's rib and created Eve. Her name means Life. According to the Bible, the serpent approached and tempted Eve to eat of the tree of Knowledge, along with Adam, although it was forbidden, thus Eve took Adam into the Fall. Therefore, later Adam blamed Eve, while Eve blamed the serpent. However, at a closer and deeper look, we will see that in the Bible it is not revealed that the serpent was Satan. It is rather noticeable that Adam and Eve resembled to today's man and woman, but at that particular level where they lived, they could not stay much longer, they needed development and experience. So Adam later became an insider, whose partner, Eve also possessed magical powers. She was the female side, that is, God's female side, because God created her in His own image as well. Adam is the Magician, whereas Eve is the High Priestess, who on one hand defends and protects the fundamental female and family values. On the other hand, Love, Beauty, Pleasure, Harmony, the Invisible Forces and the Life Force reach completion in her. We all know that if a real, complete woman does not stand beside a man, his life cannot be whole, cannot be complete, because it would miss the woman part i.e....Eve. Therefore, Eve is the Eternal Woman always standing beside and completing the man, she helps him with her intuition and visions, protects the family, on the other hand she is also a powerful Lady Magician who gives sage advice to those who turn to her.

However, the story of Adam and Lilith is an ancient Hebrew myth. According to this, Lilith was Adam's first mate, his partner, whom God created from soil as well, just like He created Adam. Soon they started to quarrel, because Lilith did not want to be under Adam, to be inferior to him. He did not want to be inferior either, he wanted to be much rather above, superior, because he argued that the woman deserves to stay at the bottom, and he above. The woman claimed that the two of them were the same, equal, because they had been both created from dirt, thus they started to fight and did not listen to each other. That moment Lilith uttered God's special name and rose into the air. Consequently Adam, the man, cried out to his Creator, to complain that the woman whom He gave, had left. Therefore, the Almighty sent three angels to bring her back. But he told Adam that if she came back, the order would be restored, but if not, then a hundred of their sons would die every day. The angels reached her in the depths of the great water, in which the Egyptians drowned. They told her the words of God. Lilith did not wish to return, saying that she (also) was created to take babies away. Since then mothers are scared of Lilith, they worry for their infants and would surround the babies with talismans, amulets and so on.

Lilith has blue eyes, and she is absolutely breath-taking. Her most important role is to show us how to convert our inactive, frustrated aggression into active, productive, creative energy. Lilith is thus the personification of knowledge and at the same time a metaphysical symbol, and lastly, she is the Great Temptress, the Great Whore, but the Holy Whore also, the priestess of the Great Goddess.

The apple was the symbol of the forbidden knowledge, forbidden love and the symbol of initiation for the medieval mystics. In numerous mythological writings it can be read that the apple is the symbol of immortality. Last but not least, it is also a popular heraldic symbol on coats of arms.

A Few Interesting Facts: Johanna, the Female Pope

I have always been interested in why the examination of gender for popes was introduced. Although it has not the value of a breaking news, it is interesting to know, that prior to initiation, it is mandatory to prove that the Pope is not a woman, but a man. Because it is certain that there was once a female pope, who was believed to be a man. Despite countless evidence, in the Church it has been a subject of debate as to whether there was a woman, known as Johanna leading the Church from 855 on, under the name of Pope John VIII.

The story says that there was a woman originally named Agnes, born in Mainz, a highly educated woman. She disguised herself as a man, was elected Pope, and held this title for more than two years. Of this particular case you can read in many historical chronicles, writings, and the oral tradition also states that in the ninth century a pope lived who was a woman. Her secret might have never been unveiled, had she not fallen in love with one of her counsellors, from who she even had a baby, according to the story. Some say she died during childbirth, others that she was exiled to a monastery when it was discovered that she was a woman. Johanna had been dealt with in the synod of Konstanz as well, in 1415, then for years, a statue could be seen in the Cathedral of Siena, between the busts of the popes, with this epigraph. 'Pope John the VIII, a woman from England'. About this unusual case countless films, books and plays have been made, many women look up to Johanna even today, a person who was not afraid to prevail just because she was born a woman.

'The beauty in a woman is not in the clothes she wears, the figure that she carries, or the way she combs her hair. The beauty of a lady is seen in her eyes, because that is the doorway to her heart; the place where love resides.' (Audrey Hepburn)

The Empress

Queen Elisabeth and the Queen of Sheba

The Empress embodies the Real Woman, standing firm, she is a loving and gentle woman with inner beauty. She herself is the symbol of fertility, shown on this card as pregnant. Dressed in a red royal gown, with a jewelled crown on her head, she sits proudly on her throne. She emanates goodness, purity, inner peace and love. Her radiation is emphasised by the approaching motherhood charm and confidence while an incredible tranquillity is reflected on her beautiful face. Nature revives around her, because she is the one who makes everything bloom. She is surrounded by Wealth and Abundance. She herself is the queen that is hiding in every woman's personality, waiting to be finally discovered.

Number: III
Letter: G
Main elements: Earth and Air

Important Symbols Appear on the Card

Half-moon: this indicates the alternation of the lunar cycle.
The three doves: refer to deep, pure love

In one hand, instead of a sceptre, she holds a lily, which is the symbol of purity and innocence, but also the symbol of fertility, transience, spiritual love, unity and hope.

Heart-shaped shield: the shield is one of the oldest information-bearer for humanity. Symbolic meanings: safety, strength, immortality, duty, loyalty. In this card it refers to love. Long ago only the coats of arms of kings, nobles, countries and authorities could appear on the shield, because throughout history, the shape of the shield was always related to things of great importance. Even today, there are some people, who are allowed to expose their decorated shield with their own coats of arms on it, in the city's distinguished place. Consequently, with this, they obtain a special place in local public awareness.

Astrology: Venus, Jupiter, Gemini and Virgo
Meditation: inner female harmony – meditation

The possible meanings of the card in a display, if you picked this

Archetype: the Mother
Negative pole: the Martyr
Psychological Interpretation: becoming uppercase Woman
Spiritual Interpretation: devotion, love

General Interpretation

This card promises total renewal and fulfilment for you. Your emotional life is being renewed and is leading you towards fulfilment. You can experience your feminine side; moreover, you are happy to realise, that through your appearance, your healthy optimism and confidence, you have a great influence on those around you. It is possible that the family will grow with a new member, or a new, creative period is beginning in your life.

Reversed Interpretation

You are unsure, something is missing from your home/environment. Perhaps infertility is also present in your life. Your creative power is reduced. Devote more attention to your family, to the roots of your family, because the key to the solution lies in this.

Identify your feelings related to family and home and bring them to surface.

Love Interpretation

If you have a partner, the next period will be fantastic for you, because your sweetheart's adoration will make you fly up to the sky. If you do not want a child, you must be careful, because the card of fertility also indicates a growing possibility of having a child. If you are single, then the Real Love is approaching, so keep your eyes open, but do not wish to be in love at all costs. Be patient, as you are going to experience how it feels to be complete, in love, no later than August.

Material Interpretation

Your efforts are going to bring the desired results, from financial point of view an increase can be expected.

Work

If you have a job, you can expect to get a promotion and a wage raise. If not, within three months you will find that particular job which you have been dreaming of for quite a while. However, one thing is certain, financially speaking, you are going to stand better.

The Question of Study

You are going to complete your studies with successful exams if you have been preparing constantly and if you have helped others too.

Health Interpretation

In case of illness it would be worth visiting a senior female doctor or therapist, who, with her experience and sensitivity, may help you trust in recovery and/or yourself again.

Family Interpretation

The arrival of a new family member can be expected, either as a child, or in the form of a new relationship. Whoever is coming, you have been waiting for his/her arrival for a long time, therefore you are going to welcome them with love and they will be real blessings in your life.

Task

You must see life in a more mature way, perhaps you need to become a mother or a grandmother.

The Message of the Card

Be wiser and more moderate. This card is the card of devotion, you must learn to give and also to accept selflessly. Be careful, do not fall over to the other side of the horse, avoid becoming a martyr!

Emotions: love, dedication and generosity
Stage of life: fulfilment, maturation, being a mother

Personalities Illustrated on the Card: Sissy and the Queen of Sheba

Queen Elisabeth, Sissy

In my view, there is no man out there, who does not know the story of Sissy, because a lot of adaptations have been published already: books, movies and tales. Something has been produced about the life of Queen Elisabeth for almost all age groups. There is nothing surprising in this, since Sissy, the 'Queen of the Hungarians', has still been alive in the heart of many people. This is why I have chosen this mysterious and beautiful Woman to be on the card of the Empress. Her life was eventful, a life filled with deep emotions and a real woman's secrets.

The mesmerising, beautiful Sissy was born with an already-grown tooth, just like the Táltos (shamans); people with supernatural power in Hungarian folk beliefs. The Táltos (shamans) mission is a task received from God, that is to save the world or a nation. Consequently, perhaps it is less surprising that, besides several Hungarian politicians, we owe Sissy the founding of the Austro-Hungarian Empire. This exceptionally beautiful woman with her unique sense knew how to impress her husband and she did a great deal to press the monarch to forgive the Hungarians. All this lasted only four years, but in the end, Sissy became the crowned queen of the Hungarians. It was then, when she received her favourite castle of Gödöllő as a gift from the Hungarian people.

Sissy received the name Elisabeth Amalie Eugenie, but among family members she was simply called Sissy. A name that later imprinted in the public mind as well. In 1853 she accompanied her sister to Austria, because her sister was the Austrian Emperor Franz Joseph I's future betrothed. However, at the meeting, the young monarch fell in love with the fifteen-year-old Sissy instead of the designated bride. It was an encounter of destiny, a love at first sight, sealing the fate of empires. Within the Habsburg dynasty, this was highly unusual, since no one could conclude a marriage out of love, but Franz Joseph persisted with his decision, and within a year, he married that charming girl in Vienna. From then on, the fairy-tale princess found herself in a world where the externals and the origin were the most important. Maybe only at this point, her lifelong vanity can be understood for which she was criticised later by a lot of people: in some books we can actually read about a vain, self-centred woman, whose main objective was to preserve her 50-inch waist. By the way it was perfectly understandable in case of a young woman, especially an empress, because in that era, few people cared about their figure or their looks. Although the Viennese court put lots of emphasis on the externals, all that was very far from what Sissy believed in: the etiquette seemed strange, the rules ridiculous and unnecessary. Thus, the young woman could never comply with her mother-in-law or with one of Europe's most conservative court and later she did not even want to.

She and her husband could spend less and less time together, because Franz Joseph was seized in the affairs of the state. However, she more often met her constantly criticising mother-in-law, of whom she was more and more terrified. Their conflict, the Sophia-Elisabeth conflict, determined the later life of the Empress. Additionally, her loneliness was increased by hostile behaviours, her health was weakened by the fact that within four years she gave birth to three children. Moreover, Sophia almost 'immediately' took the children away from her, and appointed the children's room next to her own suite, far away from their mother's; Sissy was not allowed to get involved in her children's upbringing. However much the beautiful queen admired her beloved husband, the numerous negative experiences drifted them further and further apart.

Franz Joseph did not understand Sissy's sufferings, could not comprehend why his wife did not like the Burg and the imperial magnificence, why it was not enough for her that she could be the Empress of Austria. He himself was completely happy, and after the birth of the little heir to the throne, the emperor felt his marriage had been fulfilled. He did not understand why all of this was not enough for his wife. He continued to adore Sissy, but all his efforts to please her were in vain. Since he never liked family conflicts, he did not care about the duel between his loved ones either, therefore he never took Sissy's side openly.

In 1857, with the occasion of traveling to Hungary, Sissy insisted upon taking little Sophia with her. In Buda the child, however, became seriously ill and a few days later died of dysentery. Due to this horrible experience, Sissy almost gave up the education of her children. She blamed herself for the death of the little one and considered herself a bad mother for the rest of her life. Due to her deteriorated mental state, she soon became seriously ill and on the advice of her physicians, she went to Madeira for several months. Here she closely befriended with a Hungarian brother and sister, Count Imre Hunyadi and his sister, Lili, from whom she learnt a little Hungarian. This experience led to the fact that later she hired a Hungarian teacher, and learnt the Hungarian language perfectly. She met Ida Ferenczy also, who became her Hungarian lady companion and with whom she remained true friends until the end of their lives. Ida told her first about for the suffering Hungarian people, about their history and the Hungarian landscapes. She was the one who planted the wish in Elizabeth to become the Queen of Hungary. The years spent away from Austria had been beneficial: she became mature and changed to be determined and self-conscious. Moreover, she became aware of her beauty and the inherent power, and learned to enforce her will as well. She realised that she was the first lady of the empire, therefore her will is well over Sophia's will, and she was prepared to stand her ground.

She met Count Andrassy for the first time in the Marble Hall of the Burg, at the reception organised for the Hungarian diplomatic delegation. Their meeting was a historical encounter. This moment was not about rank and wealth, nor diplomacy. It was like a lightning strike. In the life of Sissy, the Count was love at first sight also, just like Franz Joseph before.

Sissy, out of her sincere love for the Hungarian people and by this new, special love, founded the Austro-Hungarian Empire together with the Count and became the Hungarians' much-adored queen. The country's gift for her was the Grassalkovich Castle of Gödöllő. This place later became the Queen's true home, besides Corfu.

On the 22nd of April 1868, her favourite child was born, with the name of Archduchess Marie Valerie, who was mocked as the 'Hungarian child' at the Viennese court. Because by that time, rumours had already been spread, hinting that there was a romantic relationship between Sissy and Andrássy. Until today, the love relationship has still been a matter of debate, however, one thing is certain that, for the first time after 328 years, a Hungarian monarch's child was born under Hungarian sky.

Sissy was not allowed to raise Sophia, she could raise neither Giselle nor Rudolph, but on this occasion, she informed the Emperor, with a forceful voice, 'I want to have absolute power in all things, as far as my child is concerned.' Therefore, Marie Valerie grew up in Gödöllő and at the beginning she was speaking only in Hungarian.

After years spent happily, her son, crown prince Rudolf died in 1889, and Count Andrássy in 1890. Sissy was devastated by the losses, and she wore only black. She tried to ease her pain with a lot of travelling, and returned to Hungary less and less often.

She died under tragic circumstances, on the 10th of September 1898, being a guest in the Beau Rivage Hotel in Geneva, which is considered an aristocratic place even today. The owner's grandmother witnessed the fact that Sissy, who was traveling incognito, was stabbed through the heart by an Italian anarchist. The empress did not know what happened to her, because she did not realise that she had been stabbed. At the beginning, due to her tight corset, she felt no pain. She was bleeding to death slowly and quietly, within two and a half hours. Simultaneously with her death, the myth of Sissy was born, which perhaps is stronger today than ever before. In Geneva, there is a statue that guards the memory of the beloved queen of the Hungarians.

At the card of the Lovers, more details can be read about the much-disputed love story between the Queen and the Count.

The Queen of Sheba

Another determining character on the card is a mysterious and beautiful woman, known as the Queen of Sheba, who appears in the Old Testament and in the First Book of Kings as well.

The legendary queen of Sheba was considered a mythical figure for a long time, but a group of American archaeologists insist that they have found her palace. In the palace, her name can be seen carved in stone in several places.

Following the instructions of an Arab chronicle, researchers have found the place where the queen, that is Bilkis killed somebody, in order to regain her throne. Bilkis was the only child and first counsellor of her father, King Hadhad ben Sarh. When her father died, a distant relative emerged victorious from the struggle fought for the throne. The courtiers supported him, and made the people do the same. However, he could not enjoy his popularity for long, because the reputation of his cruelty soon spread and also many people became aware, that the new ruler would do anything for a beautiful woman. Bilkis recognised that the king's bad qualities played right into her hands. Thus, she approached the king, who joyfully welcomed the beautiful girl in his bed. Bilkis made him drunk and stabbed him on their wedding night. The next day – according to the chronicle – the people acknowledged Bilkis as their queen. This is how Bilkis became the beautiful queen of one of the greatest powers of the first millennium BC, and her people's saviour.

However, many Yemenis believe even today, that Queen Bilkis was a Witch also, because she served the chief Sabean god, Ilumkuh. In her quality as Priestess, the queen possessed magical powers too. This included the ability of divination as well. Legends about the Queen's thousand-year revenge have been known in Europe as well; just like the rumours around the death of some English expedition members who were exploring the tomb of the pharaoh Tutankhamen; the mystery-loving people were also eager to spread rumours about the former grand dame of Sheba as well, according to which the already long pulverulent queen has still been killing, long after her death. The Arabic workers who feared the beautiful woman's curse, tried to get rid of the Americans, but they insisted that this place was one of the largest existing archaeological treasure troves in the world, and the monumental circular temple, built in honour of the pre-Islamic Moon-god Ilumkuh, is an almost completely unique construction. The wealth of the Sabean people was indeed unimaginably great. In wealth and wasteful lifestyle these people not only surpassed the neighbouring tribes, but other people as well. They had countless gold and silver drinking vessels, their rooms were held by a mass of gilded columns, and the main pillars were decorated with silver figurines. Ceilings and doors of their houses were divided by shield-shaped indentations, which were jewelled or gilded. Furthermore, the house furnishings were also admirably valuable: partly made of silver and gold, and partly of ivory and precious stones. These people, actually, found joy in splendour. They believed the earthly riches were an honouring gift from the gods and that they were praising the gods by showing the riches to others.

According to the biblical story, the Queen of Sheba, hearing about the wisdom and manfulness of the King of Israel called Solomon, she almost immediately travelled to him, fuelled by her inner curiosity. With chariots richly loaded with herbs, spices and gold, and with full glory of her beauty, she arrived at Solomon's court, where she spent a lot of time. Among other things she tested the King with riddles and questions, because his intelligence, magical powers and wonderful stories impressed the queen. In addition to his wealth, Solomon had a big influence on her as a man; that is why she was practically unable to return home immediately. At her arrival, she gave plenty of gifts to the king: gold, spices and gems, therefore later, when she was leaving, Solomon lavished her with lots of special things, thus the Queen of Sheba returned home laden with special presents. (At that time, the Sabean people traded with the things that the whole world was in dire need of: their caravans transported frankincense and myrrh to distant lands).

In 1320, an Ethiopian monk named Yetshak wrote a compendium of legends entitled 'Glory of the Kings'. It is written in it, that when the Queen of Sheba – referred to as Makeda in Ethiopian – visited Solomon, the great king was completely under the effect of this beautiful woman and decided to seduce her. A man accustomed to reign, said to her that she was very welcome, but must not touch anything without asking. During the night, the beautiful lady suffered a terrible thirst caused by the spicy meal Solomon had fed her and she drank from the water carafe placed by her bed. Thus, she broke the rule. The next day, the king summoned her in his bed, telling the punishment: she must sleep with him as repayment. Most likely the Queen did not protest for long.... According to the legend, the next morning Solomon gave her a ring and let her on her way with these words: "If my successor should have conceived in you, this shall be his/her sign. If it is a boy, tell him to come and see me."

The Ethiopians believe King Solomon got the Queen of Sheba pregnant right that night, and a son was born soon. The prince was named Menelik, i.e. the son of the wise. From then on, the Ethiopian caravans were able to cross Israel smoothly and Solomon's ship could anchor at the southern Arabian coasts to purchase water and load the shipments of the Ethiopians. Evidently, Solomon ensured free passage through his country for the caravans of Sheba.

At the age of 20, Menelik travelled to Jerusalem to meet his father and his court. Solomon's priests were not thrilled with the encounter and demanded him to return home to his own people as soon as possible. Solomon finally succumbed to the jealous claim, but let Menelik home only with the condition that the first-born son of each elder (temple priest) shall accompany his son to his mother's kingdom. According to the legends, it was then when King Solomon handed over the famous Ark of the Covenant secretly to his son, the first ruler of the Ethiopians.

This story has been equally inspiring the Christian cultural area, the Turkish and Persian art, and is also one of the first love stories of the world.

***'When a man is that special, you know it sooner than you think possible. You recognise it instinctively, and you're certain that no matter what happens, there will never be another one like him.'* (Nicholas Sparks)**

The Emperor

Franz Joseph and King Solomon

The Interpretation of the Picture

He is the consort of the Empress. He is the possessor of the outward and visible power, who has already entered manhood and is getting ready for fatherhood and who is also aware of his own responsibility. He wishes to protect and guard his loved ones, protect his people, because it is very important to him that besides his family, his subjects too can live contentedly and in safety. He is surrounded by respect that is rightfully his as a Ruler, his noble face is motionless. Only a few people can tolerate his penetrating gaze without being obliged to cast down their eyes in front of him. This huge power radiating from his eyes is the power of love and wisdom. He sees and understands everything. The Emperor has arrived with the mission to guide people in their earthly lives, therefore he dedicates his entire life to this task of showing how a country should be governed so that all of its inhabitants would evolve happily. Meanwhile, he is also well aware of the fact that he should never abuse his own power.

Number: IV
Letter: D
Main element: Earth
Astrology: Jupiter, Mars, Venus, Taurus, Aries
Meditation: Conscious Creation

Important Symbols appear on the Card

The Emperor's royal blue dress shows that he is no longer controlled only by his ego and the red colour of his mantle symbolises the active male strength. His figure indicates earthly power, the laws of nature and society.

Sceptre: The Emperor holds the orb in his left hand and the sceptre in his right hand. These are the symbols of the royal power and fire, which also refer to the fact that the Emperor dominates the forces of Heaven and Earth. The sceptre is the symbol of judgment, justice and the service of justice, so it is an ancient insignia of power. It is the oldest remaining essentially unchanged piece of crown jewel sets and was brought to Europe from Egypt. Egyptian initiates knew it as the wand of life and attributed magical power to it. The wand was taught to lead on that force which the initiate channels inward, therefore the wand used to symbolise the power over all forces of nature. Subsequently also this sceptre held in hand symbolically confirmed the ruler's power. (The crystal ball itself could have originally been the sceptre's top).

The crown: From the beginning of the first millennium, the coronation became the most important moment at the inauguration of monarchs and among the rulers' symbols the crown has become the most important one. In England, in 1176 the king had already ordered the judges to enforce his rights, which were also the crown's rights. In France, a document dating from 1190 stated that the city of Amiens could not be alienated from the Crown. To this day the Holy Crown of Hungary has been one of Europe's oldest and entirely preserved initiatory crown. According to the historical tradition, on the 15th of August 1038, on the day of the Assumption of Mary, the Hungarian King Stephen I offered Hungary to the Virgin Mary symbolising the country with the Holy Crown. Accordingly, for centuries it has been perceived as the crown of Saint Stephen, still known so nowadays in many places. The Crown of Charles the Great was the ancient inauguration (coronation) crown for the Frankish kings and later for the kings of France. The crown is a strong symbol of power. Thus, on the Emperor's head there is a huge, jewelled crown.

Above the Emperor's head a part of the sun disk is visible, which ensures the life-giving energy. You can also see an eagle indicating the Emperor's reign. His throne demonstrates his massive, mighty solidity. On the Emperor's card fiery, strong colours dominate, whereas pastel colours cover the card of the Empress. The two of them are the Magician and the High Priestess' mature form of parenthood.

The card's meaning in a spread, if you picked this

Archetype: the Father

Negative pole: the Egocentric (Egoist)

Psychological Interpretation: becoming uppercase Man

Spiritual Interpretation: healthy self-consciousness, self-confidence, self-awareness

General Interpretation

Now you will get the chance to understand the context of your life. Because you have reached a period in which you must settle your life. You must learn to create safely in order to achieve harmony. At present, it is important for you to listen to your mind when making decisions, rather than to your heart. Clarify your relationships, make sure you place them on proper 'foundation' and although you have to decide with your mind, listen also to what your inner voice is telling. If you succeed to make your life perspicuous, your dreams may come true and your relationships would also strengthen. This card also shows a supporter, a well-wisher. Therefore, within three months a mentor may enter in your life, who can help you most effectively if you have already learned to control yourself. On the whole, it is crucial for you to accept his or her help because the card also warns that you cannot complete the changes in the following period alone.

Reversed Interpretation

The reversed card indicates assertive difficulties. Control has slipped out of your hands, you have lost your powers. It is important to feel safe again, because you can solve the problems only if you get this balance back. Think everything through carefully, analyse situations before you make decisions. You must learn to control your life correctly. The card can mean temporary poverty, in material, psychological and spiritual sense as well. In order to recover from this, you need to reconnect with your old self-confidence and also to take responsibility for your actions.

Love Interpretation

In terms of relationship, stability can be expected. Old desires may reappear, desires from which you have to choose the one that can be attained and focus on it. During an intimate dinner answers may come up to questions such like 'where to?' and 'how?'.

Material Interpretation

The Emperor indicates stability and predictability in financial issues also. This however does not mean that everything is falling into your lap, but in the long run, you will not complain. Thanks to your persistent work.

Work

Here also concentration and self-discipline are coming into focus. The period of action is greeting you. Your achievable plans are going to be attained now, thanks to your discipline and persistence. Do not let the control slip out of your hands, but always analyse the situation before you make a decision. It is possible that the mentor who can help you will find you at your workplace. Finally, if you are looking for a job, now you have the chance to prove successfully to your employer that you're the most suitable person for the position.

The Question of Study

You obtain great results only through hard, diligent work. There is nothing else left, but to set up the order of priority and learn persistently.

Health Interpretation

For your recovery you need to do the following: change your lifestyle and adhere strictly to medical regulations. If you consistently pay attention to yourself, the healing process will start quickly.

Family Interpretation

This card indicates our own father, who is our protector and the creator of the family rules as well. If your father was/is highly present in your life, then the card refers to that authority which he has achieved for himself in life. If he was not present or was just a negative example, then it indicates that you must unlock the paternal blocks to let the traditional male pattern fully take their place. If you do this you will be able to attract such friends, advisors and maybe a partner, who is reliable, enjoys public recognition and will ensure a real protection for you.

Task

Now it is time to take more responsibility. (become a husband, a father)

The Message of the Card

Be disciplined and persistent. Never forget that the measure of intelligence is nothing more than self-control.

Emotions: vitality, strength, discipline
Stage of life: stability, being/becoming a father, fatherhood

Personalities illustrated on the card: Franz Joseph and King Solomon

Franz Joseph emperor and Hungarian king

(18th of August 1830 Vienna – 21st of November 1916 Vienna)

Franz Joseph's reign has great importance in both Hungarian and world history. A whole library could be filled with literature only about his reign, therefore here I shall mention only some facts about him briefly. Franz Joseph's upbringing was hugely determinant as far as his long life and reign were considered. His very close relationship with his mother, the Archduchess Sophia had a decisive influence on his youth. The teachers chosen by her mother, people serving as role models (especially soldiers) had an impact throughout his later life. He came to the throne at the age of only 18, in one of the most difficult periods, during the precarious political situation of the 1848 revolutions. With Russian help, he suppressed the Hungarian Revolution, which, due to his upbringing, he perceived as a rebellion of a rebellious nation against its ruler and then he took part in its brutal reprisal. Due to the influence of his wife, Sissy, he later eased many punishments and then declared amnesty. In 1867 with the Compromise, the dualist Monarchy was established wherein Austria and Hungary received equal rank. This triggered the displeasure of the nationalities in the Balkans, because in this way the influence of Hungary increased significantly within the Empire. With the occasion of the Hungarian coronation on the 8th of June 1867, the ruling couple received the Gödöllő Castle and the surrounding estates as gifts from the nation. From then on, horse races and hunting were organised, then, according to the English model, coursing was also organised, for which the most important representatives of the Hungarian aristocracy were invited. In 2014, the exhibition of the Royal Palace of Gödöllő was about Franz Joseph's life, but it only showed a few phases of his life, emphasising the relationship between the king and Hungary. The assembly from contemporary press, recollections and personal letters presented the monarch as a person. It highlighted the values which the Emperor considered important, emphasising the fact that in order to preserve and strengthen his royal status, Franz Joseph considered it fundamental to maintain traditions and representation. As a king, he carried on Maecenic activities from his own fortune.

Because of his son's death, the heir of Franz Joseph was his nephew, Franz Ferdinand who was killed by a Serbian nationalist, Gavrilo Princip in Sarajevo in 1914. Franz Joseph, who had the army as his main support all through his life, declared war on Serbia. The old monarch, who entered the war with Serbia as a protector of his country and his family, did not suspect that with this decision he would start the First World War.

Sissy and Franz Joseph

In 1853, Elisabeth accompanied her mother and her sister, Princess Helene to Bad Ischl, in order to meet their cousin, Emperor Franz Joseph, who wanted to marry Princess Helene. However, the prince saw his little princess in Elizabeth; and this was certainly love at first sight. So it happened that instead of the already chosen girl, he chose Princess Elizabeth. Sissy – as Elizabeth was named within the family circle – immediately became the queen of the handsome prince's heart. The groom did not hide his deep love under a bushel not even for a moment, even in spite of the consternation of the imperial court and the Bavarian family. Sissy was considered an ugly duckling compared to her shining sister, she had not received as thorough an education as Helene. Sophie tried to dissuade his son, but although Franz Joseph followed the rules imposed by his mother, this time he did not give in and he chose Sissy.

Therefore on 24th of April 1854, a true love-match took place between Franz Joseph and Elisabeth Wittelsbach. However, after the wonderful wedding everyday life began soon. They spent very little time together, the man was busy with politics, thus Sissy felt more and more desolate in the royal court, where everyone was just watching when and how she would make a mistake. The detachment from her husband really began when her children were taken away from her, and Franz Joseph was not sticking up for her, because he did not want to interfere in his mother and wife's discussions. The situation became even more burdening when they lost little Sophia and Sissy blaming herself plunged deeper and deeper into depression. Then, at the advice of her doctors, she began to travel and became less and less involved in the Viennese court and her husband's life.

At the same time, during a morning walk, the lonely Franz Joseph met Anna, who became the Emperor's secret mistress for more than a decade. She was followed by actress Katharina Schratt, who was rumoured to be recommended for her husband directly by Sissy, so he would not be so lonely. Franz Joseph lost his wife and their true love quickly. Although he loved Sissy with adoration, he could never actually understand her and he never really stood up for her either. Later the family was struck by a series of tragedies. They lost their firstborn daughter, the heir to the throne committed suicide and there was an assassination against Sissy in Geneva, in which she lost her live. The losses made the Emperor deeply depressed, thus he devoted himself exclusively to politics until death.

Franz Joseph was chosen on the Emperor card because of the true love he felt for Sissy, as a warning to say: we always have to stand up for our beloved spouse, our partner, we should pay attention to how they feel, what they are going through and if they are really important to us, we really must become a part of their life. In conclusion, this man is present on this card as an admonitory example, who had a tremendous power, but lost everything because he did not stand up as a real Ruler for his family and his love.

King Solomon

The King of Kings, the Wise of the Wise

'The world can exist only through secret' (Sefer ha-Zohar)

Everyone has already heard more or less about King Solomon. To this day, he has been the paragon of the wise and righteous ruler, who was also one of the great figures of the Old Testament. His father, David, himself appointed him as his successor, at his mother, Bathsheba's, request. Since David's firstborn son could not take the throne because of the putsch (he had already proclaimed himself king during the reign of King David) therefore King David's loyal leaders also supported him in making Solomon his successor. The four-decade reign of King Solomon was the zenith of the Jewish kingdom.

While he settled accounts with his father's opponents, as David had instructed him as his last will, one night he had a strange dream: a dream in which the Lord appeared to him and asked what it is that he wanted the most. Solomon did not think much about the answer, he asked to be able to distinguish good from bad. According to the story, thus Solomon received the gift of clairvoyance, in addition to amazing power and wealth. Contemporary locals respected him for being the one who understands the language of trees, wild animals and birds, for being a song performer, a solver of riddles and puzzles. Solomon's wise judgments were widespread and became proverbial among the surrounding nations. The stories introducing him are about his royal, governing, foreign policy and economic manager abilities and actions, his administration and about individual cases of his evaluative just decisions.

Solomon however was considered primarily a wise judge. The best example for this is the widely known case about the two women of bad morals and the child. The two women lived in the same place and gave birth almost at the same time. However, one woman crushed her son to death in her sleep and then switched it with the other woman's baby. When Solomon was requested to judge the case, the king turned to the servants asking for a sword. When it was brought to him, the king ordered his servant to cut the child in half. The real mother instantly began to beg for the little one's life, while the thief woman stated that it was the only fair thing to do, if the child could not be hers, he would not be anyone else's either. Therefore, the king immediately knew who the child's real mother was.

Solomon had a special royal authority. Although his kingdom was part of the religion, he himself was a sacral king. He supervised religious ceremonies, he also showed sacrifices and blessed people just like the high priests. He performed the consecration of the royal court as well and was interested in astrology and magic too. *The Key of Solomon* is regarded as an important work of art by the insiders although the great majority are rather familiar only with the Canticles, the Proverbs and Ecclesiastes which originate from him. However, *The Key of Solomon* is still one of the most popular grimoire, i.e. the textbook of magic. In this he himself, the religious king refers to the fact that in occultism knowledge, rather than virtue, supports spiritual progress and knowing everything means power over the universe.

The most famous king of the Jews built the renowned Temple sometime in the tenth century BC. The construction of the temple was one of the major events of the Old Testament because according to the Bible, (in the Sacred Shrine – Holy of Holies) the Ark of the Covenant was stored here (in which the original Ten Commandments were protected and which supposedly possessed supernatural powers). The construction of the temple lasted seven years and it was followed by the construction of the palace which lasted for 13 years. Four hundred years later the first Temple was destroyed by the Babylonians, who also banished the Jews, and regarding the future of the Ark of the Covenant there has not been any credible information ever since. According to some people, the Babylonians did not find the relic because it had been hidden on time, others say the Babylonians took it away and still others claim that Solomon had already given it to the Ethiopian king Menelik, whose descendants have still been carefully guarding it in a monastery in Axum.

There is also a Masonic legendry related to the king. According to the 'tale', Freemasonry is a three-thousand-year-old secret alliance, which was founded by King Solomon himself. This is suggested also by the fact that the five-pointed star was his seal, which later was used by the members of the association. The members of the former Order of the Knights Templar later hid in this temple built by Solomon (more precisely among its ruins) and here they began their astonishing (ecclesiastic, political and economic) careers.

King Solomon's love life was protean to put it mildly (and morally controversial even to this day). Allegedly he had 900 wives, but only one true love: the gorgeous Queen of Sheba. He adorned her with precious stones, respected her as an equal partner and later he entrusted the Ark of the Covenant to the son she gave to him. Since then many kings have reigned, but the memory of king Solomon's wisdom never fades, nor the way this mighty king treated his loved one. Exactly the way every woman should be treated by her loving man: as a real queen. All in all, that is why he belongs right here, on this ruler's card.

'Whatever you are towards yourself, you will be towards others. If you love yourself, you will love others. If you are able to flow within your being, you will be able to flow in your relationships also. If you are frozen inside, you will be frozen outside also.'
(Osho)

The Lovers

Sissy and Gyula Andrássy/ Siegfried and Brünhild

The Interpretation of the Picture

This card is the obvious symbol of love and choice. In old decks a young man is between two women who wish to call him towards themselves, above them Cupid flies around. Here, however a woman stands in the middle and two men want to lure her in two directions. In general, the man on the left is the sin and the one on the right pulls her toward virtue and she has to make a decision. Furthermore, on some old tarot cards we can also see a young couple who are being united in matrimony by a senior person. In Love tarot this card shows the different aspects of love, marriage and choice.

I have recently read an interesting reflection, which was about love and marriage. It has deeply ingrained in me, because I live in a marriage too, and most importantly love also is my vital element. The reflection is based on the thesis that love is nothing more than two halved souls' experience of unity in which one part wants to embrace the other, it wants to become one with it. Today's people mostly marry out of love, and then later some do not understand what had happened, why everything changed. The only secret is that another mystery has entered into our lives. To put it another way, once the family is established, we cannot speak solely of a love story. It is about another thing already. Yes, the love drama, which is meant only for two souls, is no longer possible to experience, because the whole thing is about something else. Individual experiences become destiny, marriage is forged into commune destiny. Its foundation is indeed the male-female relationship but it is no longer solely about that. It is also about the children, relatives, friends and means of living, one should not forget that there is a lot of work in order to have a good family, a good marriage. From both sides. In a good marriage good self-knowledge is indispensable, because if we live in a bad relationship with ourselves, how could we live well with others? Family is a community, which we create and shaping it depend on us.

However, if we allow outside love to invade this common fate with great intensity, it will have a tremendous power. Some are capable to sacrifice their family for it. They do not become aware of the difference. They cannot separate the spiritual quality of the two types of love, since they believe that they have the right for love in every case. They forget responsibility. They forget that in this common fate mother and father are 'God' and that they are responsible for the world they created.

Then again one cannot walk on two roads. One must decide. Making a decision is difficult, because in every case it entails betrayal. For this reason, self-awareness is important when starting a family: because we need to know which path is ours and we need to stay on that one. Who really wants a family, no one has an easy task today. They must create protection around it and must filter everything that flows in. One should know that belonging means we are responsible for each other's fate as well.

In the Love Tarot, the woman stands in the middle (Sissy), on her left there is a man (Andrássy), on her right there is a much older man (Franz Joseph), who is much older. Here the woman chooses! This card shows the difficulty of choice: the woman reaches out her hand to one side, but already turns towards the other.

From farther away the older man helplessly watches the new couple plunging in the state of love with a 'not seeing anyone else', blind love. He waits patiently and lovingly.

This card connects two themes, it refers to duality and also to the difficulty of choice. It shows that you have to give up the boundaries of your previous life and you must finally commit yourself and stick to your decision. Not an easy task.

Number: VI
Letter: V
Main element: Earth
Astrological connections: Virgo, Gemini, Taurus, Moon, Neptune and Mercury
Meditation: Love meditation, Decision meditation

Important Symbols Appear on the Card

The symbols accompany our human history regardless of age, culture or geographical location. Thus, it is obvious that they are quite general and their use is linked to the 'eternal' man. A sense of order is created in the mind through the use of symbols. It is filled with the qualities of each particular symbol, it replaces and transforms the profane content and it also raises ordinary consciousness to a higher level, thereby raising the quality of human life experience.

Yin-Yang: Understanding the Yin-Yang theory is absolutely an imperative.

Yin and Yang are the names of the unity of existing opposites in nature, environment and the world's every phenomenon. Accordingly, the world is a unified whole and this whole is the consequence of the two opposites in equal proportion. The Yin-Yang theory is a system that is based on the unity formed by the two poles.

Every phenomenon in the universe contains the Yin and Yang character, for example: cold and warm, day-night, motion-stagnation, active-passive etc. According to the Tao principle, nothing can exist merely on its own or for itself. Nothing can exist without its opposite, because they keep each other in motion.

Everything that is passive, feminine, small, receiving has the Yin character and also what is calm, the night, the shadow and introversion

Everything that is active, masculine, tall, hectic, the day, the light and extroversion, have the Yang character.

The doves: dove symbolises peace, motherhood and the female energies of augury. It also refers to love and security of home fertility and ancient energies. It is the bird of soul to put it another way. Furthermore, it is the symbol of affection, love and supernatural things.

The possible meanings of the card in a display, if you picked this

Archetype: Crossroad, Choice

Negative pole: Quitting, Resignation

Psychological Interpretation: Choosing a mate

Spiritual Interpretation: Experiencing emotion-driven behaviour

General Interpretation

In addition to the love interpretation this card especially warns that you have to make an important decision within three months. You always have the option to choose the easy way however this time the hard way is the one that takes you closer to your goals. Be circumspect and ask the opinion of others, if you feel the need.

Interpretation of the Reversed Card

You feel confident because you believe that your personal relationships are based upon solid foundations. You are mistaken. The card draws your attention to the fact that soon you will have to make a decision that affects everything. Be very cautious, otherwise conflicts may occur.

Love Interpretation

Your current relationship is either deepening or ending. The card may also show that you have to choose between two candidates and also that after long waiting someone is going to step into your life. Every interpretation depends on the card's placement in relation to other cards. If it stands together with the Hanged man, the Unnamed card and the Tower, then it warns that on account of a misunderstanding even a breakup can take place.

Material Interpretation

The card indicates a serious decision. It suggests that you should be more thrifty, save some money because unexpected expenses may arise. If it stands together with The Hermit, The Hanged man or The Tower, it shows that your financial situation is very bad currently. The circumstances cannot be solved easily, but in order not to last for long, a change is necessary. Take the advice of your more experienced friends.

Work

Here too the card refers to the situation of choosing. It is conceivable that more job offers are coming to you. Prudent decision-making is very important. If you are unable to make right decisions, you will have to face serious occupational problems. You will make no headway in your business deals until this crisis situation is solved.

The Question of Study

Be honest! Do not cheat on the exams, rather learn and prepare for them. You can be successful only this way. Otherwise you can expect serious complications.

Health Interpretation

This card indicates that you are experiencing a more exhausting period, but soon your health and activity are going to return. However, if the card stands with the High Priestess, The Hermit, The Unnamed card and The Tower, then you should be very careful because a number of different medical complaints may indicate a more serious illness. Health is not to be played with! Consult a doctor!

Family Interpretation

The card alerts you for a difficult decision. You have to accept that relationships change over time, that love ecstasy which you longed for before marriage, is not always possible to experience within the family. The passionate story of two cannot continue in the usual way. To maintain the relationship, you must have persistence. If the card is together with the Magician, the Empress, the Chariot and the Wheel of Fortune, then it refers to a joyful change.

Task

You must learn to cooperate with others and make decisions consciously.

The Message of the Card

The card means love, beauty, carefree, optimism. In an opposite case it refers to failure, disappointment, hesitation and infidelity. In all cases, it draws the attention to prudent choice.

Emotions: love, affection, fear, worries, disappointments

Stage of life: Commitment

Personalities Illustrated on the Card

Sissy and Gyula Andrássy

Sissy and Franz Joseph's marriage deteriorated after two decades. Perhaps they were not exclusively to blame for this; because family tragedies struck them, which often cause disintegration of marriages even today. In 1857, their two-year-old daughter, Archduchess Sophie got sick with typhus and died. In 1867, Franz Joseph – partly through his own fault – lost his beloved brother, Archduke

Miksa was sent to Mexico at the persuasion of Napoleon III after the French intervention and the local freedom fighters executed him. The real tragedy reached the royal couple only after that: in 1889, as a result of the frequent conflicts with his father, Crown Prince Rudolf committed suicide. Elizabeth almost died from the loss of his only son, she could never really forgive her husband whom she blamed for the death of Rudolph. Under these circumstances, it is not so extraordinary anymore that Franz Joseph and Sissy estranged from each other. The Emperor secretly sought comfort in the company of famous Viennese actresses, while Sissy openly befriended with one of the finest man considered in that period: Count Gyula Andrássy, the Hungarian Prime Minister.

Already on their first meeting the Hungarian count enchanted the Empress, famous for her beauty, which is not surprising, since Andrássy's charismatic essence and good speaking skills had achieved great successes in politics as well as among women. According to the Habsburg point of view the Empress and the Count were hardly able to have a physical relationship, since they never even talked in private due to the strict court etiquette, but this is still controversial even to this day. There is indirect evidence of the time they spent together: in 1872, Sissy, at twilight, travelled from her Gödöllő Castle to the station in Andrássy's carriage. Sissy later remembered that ride as an exciting secret, it is likely that then something significant had happened. The fact is that Sissy is one the most controversial personalities in history and her love for the count makes us guess a lot. Whatever the truth is, we will never know. Sissy cannot tell us about it anymore. The figure of the Empress has been surrounded by a divisive kind of magic, up to this day. Some people hate her and think of her as a person exploiting the nation who looked only at her own interests, a capricious and selfish Empress, and there are people who just adore her. (About Sissy you can read more on The Empress card, about Franz Joseph on The Emperor card, and about Count Andrassy on The Hanged Man tarot card.)

Siegfried and Brünhild

The personalities on the card are the famous characters from The Song of the Nibelungs, knight Siegfried and Brünhild whose fate is mostly known through Wagner's Ring of the Nibelung opera tetralogy. The story is at least as diversified as the Holy Grail's legend and is differently known from country to country. I am sure however, that if we look into the depths when we encounter a legend, sooner or later history will also show up. That is why I have chosen this love story for this card.

The Antecedents

The tale begins with Odin, Loki and Hœnir. They glimpsed an otter at a waterfall who was no one else but a dwarf named Otr. Loki hurls a stone at the otter, killing it instantly. The gods flayed the otter's skin and with it they arrive at Hreiðmarr, a famous wizard. He immediately recognises his son in the otter and along with his two other sons Fafnir and Regin he asks ransom for him. The gods must pay: they must fill the otter's skin with gold and cover it with gold on the outside as well. Hence Loki sets off to get gold at the Andar Falls, where an enchanted dwarf in the guise of a pike guards a lot of golden treasures in the river. He catches the pike, who gives Loki the gold in exchange for sparing his life. Nevertheless, he casts a curse on the last ring: whoever the owner of the ring is, they should die a violent death. Getting back at Hreiðmarr the gods immediately fill the otter's skin with gold, and with the magic ring they cover the body too. Loki says laughing that the gold is actually cursed, but the wizard does not care.

After the gods leave, the two sons stand in front of their sorcerer father demanding their part of the gold. The father does not want to share it, so after he falls asleep, Fafnir kills him with his sword. His brother, Regin also asks for his share but Fafnir hides it in a cave laughing, he himself changes into a dragon snake guarding the cave. After that Regin decides to look for a knight who helps him take away the gold from Fanfir. That is how he meets Siegfried.

Siegfried

According to the German tradition, Prince Siegfried was born near the river Rhine in Xanten. His mother died early and his father raised him to be a true valiant. Siegfried is the prominent figure of the ring's story and of the entire German-Scandinavian mythology. His heritage is a broken magic sword which he welds with the help of Regin. The sword is called Gram, with it he defeats Fafnir the dragon snake, and obtains the ring along with the helmet of invisibility from him. Then befitting a hero, he bathes in the dragon snake's blood that makes him invincible, but he does not realise that a leaf sticks on his back, thus in that particular spot he remains vulnerable. He also kills the double-dealer Regine and continues his adventurous journey.

One day during his wanderings he sees a strange light from a distance. When he gets closer, he sees that it is a castle, which is guarded by flames. He hurdles over it and in one room he finds a girl sleeping in armour, who is no one else but the beautiful Brünhild, who was bewitched as a punishment by Odin. The hero wakes her up and they immediately fall in love with each other. The girl tells him that she has been a fairy (Valkyrie) and 'ready for victory, hence the name Brünhild. The Valkyries belong to Odin's retinue, they help the one win whose name Odin whispers in their ears. However, Brünhild once disobeyed Odin's orders and helped a warrior to whom the main god ordered a heroic death. As a result, Odin turned the fairy girl into an earthly mortal whose punishment is to marry a mortal. Brünhild requested however, that the main god would at least allow her to be the wife of the bravest and most valiant mortal. For this reason, Odin hid the bewitched fairy in the flame-surrounded castle. Siegfried cannot get enough of the girl's beauty for a long time and she also teaches him much wise science. Among other things, they study rune reading too. Before the hero sets off again, with the Andar dwarf's cursed ring he vows loyalty to Brünhild, promising to return soon to his sweetheart. However, as soon as he crosses the gates of the castle, due to the curse linked to the ring he immediately forgets her and the oath made to her.

Therefore, it is possible that immediately after returning home he falls in love with Kriemhild, who sees a dream before the arrival of the hero, wherein she sees her future husband and also that their love cannot be long lasting due to a conflict. Siegfried asks the girl's brother, Gunter for his blessing on the matrimony with his sister. But the brother imposes conditions regarding the marriage: in return Siegfried must help him get Brünhild with tricks. Heroes are competing for her hand and she is desperately waiting for her unfaithful sweetheart who woke her from bewitched sleep.

Siegfried boards a ship with Gunter to endure three tests for Brünhild. Siegfried helps his future brother-in-law in the invisibility helmet. Brünhild however, immediately recognises her sweetheart and when she realises that the hero clearly does not remember her, she can hardly hide her pain. The plan of the two men works, they craftily defeat the girl and Kriemhild will be Siegfried's. But Brünhild will not give herself so easily, thus the unfortunate Gunter has to ask Siegfried's help on the wedding night too. The false lover in the invisibility helmet forces her to the ground, takes away her ring and magical belt and then switches place with the rightful husband. He gives the belt and the ring to

Kriemhild as presents, he makes her swear that she will never tell anyone how he obtained them.

However, 12 years later, Kriemhild has a dispute with his brother's wife before the church service. As for long minutes they cannot decide which one of them is higher in rank, Kriemhild furiously shouts the truth at Brünhild. The amazon-natured woman turns terribly angry and asks her servant Hagen to take revenge on Siegfried. The servant discovers the hero's vulnerability and kills Siegfried. He throws his treasures (including the invisibility helmet) into the Rhine.

After 13 years of mourning, Kriemhild is getting married again, she chooses Etele (Attila), the king of the Huns as her husband. The new marriage is not about love, but revenge, and soon Kriemhild invites the Burgunds for a feast. During the visit, the Burgunds confront the Huns, who slaughter their arrogant, haughty guests in anger. Only Gunter and Hagen survive of the team. Kriemhild calls Hagen to account for the death of her former husband and tries to find out the secret hiding place of Siegfried's treasures. When she sees that the interrogation is useless, she gets them killed. However, for murdering her brother, Kriemhild also faces doom: a valiant Hun wounds her fatally amid the massacre.

Brünhild, the Valkyrie

The fairy girl is a real mystery. We do not know exactly who she is, all we know is that Odin, the Father of All had chosen her to lead the Valkyries, a team consisting only of women. In addition to goddesses, mortal warrior women also serve in the team and Odin only turns to them when all other options have been exhausted. Brünhild is the number one leader of the Valkyries for thousands of years.

About Odin, we know that he often teaches his son Thor a lesson by erasing his memories and then sending him as a mortal in the earthly world. One day Thor travelled the world as Siegmund. However, one of his decisions provoked the wrath of Odin, who decided to put an end to Siegmund's earthly life and brought him back to Asgard. Odin thus stated Siegmund's death sentence, which was to be implemented by Brünhild. However, the warrior woman felt sorry for Siegmund (did not suspect that the man was Thor himself, who would not die after the execution of the judgment), and hid the man and his pregnant partner, Sieglinde. Therefore, Odin deprived her of her divine power and immortality, then put her in a coma. The girl was awakened by Siegfried, who was

Siegmund's son, that is Thor, because after Siegmund's natural death his soul transferred into his son Thor's body.

The warrior woman and Siegfried fell in love with each other, but Siegfried betrayed her. When Siegfried/Thor was killed, Brünhild threw herself on her love's funeral pyre thus following him into the afterlife. Odin took pity on the lovers and gave back their lives. In other words, Thor returned to his original personality, Brünhild became the leader of the Valkyries again, Odin erased all her memories about her stay on earth, so the girl would not be tortured by her love for Siegfried. This event was introduced in The Scandinavian-Germanic mythology as the Niebelung legend, as a real pearl.

'Whatever you do, you need courage. Whatever course you decide upon, there is always someone to tell you that you are wrong. There are always difficulties arising that tempt you to believe your critics are right. To map out a course of action and follow it to an end requires some of the same courage that a soldier needs. Peace has its victories, but it takes brave men and women to win them.' **(Ralph Waldo Emerson)**

THE CHARIOT

JÁNOS HUNYADI and NIMROD

This card is the symbol of victory when the soul triumphs. A crowned man drives a richly decorated chariot, like Roman warlords celebrating their glory in the triumphal march, but here it is night and there is a woman sitting in the chariot. The woman and the man in the chariot are signs of duality, indicating that the wise leader shares his victory with his dear one, and on the night before the invasion he seats solely her at his side, to share the details of the path to victory as well. This card is also about togetherness and the power of love. It is about all true Kings/Men who must have a real Queen/Woman behind and she is raised to become a ruler by the man's love and respect. A queen, at whom he only has to take a quick glance if he loses confidence, because the alliance between them allows the Woman to signal merely with her eyes or with a nod: whatever happens, the two of them belong together. Thus, the man is able to face any challenges with renewed strength as he is aware of his unquestionable power and faith. Because it is neither money, nor power that gives him strength, but a special woman. The one who looks up to her love, respects him and is able to stand beside him in the midst of difficult decisions. The one who can offer consolation, can encourage and love him from the depths of her heart, who lets the man go to fight, so that he could remain faithful to his principles.

Number: VII
Letter: Z
Main element: Air
Astrology: Gemini, Libra, Sagittarius, Cancer, Mars, Venus
Meditation: 'In front of the throne of God'

Important Symbols Appear on the Card:
The blue colour: the blue colour dominates the card. This indicates that man already dominates and controls the soul's energies.
Letters 'V' and 'T': on the front of the chariot letters 'V' and 'T' if you read them from right to left, they give you the Hebrew letter Tav.
Half-moon: The fertile half-moon is a crescent-shaped area of the Middle East, this concept was introduced by the Egyptologist James Henry Breasted in 1916

as the cradle of civilisation. It also shows that every lunar cycle is 7 days long and that the number seven governs the rhythms that form the foundation of the universe. Seven is the number of holiness and of the mystique. It symbolises the days of the week, the duration of holidays, the spectrum shades, chemistry and the seven tones of the tone sequence. As the sum of three and four it represents the two most simple geometric shapes the triangle and the square. The mythological ladder had seven steps, the tower of Babel had seven stairs too, the shaman tree and the Hebrew sacred candlestick were both seven-branched as well. In medieval Europe, the half-moon on the coat of arms was considered a great honour; many Templar Knights used it while returning home, mainly in France.

The four elements: In ancient times, it was believed that the world was built up of four prime elements: Earth, Fire, Water and Air. These elements support the chariot's four-poster.

The two horses: (white and black) represent the soul and the body, the mind and the reason.

The Possible Meanings of the Card in a Display, if you Picked This

Archetype: The Hero

Negative pole: The Loser

Psychological Interpretation: Mission, task

Spiritual Interpretation: the triumph of the soul, finding the true vocation

General Interpretation

Rivalry between two people is completely natural, fighting spirit was born along with humanity. You shall face many rivals in the course of your life. This rival may be a colleague, a relative or the one who laid her/his eyes on your loved one. You are fighting for something that is important for someone else too. Do not forget that two people who want exactly the same thing, resemble a lot. This gives you a slight advantage, because this way you can see what tactical train of thought your rival has and you can turn that to your own favour. Your boldness will be rewarded, you are under spiritual and divine protection. This card means success and victory, your tenacious work is going to bring the desired result. The card thus symbolises a great power and draws your attention to the path towards success.

Interpretation of the Reversed Card

Right now, you are finding it difficult to hold on. You are already weak to fight and many times you want to give up. Maybe the fight has been going on for too long and too hard and you cannot find a way out of the situation. Rest, gather strength, believe me, if you relax you can judge better whether it is worth to keep fighting. The card's reversed pick shows confusion, escape, unexpected travel and also refers to failure and disappointment.

Love Interpretation

This is the time for knotting your love and family ties and place them on the solid foundation. If it stands together with the Sun, the Truth and the World, it indicates that it is time for you to settle down and to legitimise your relationship. On the other hand, if it is together with the Lover, the Moon and the Fool, they warn that your current love affair is going nowhere, a breakup is expected if you do not change. If you heat two irons in the fire, you have to decide firmly now.

Material Interpretation

Your previous plans are bearing fruit, your financial situation is constantly improving. In both personal and professional sense, you can only expect success, thanks to your determination and confidence. Be careful however, these should not change into excessive ambition.

Work

A fortunate period is starting, due to your persistence you can achieve greater financial security and your new investments are paying off. You can be sure that your future will be secure and balanced.

The Question of Study

The card promises successes only if you do not let the control out of your hand. All you need to focus on is that love should not take away your attention completely from preparation. If you stay self-consistent, thanks to your creativity and susceptibility everything will go great on its own course.

Health Interpretation

The card promises healing, if you do not let stress overwhelm your life. Take enough time to relax and do not try to push your strength over the edge. Then everything will be alright. If you suffer from a serious illness, the card says that right now you can choose the successful cure. Even from the most hopeless situation there is a way out.

Family Interpretation

Whether you are solving an old family dispute, buying a property or taking care of a child, this card promises success in all aspects. Every aspect of your life is imbued with Harmony.

Task

The card indicates a huge jump. You have to find new goals and carry them out successfully.

The Message of the Card

It is high time for you to deal with your own spiritual and intellectual development. You have to change your usual way of thinking and you must walk your own path.

Emotions: power, freedom, self-reliance

Stage of life: New beginnings, independent decisions

János Hunyadi (1407-1456)

János Hunyadi was one of the biggest figures of the Hungarian history in the 15th century, he was famous for the successes he achieved in the battles against the Ottoman Turks. He is the great *Ottoman Turk beater*. Also King Mátyás' father.

By the middle of the 15th century, the clashes of the Christian and Islam civilisations had already a long history in Europe and in the Middle East. The Balkan nations resisted for a long time, but by the middle of the 15th century every state had come under Ottoman Turkish rule for more than 400 years. The Ottoman Turks crowned their conquests with the fact that during the reign of Sultan Mohammed II (1451-81) in 1453 they occupied the former capital of the Eastern Roman Empire, the more than one-thousand-year-impregnable Byzantium. The curiosity of the siege's military history is that fire weapons, especially the cannons here at the castle siege, received their first major military role. Mohammed II's political creed was: 'One God in heaven, one monarch reigns on earth!' Three years after the incorporation of Byzantium this Ottoman Turkish sultan set off for the invasion of Hungary with his unbeatable, world-conquering army and equipped with modern fire weapons. János Hunyadi's army fought against the Ottoman Turkish corps that offended the country. Fortunately, in 1456, Hunyadi had already been well experienced as a military leader and politician's past, therefore after the victory at Belgrade the whole Europe celebrated him, because Hunyadi, beyond the protection of his own country, defended the entire Western Christianity too.

(In mid-June 1456 Pope Callixtus III issued a bull in which he asked the universal Christian congregation to pray every day to God to turn away the Ottoman Turkish peril from above the head of European Christianity, to give victory to the Hungarian weapons and as a sign for this, he ordered the Christian church bells ring every noon. Since then, the bells have been ringing at noon in memory of the 1456 triumph.)

The origin of the Hunyadi family has not been elucidated up to this day. Earlier there was a stubborn tradition, according to which János Hunyadi would be directly King Sigismund's (1387-1437) illegitimate child born from Lady Elizabeth Morzsinai outside marriage, according to another version the Hunyadi family's ancestors came to Hungary from Wallachia, the territory of today's Romania. In connection with this usually there is a reference to a charter from Sigismund dated 18th of October 1409, in which he had bestowed the Transylvanian Hunedoara Castle and the belonging estate to Voyk – the king's knight – for his loyal services and merits. The mentioned Voyk could be János Hunyadi's father.

János Hunyadi, due to his brilliant talent, quickly moved forward in the rank of national dignitaries. Before 1456, he had already won many significant victories against the Ottoman Turks. Consequently, it is no wonder that, thanks to his talent and extraordinary career, he was well-known in contemporary Europe, and this widespread interest sustained after his death also. The image created of him is quite variable. Hunyadi is primarily known as a legendary general and the terror of the Ottoman Turks. However, in Hunyadi was not seen 'only' the hero of Hungary, but also the champion of the whole universal Christianity. His career was not effortless. Some noblemen who were against the Hunyadi house were responsible for his hardships. Out of envy they made Hunyadi's job difficult and they did not even refrain from murder and highlight his military leader skills and talents. He is presented as a real hero with European reputation, the terror of the Ottoman Turks. His merits are not disputed even by the fact that he was defeated in two huge battles (Varna and Kosovo), because he was not responsible for these defeats. On the other hand, curbing the Hungarian civil wars and restoring internal peace are considered his merits.

Nimrod

Medieval Hungarian chronicles present the legendary Nimrod as the first forefather of the Hungarians. Nimrod first appears in Hungarian historiography in Simon Kézai's Gesta Hungarorum, written around 1282. In this, Kézai points out that the giant Nimrod began to build the Tower of Babel with his entire nation. After the linguistic cacophony he moved to the land of *Evilat* and there his wife, Eneh, bore him twin sons, Hunor and Magyar (aka Magor). The Huns and the Hungarians are descended from these two boys and from the valiants standing in their service. This story is repeated in more than twenty medieval Hungarian chronicles, and even a German chronicler also adopted it.

The modern historical science declared the Hungarian Nimrod legend, 'a nice tale', without any investigation accusing Kézai that he simply borrowed Nimrod from the Old Testament to obtain an acceptable Biblical ancestor for the Hungarians. However, the borrowing hypothesis has many obstacles. In other words, Nimrod is mentioned in the Bible as the descendant of Kam, but the Christian church fathers, whom Kézai knew very well, stated unanimously that the Huns and the Hungarians were descended undoubtedly from Noah's other son Japhet. Therefore, if Kézai had simply picked Nimrod from the Bible, he would have acted against the teachings of the Church and would have searched for his nation's ancestor in Kam's kindred. This is something he could not do as a Catholic priest, especially the king's own pastor.

Furthermore, Nimrod is a great Mesopotamian king in the Bible, a person described with rather vague outlines. The beginning of his kingdom was the towns of Babel, Uruk, Akkad and Calneh in the land of Shinar. From this land, he went to Asshur and built the cities of Nineveh, Resen, Rehoboth and Calah. Moreover, he built the tower of Babel mentioned in the Bible. I have chosen him on his card.

The Arabs also have an ancient saga, in which it is said that the tower of Babel was built by Nimrod, because he wanted to see Abraham's God. Similar legends have been preserved among other peoples also in Mesopotamia and the Middle East. However, Kézai could not have known about these.

***'Basically, courage is risking the known for the unknown, the familiar for the unfamiliar, the comfortable for the uncomfortable, arduous pilgrimage to some unknown destination.'* (Osho)**

Strength

Countess Lajos Batthyány born Countess Antonia Zichy and Mary Magdalene

The Interpretation of the Picture

The image of Courage appears in this card, it is one of the main virtues and the card of discipline as well. The card is also related to Union and to the Divine Mystery of Desire. To this day it has been a subject of serious debate as to which card should follow the Chariots. In old decks, the eighth card was the Justice and the eleventh one was The Strength. However, the mystical order of Golden Dawn has swapped them because The Strength is a better fit for the Leo Zodiac while the Justice is better for the Libra. In the card it is summer, the time of Leo, the card itself is filled with erotic charge, so The Strength is perfect for the eighth place.

In general, in other tarots, in The Strength card there is an Amazon-like female figure, who defeats the Lion (a bit like St George, just not the dragon). But here is a beautiful Amazon in the card, who emanates The Strength and who does not fight with the Lion but cooperates with it. Because now the goal is rather turning inwards. We should not overcome our 'instinct self' but become one with it. We need to dissolve in it, we have to accept it and must build it into ourselves.

Number: VIII
Letter: K
Main element: Fire
Astrology: a card under the influence of Leo, Aries, Mars and Sun
Meditation: the acceptance of fear and becoming one with our desires

Important Symbols Appear on the Card

Beside the woman, a majestically standing lion appears which accepts the power of the Amazon. The sign of infinity connects them and the Kundalini energy is embodied in the serpent. The card is fiery therefore the Amazon's dress is red.

Lion:

The lion, as a symbol, represents the Sun above all the visible and the spiritual light, the external and inner radiance, the heavenly and the earthly fire, the glory, the splendour, power, dominion, the kingdom, tranquillity, solidity, perseverance, justice, honesty, generosity, shrewdness, alertness, dignity and wealth. In the negative case however, it symbolises tyranny, cruelty, violence, threats, temper and insatiable greed.

The sign of infinity: refers to endless possibilities. Additionally, it is also a symbol of balance and internal harmony – a symbol of the Woman, who is longing to reach equilibrium with herself. Eight is also the number of new life. The woman in the card can also be Eve who tames Adam, the fruit of this embrace will later result a child.

The serpent: The presence of the serpent refers to the Kundalini energy. Three types of forces keep the human body alive. The first is the Fohat, which is manifested as electricity, heat, light and movement. The second is the Prana, which we otherwise regard as Vitality and the third is the Kundalini, i.e. the serpent fire.

The Kundalini is our inherent, slumbering energy which can be evoked and is hidden at the bottom of our vertebral column in the form of helix. It is also referred to as the Mother of the World, because through Kundalini we can revive our silent, slumbering senses and even the Higher Worlds may open up for us.

It can be found at the root chakra i.e. at the bottom of the vertebral column. It never wakes up in the average life of an average person, thus he or she cannot experience the existence of it. This is so because this energy can only be processed and directed through adequate moral and spiritual development and can only be used for good purposes. No one should experiment with it without having received a rigorous instruction from a knowledgeable teacher, because it is very dangerous.

However, in some cases, the Kundalini awakens by itself, then you feel a dull glow, what is more it may even start to move by itself, though this is rare. In the latter case it causes excruciating pain because the ducts are not prepared for it and this is a painful process. When it wakes up by itself or is accidentally woken up, it usually tries to race up the inside of the spine instead of following the spiral path, in which occultists learn to lead it.

During Chakra Meditations, when the cleaning of different chakras is performed and we 'call upon' each chakra to function through breathing techniques and mantras, it is possible to succeed in setting of the Kundalini.

The main task of the Kundalini is to open the path – in a spiritually matured personality – between the astral and the physical body through the chakras, and this acts as a link to the higher spheres.

The Cards Meaning in a Spread, if you Picked This

Archetype: Hercules, the brave reliable hero who persists in spite of the dangers lurking at him. Who is respected, because he is courageous or did noble deeds.
Negative pole: The Coward (man), who, by nature, is afraid of danger, potential difficulties as well as inconveniences, and he behaves accordingly.

Psychological Interpretation

The Strength in old decks also was the image of Courage, one of the main virtues. The card is in strong relationship with the Magician, the only difference is that while the power of the Magician results from the domination and harmony of conscious and subconscious forces, The Strength symbolises the vigorous, everyday people's courageous confrontation with their sometimes-archaic forces living inside them. These can be 'tamed' only by love and acceptance.

Spiritual Interpretation

This card is often referred to as St George the dragon layer's female equivalent. The woman taming the king of beasts is a symbol of victory over the cruel and evil. The Amazon does not kill the lion but cooperates with it. This symbolises the spirit, the awareness of temptations, audacity and verve. It encourages you to look deep inside yourself and decide which area of your life you want to live to the fullest. Another also important teaching is to recognise what exactly has prevented you so far from making this area come true.

General Interpretation

It requires strength and courage to face your fears. Love is always stronger than hatred, therefore courage may spring out of love too. Confronting your fears will help you in your development. If you get rid of your fears, you will be free, thus you will be able to accomplish even greater things. The Amazon does not have to fight simply because she accepts the fact that she has fears, by becoming one with them, the fears disappear suddenly, because she has realised that they spring from her. You have very intense and much more inner strength than you thought. Use it. Learn to accept your instincts and desires, transform the force emanating from these into creative power. The point is that you dominate them, not vice versa; do not let them dominate you.

Reversed Interpretation

You have the feeling that you are not controlling your own life. As a woman, you have the strength within you, yet you cannot use it in this situation. Fear has taken control over you. You must be careful not to be confused. This card may also indicate for you the overwhelming passion and fear of intense emotion, which are dangerous because control may slide out of your hands. Perhaps you are paying too much attention to the material things of life, or are lacking the courage to face a timely issue. Calm down now, observe your fears and your desires. Let them spread within you, become one with them and thus the spiritual power will return. It was within you all along but eclipsed by your fears was not used.

Love Interpretation

The card of Strength suggests that every tool is in your hands (or is going to be within 3 months) in order to be able to dominate even the most difficult situations. This is an excellent period to dedicate more attention to your personal life. Now is the moment to strengthen bonds and relationships. In case it stands together with the Emperor, the Devil and the Chariot it shows that if you get married you will be very happy and experience wonderful moments with your loved one. However, if it stands with the Lovers, the Fool and the Moon, it indicates that you are expecting too much from this relationship and unfortunately things are not turning out the way you want. You have to wait patiently for a more appropriate period.

Material Interpretation

Everything is going excellently on its own way, now you can achieve anything if you are emotionally strong enough and mature. Momentarily you are capable to organise and manage everything well. Accordingly, your ambition is going to be crowned with success, but pay attention to your decisions. Now you can implement your long-cherished plans.

Work

The Strength symbolises vitality, spirit, success and the fulfilment of wishes. You are going to be supported in each new initiative, but bragging is forbidden because this may cause tensions in your relationships. Now you can really prevail only through modesty.

The Question of Study

The Strength encourages perseverance. Plan carefully how, what and when you want to study. The reward is going to be a successful exam.

Health Interpretation

The card symbolises the healing forces. It is time to regenerate and recharge yourself physically, mentally and spiritually.

Family Interpretation

Now you can strengthen your family life and friendly relationships and you can also easily undo the mistakes you committed in the past. However, if it stands opposite the Hanged man, The Unnamed card and the Tower, you will face problems which you may find difficult to handle. At present it is also conceivable that a friend may walk out of your life. Keep calm, meditate and things are soon going to be re-established.

Task

Face your old fears and obsessions and accept them with love. This way the Mind and the Instinct are going to be able to work in harmony within you.

The message of the card

Enjoy life! Treat every emotional situation with more awareness.

Emotions: vitality, courage, pride, passion, intuition

Stage of life: The preservation of your self-control is requiring inner strength, determination and courage. If you have willpower and are able to control yourself, then you can overcome every obstacle.

Persons illustrated on the card are Wife of count Lajos Batthyány born Countess Antonia Zichy and Mary Magdalene

Wife of count Lajos Batthyány born Countess Antonia Zichy (1816-1888)

We often write about the life and deeds of our national heroes and historical figures, but much less is said about the women who stood by the side of the heroes. To put it another way, the role of wives was absolutely not secondary at all because they often influenced their mate's decisions and thus the fate of the nation. For example, such an important woman was Countess Antonia Zichy, who was one of the most prominent figures of the Reform Age; she was the wife of the Prime Minister of the first independent Hungarian Government, Count Lajos Batthyány, who was a martyr of retribution following the war of independence. Her parents strongly shaped her personality. Her father, Count Károly Zichy, played a prominent part in her life as thanks to his important position he did a lot of charity, helped the ill, supported the poor and even founded a Hungarian school as well. He was the deputy of the first steward of Vas County and the imperial chamberlain. Thus not only fortune did Antonia inherit from him, but also helpfulness, deep religiosity and national commitment.

Antonia and Lajos Batthyány first met in Bratislava, in December 1833. They immediately fell in love with each other, and the Count, after just one year, asked the countess, who was then only eighteen years old, to marry him. Afterwards the young couple travelled throughout Western Europe. While Batthyány spent his time listening to prosecutions in the French courts, his young wife got acquainted with the French fashion, shopping a lot while admiring hairstyles, and expensive fabrics. Three girls were born from their love, but only two survived and reached adulthood: Helena and Emilia, but little Antonia died at the age of two. When they also lost their firstborn son, little Akos, this tragedy was really hard on Batthyány. However, two years later, Antonia gave him a son once again. Therefore – although they could not forget the loss – their love and togetherness became much stronger.

Antonia, in addition to caring for her family responsibilities was also her husband's political helpmate. She visibly stood by the political views of Lajos, whether on the National Assembly or in the Theatre of Pest. She supported her country's economic initiatives, she regularly made donation to charity. She proved to be a loyal companion during the joyous period, when her husband was the Prime Minister and later amidst hardship, during his imprisonment in Austria. Then she followed him and with her letters she kept the strength in him and consoled him.

Her immense self-control and amazing strength are exemplified by the fact that on 5th October 1849, on her husband's instruction she smuggled a dagger into his cell. Batthyány caused wounds on his neck with this, thus eluding hanging. Even after this, Antonia did everything to obtain a petition for reprieve, but could not help Batthyány: her husband was sentenced to death by shotgun and was left into the hands of Haynau. The 'hyena of Brescia', of course, did what the monarch ordered: implemented the verdict regarding Count Lajos Batthyány, who suffered a martyr's death in a symbolic way, precisely on 6th October 1849, the anniversary of the revolution. After Batthyány's wealth was confiscated, the only legacy this inconsolable woman had was a farewell letter left by her husband, which she held onto for the rest of her life. However, her tribulations did not end with the death of her love: from the continuous harassments Antonia was forced to move abroad with her children and their livelihoods were provided by the substantial Zichy wealth.

First she travelled to Bavaria, then to Paris and eventually she settled down near Zurich. After this however, the Austrian secret police were constantly watching her, because her house was regularly visited by leading figures of the Hungarian emigration, led by Count László Teleki. Although the Countess did not interfere in the emigration policy, she often helped the poor wanderers. At the beginning of 1856, she moved back to Hungary and bought a small mansion in Daka. Adhering to her husband's will, she did not request anything back from the Austrian state. Bearing the heavy role of a widow, she was surrounded by love and respect not only for the respect she had for her husband, but also for her charity and patriotism, as well as for setting a good example. Wherever she appeared, it was considered as a protest against autocracy. In the last stage of her life she continued charity, for example, with the widow of Janos Damjanich she founded the Association of Hungarian Housekeeping Ladies. Moreover, together with the wives of the martyrs of Arad she held a requiem on 6th October each year. She passed away on 29th September 1888. According to her wish, her husband's farewell letter was placed on her chest, above her heart and she was buried with it. (About Count Lajos Batthyány you can read more on the Unnamed card.)

Mary Magdalene

Mary Magdalene, to this day, has been a mystery and not only for Christians. She is perhaps the most controversial female figure in the Bible. A lot has been written about her in contradictory evangelical texts, in fact many researchers agree on the fact that Jesus spent the last week of his life in Bethany, probably in the home of the two sisters, Martha and Mary Magdalene. This was unusual because at that time, according to the contemporary Jewish moral laws, women living without paterfamilias could not welcome men, not even as visitors. Therefore, it is no wonder that nowadays in every educated man the question arises, exactly what kind of a relationship Jesus and Mary Magdalene had. Was he the Master or the paterfamilias returning home? This question has kept me preoccupied for a long time, this is why now I am writing you about Mary Magdalene in an unusual way.

You most certainly remember Dan Brown's book, *The Da Vinci Code*, which was leading the U.S. sales charts for more than forty weeks. The author was contested by many people for claiming in his book that a completely false Jesus image has been mediated to believers by the Church. According to him, the Saviour's true face is revealed from those coded messages that the great Renaissance painter Leonardo da Vinci concealed in his fresco, the Last Supper. According to *The Da Vinci Code*, which is a tale in a scientific disguise, Jesus Christ did not die on the cross, thus he could not resurrect from the dead, but married Mary Magdalene, from whom he had children, and they lived happily ever after. However, the Roman Catholic Church has protested against the book's statements.

The fact is that while crucifixion was alien for the Jewish people, for the Romans however it was an everyday mode of execution. Instead, the Jews burned, beheaded, strangled to the death and threw stones at the condemned ones. So perhaps, it is not strange that throughout history, only one crucified man's skeleton has been found in the Holy Land. The alternative notion in the book may derive from this, stating that Jesus and Mary Magdalene were married and their descendants were the founders of the Merovingian royal dynasty. All this was kept a secret for centuries, because this secret was defended by a multitude of esoteric societies, including the Knights Templar and the Priory of Sion, one of the Great Masters of which was Leonardo da Vinci himself. The secret was known only to the initiated, including Leonardo who actually painted the mystery onto his fresco the Last supper: the person seen next to Jesus is not John – as previously thought – but Jesus' alleged wife, Mary Magdalene.

(As it is becoming generally accepted, the Old Testament had been created by some scribes in an extremely long time, i.e. different sources were skilfully compiled in one work.* Therefore it should not be a surprise if writers and directors' imagination is tickled by Mary Magdalene and Jesus' relationship.)

I have recently visited a small French settlement, Rennes-le-Château. The temple located there has painted windows, on which the French ancestors portrayed a pregnant Mary Magdalene. This launched a major controversy. Many books have been written regarding this, since local legends say that the small town belonged to none other than the Knights Templar. Of course, as usual, several people questioned the story, especially when decades later it was also revealed, that in January 1956 its fictional versions appeared in the French press as tourist baits. This advertisement came from a man named Noel Corbu, a restaurant owner in Rennes-le-Château.

***

The base of Rennes myth was established by the death of Marie d'Hautpoul de Blanchefort. She was the last descendant of the d'Hautpoul family who died without having children. The family members belonged to the Order of the Templar and built a family castle in Rennes, centuries ago, around which a small village was established. They were told to be the ones who had guarded the secret of the Templars' for centuries, which eventually Marie entrusted to her confessor abbot Antoine Bigou, who was then the parish priest of Rennes. Bigou supposedly hid all the information about the secret and the fortune inside a Visigoth column in the local church. This was found by the latter abbot Saunière, who out of the 'found' treasure paved the streets, renovated houses, granted loans to those in need, which they never had to pay back. He also renovated his church and decorated its interior with cryptic guidelines toward the treasure he hid. He had a companion 16 years younger than him. She remained with him until his death and later he entrusted his greatest secret to her.

Of course, the odd restoration work struck the bishop of Avignon so he summoned the priest to demand explanation from him, namely how he had gained so much money, since the work around the temple had cost a significant amount. An abbot of such a small village could not have obtained this much wealth, just like that. The materialistic bishop had no luck, Saunière denied the fact that he had found any treasures. He constantly insisted on the fact that he had received many personal donations and covered all expenses from that. The disgruntled bishop decided to suspend the abbot and wanted to take the matter to the Ecclesiastical Court. Saunière however lodged an appeal and turned to Vatican, but he died before the trial could have been scheduled. Nonetheless, before that he had withdrawn from the church and held the sermons in Villa Bethania, which he had built in Rennes. Consequently, as he knew the bishop of Avignon's materialistic nature, he transferred the authority over the area around the church, including the villa as well as his bank account to his mistress. Thus the Church was helpless, because it was impossible to take anything away from her. Of course, the books that are currently available are about 95 percent fiction, but stories can always be well built on these basics, if the story captures our imagination.

Thus it is not surprising that when Corbu met the writer Plantard, he immediately got the idea to flourish the place. As soon as Plantard heard the Saunière story, he began to write a book. He also included new details about parchments found inside the Visigoth column which lead to the bygone Merovingian dynasty, who he derived from Jesus and Mary Magdalene. Plantard's friend, Philippe de Cherisey – a tippler, but a smart aristocrat – for Plantard's sake also created fake parchments, which were immediately placed in the Bibliothèque Nationale and could be discovered as evidence of Plantard's story. This has inspired Dan Brown as well. Although later, Plantard confessed under oath that it was all a lie, because the idea that he would become an organiser of the world as a member of a secret society seemed appealing, regardless of this there are certain facts in this small town that are true. For example, the relationship between the d'Hautpoul family and the Knights Templar. Furthermore, each building exists, every modification on the church conducted by Saunière is real, the interior of the building is like a colouring book of religious history.

With reference to Mary Magdalene: the Gospels all agree upon the fact that Jesus' teachings and charismatic personality were a magnet for female parishioners. His teaching amazed everyone because his word had power. Thus on women he had a particularly great influence. Although Mary Magdalene is mentioned twelve times in the Gospels, it has not been specifically revealed what kind of role this open and sensually devoted, during the tragic fate steadfastly persistent, enigmatic female figure filled in the life of Jesus.

***

Regardless of what I have written, everyone believes in whatever they want and in whatever they choose. I think this is good, as long as someone does not force, manipulate, or intimidate others just to extend what they consider to be good or holy. I shared a different version with you, according to which Mary Magdalene might have stood closer to Jesus than as it was taught to us. Nevertheless, her merits cannot be disputed, I know that she was the woman who was given the unusual task of announcing the death and resurrection of Jesus. And who was later named 'the apostle of the Apostles'. In fact, no one knows what documents the Vatican really guards.

* In many parts, the biblical stories were shaped by latter influences, they were extended and of course at each amendment the original meaning of the text was chipped. There are plenty of examples regarding this. In Genesis, for example, two conflicting myths about Creation can be found. There are two different stories about Adam's descendants as well. About this there are already a number of professional literatures, so I will not refer to it furthermore. What is important: the Old Testament, as we know it today seems to be the result of translation. The Hebrew language of the original text was extinct around 500 B.C. Those Jewish scholars who interpreted the text between 500 and 900 BC, did not know the Old Hebrew, so the reconstruction was based on guesswork.

** Corbu at that time was the owner of Saunière's estate and racked his brain on how he could make his isolated hotel more known. Finally, he invented a more colourful tale than the original about the treasure of the Templars and the blank columns of the church. However, all this has not affected the local tourism, the church of Rennes is still visited every year by tens of thousands of visitors, hoping to get some insight into the legend about Rennes.

*** Matthew and Mark report for example, that during a dinner in Bethany, a woman appeared and poured expensive spikenard on Jesus' head from an alabaster vessel. If we put together the Essene marriage laws and the section about the woman pouring oil, we can assume that their relationship was not purely of spiritual nature. How could a suddenly appearing woman participate at this private gathering if she was a stranger? If she had been just a stranger dropping by, probably she would not have been criticised by the disciples as to why not spend her unnecessary money on the poor. From the described lines it is also revealed that Jesus knew his 'pamperer' and immediately cut off the reproachful disciples: "Why are you bothering this woman? She has done a beautiful thing to me. When she poured this perfume on my body, she did it to prepare me for burial," he added.

All in all, the question occurred to me (as well) how a foreign woman could have known about the impending sacrifice of Jesus? Therefore, who was this woman who in a previous scene 'was crying; and when her tears started landing on the feet of Jesus, she wiped his feet with her hair, covered them with kisses and anointed it with fragrant oils?' Probably none other than the closest person to Jesus, Mary Magdalene who, without any shame, shows her emotions and sensual feminine self.

'A wise man does not have to leave his own room to understand what is happening in the world, because he knows himself.' (Lao Tzu)

THE HERMIT

Géza Gárdonyi and Christian Rosenkreutz

The Interpretation of the Picture

The Hermit is the card of introversion, looking inward, withdrawal, abstinence and the card of concentration on purity and spirituality. Long ago this card illustrated the Time, however today the card is mostly interpreted as a wise man in search for the truth and the bearer of clarity and light.

Number: IX
Letter: T
Main element: Fire
Astrology: Leo, Virgo, Sagittarius, Neptune, Jupiter and Saturn
Meditation: Wisdom (Understanding) Meditation

Important Symbols Appear on the Card

The Hermit's lamp is the light of intellect and knowledge, his habit is the robe of self-control, moreover his stick suggests that the eternal and mysterious forces of nature help him. He has a long beard and he is a calm master, the wise man who possesses immense knowledge. He himself chooses his disciple, not the other way around. Because real masters are not chosen, they 'just are' and with their consciousness they attract seekers, like honey attracts wasps. You must know the saying: 'When the student is ready, the teacher will appear'. The encounter with your master always happens out of an internal impulse, not as a result of long thinking and selection. *'The true master does not educate disciples but only masters them.'*

(Robert Schumann)

Lily and daffodil are present on the card, these are the symbols of purity and self-love. The snake crawling upward on his stick suggests healing and at the same time the male power in reserve. (The Chariot, the Strength and the Hermit are the symbols of life-death-reclaimed life.) Number nine is also mystical. As the last digit of the unary numeral system, it has the highest vibration value, finished and prepares a new manifestation. When you add nine to itself or multiply it with itself, the result always shows nine again. It shows the strength of maturity and wisdom.

If this number appears to you within a spread, you should fill a kind of serving role for people throughout your life. This role manifests itself in most cases, as a request to help solve a problem, to which only you have adequate knowledge. (The duration of foetal life is measured in nine months, there are nine Muses and nine angels as well in the mythology.)

The cards meaning in a spread, if you picked this

Archetype: the Master, the Teacher who does not turn to the masses as the High Priest does

Negative pole: The lonely, desolate man

Psychological Interpretation

The Hermit card always invites us for introspection. This, however, is a deeper introspection in an introverted stage of life, which is painful and sometimes it requires a lot of self-abnegation in order to achieve wisdom.

Spiritual Interpretation

The old Master's lamp seen on the card is not directed toward the road, but inward to himself. This also indicates that now this is not an act of judgment, but an analysis of the soul. (The symbol of the High Priestess reported a similar process, the one who picks the Hermit card gains not only intuition, but also specific knowledge about him or herself and his/her relationship with the world.)

General Interpretation

Ordinary people are very curious about how someone can/will become a spiritual leader. About the kind of reactions, motivations, encounters that influence someone in becoming a Master. This card indicates that soon you are going to meet someone who has a lot to do in your life. All this is for you, as a pathfinder, to be able to find and/or re-discover the Master within yourself. This is the card of self-knowledge. You have learned many lessons and gained experience to see the path you must/should follow in your life more clearly. This road is now showing toward the period of retreat and meditation. Now you have to think through who you really are and what you believe in. All this is for you to rely on your own judgment and not to depend on other people's opinion. This retreat will not last long and when you 'leap again' into your life, you will be fully prepared to take in the world where you really belong to, with open eyes and heart, while you are giving and receiving more and more helpful advice and wise guidance.

Interpretation of the Reversed Card

Maybe you need to revise some lessons which you failed to learn properly. You have not listened to your own advice or of those who have already walked on this path you are walking on right now. Don not forget that history repeats itself and if you refuse to learn from the past, it may lead to foolish decisions and situations.

Love Interpretation

If you are patient, this infinite peace that fills you while exploring the path of self-knowledge will help your emotional relationship also to move on the right track. If you have been living in an uncertain relationship, then now it is high time for your relationship to be strengthened or come to an end. To make a decision, you have to be alone for a while.

Material Interpretation

Your financial situation is going to be solved slowly, do not despair: your perseverance and patience will finally be rewarded with success. Your incomes are going to increase soon and good fortune is going to smile upon you in all areas.

Work

Now is time for you to help others. Everyone will appreciate it. If you have picked this card along with the Emperor, the Justice, the Strength and the Devil, it indicates that now is the moment when you have to start a new business or ask for a raise. In case you have been postponing your plans, you might want to think them through, take them seriously and start realising them. If you are looking for a job, again, patience is the keyword with which you are going to be successful and effective.

The Question of Study

Now you can learn the most from the people, who do not stand out from the crowd. Be modest, persistent and patient because these lead you to success.

Health Interpretation

It is time for a lifestyle change and to fast a little. Since the Hermit card indicates the turning toward the spiritual world, this is one of the best periods of physical purification too. Through the harmonisation of body and mind you can move ahead more confidently until you reach your goals. (Relating to conscious eating there is a large scientific literature, therefore I will not get into it deeper, but it would be worth to turn to the Ayurvedic therapy, for example.)

Family Interpretation

If you have the opportunity during this current period, spend more time with the older members of your family, whose life experiences can be most helpful to you. Moreover, it is also possible that the younger members of your family may turn to you with their concerns and ask for your advice.

Task

The Hermit retreats from the world into voluntary solitude, so undisturbed and excluding any outside influence he would gain insight into his hidden self and fight his own shadows, fears and doubts. You need to do the same, to be able to teach wisdom to people later, similarly to Nietzsche's Zarathustra. Examine also whether there are any unfinished situations or relationships in your life and clarify them.

The Message of the Card

The Hermit is the symbol of wisdom, related to the archetype of the pilgrim. The goal is finding a new path, the prerequisite of which is psychoanalysis, the full revealing of personality and in order to achieve this, one needs to shut out the external world's influence. Since not everyone is willing to undertake voluntary solitude, this station is often preceded by an event, which inflicts confinement and retreat. The Hermit card demands self-abnegation and also requires the analysis of the past and the exploration of the hidden subliminal content, in order to get closer to the recognition of regularities of fate and personality.

Emotions: tranquillity, solitude, relaxation
Stage of life: wisdom, independence, withdrawal, introversion

People illustrated on the card are Géza Gárdonyi and Christian Rosenkreutz

Géza Gárdonyi the hermit of Eger (1863-1922)

In Eger, in the Kiralyszék town district there is a small house with a porch. 'The hermit of Eger', Géza Gárdonyi lived and worked here in the last decade of his life. He was one of the major writers of Hungarian literature. If I think about him, the former heroes of the Castle of Eger come to my mind, that is, his greatest work titled Egri Csillagok/ *Eclipse of the Crescent Moon.* No one would have been able to depict human greatness and altruistic patriotism of Hungarian heroes more fascinatingly than Gárdonyi did it in this novel.

Géza Gárdonyi was born in Asgárd. The ancestors of his father Alexander Ziegler were German immigrants from Styria relatives of Martin Luther according to the family tradition. Alexander acquired qualification in mechanical engineering in Vienna, and he also registered several inventions, from which he obtained a significant income. When the 1848 revolution broke out in Hungary, he offered all his money to the independent Hungarian government. In Pest, he became the friend and confidant of the revolutionaries including Kossuth and Petőfi, then he founded a weapon factory in order to supply the national army. Due to the downfall of the revolution he lost everything, his life was saved only by a fake ID. From then on, he served as machinist on different estates, thus the family often had to move. He was married to Teresa Nagy, a woman of peasant origin. Their son Géza was born in 1863 in Asgárd, but was baptised in Gárdony, that is why he took up the name Géza Gárdonyi as a student journalist.

Géza Gárdonyi's way of starting a family was as adventurous as his father's. At the age of twenty-two he married the vicar of Dabrony's niece Mary Molnár Csányi, who only married him to free herself from the shackles of the rigorous upbringing that had existed at home. As the wife of the writer, she lived more freely and she frequently travelled to Budapest, where she stayed for days to have fun. A year later Géza saw the situation clearly, which he even described in his diary: "This marriage will end in divorce or in murder." Fortunately, the latter did not happen, although their divorce proceedings lasted a long time, more precisely, thirteen years. During those ten years which they spent more or less together, they had four children, Géza Gárdonyi did not even want to acknowledge the fourth one as to be his.

After his failed marriage, in 1890, he nurtured affectionate feelings first for a short period of time toward his foster daughter, called Margaret Feszty (Masa) and then for six years toward schoolmistress Margaret Szarvassy. The Feszty's refused his marriage proposal, and his latter love was not fulfilled, at first because of the reserved conduct of the writer, then – when Margaret was about to agree – Gárdonyi shirked the marriage proposal citing his unsettled family status.

After moving to Eger, for nearly two decades Gárdonyi was bonded in a mostly platonic relationship with Mátékovics Tóth Ilona (as the writer called Mila), who left her husband and the livelihood he provided and she was his loyal soul mate and caregiver while he was sick and pinned to bed – until his death. For the author, Mila ultimately embodied the image of that female paragon, whose fragile figure and almost ethereal pure soul appeared successively in Gárdonyi's prose.

Gárdonyi graduated from the teacher training institute in Eger, thereafter he was a rural teacher for six years. During the years of teaching among miserable living conditions, the bitter feeling of neglect accumulated in him, so later he even applied to be a monk, but the head of the Bratislava Franciscan order dismissed his application. Then he became a journalist and worked for some time in Budapest. From 1897 until his death, he lived and worked in Eger, secluded from the world. The legend around him emerged immediately after moving to Eger, while he was still alive. He was addressed by his contemporaries as 'the hermit of Eger', or after his novel the *Invisible Man*. He had the reputation of being inaccessible, the reputation of a man who searches escape from prying eyes, however there was a lot of exaggeration in this.

The myth arose due to the unanimous reports of his fellow writers visiting his house in Eger. According to these reports, Gárdonyi's study room was windowless, the writer walled up the windows of the house; nevertheless, he just held the window panes closed because of the frequent and severe headache. However, it is a fact he devoted all this period to literature and the Eger solitude gave birth to his most prolific period of his art. Enjoyment of sensual pleasures was far from him, he disregarded physical delights and thought very high of the transcendental, almost religious worship. Furthermore, although Gárdonyi's soul was indeed wounded by love disappointments and he turned away from the superficial male-female relationship providing only physical fulfilment, in the last stage of his life he still found true love, and a soul mate in the person of Mila.

Although Gárdonyi was an advocate of *embourgeoisement*, his favourite heroes come from the poor villages. He asserted what János Arany did: the nation is shaped by talented men standing out from common people. He was passionately interested in the nation's past, the villagers' life and the language of the people. His style is simple and easy to understand. He preferred to write about children and young people from among the poor – especially in his historical novels, his heroes struggle themselves forward through education.

Christian Rosenkreutz, the founder of the Rosicrucians (1378–1484)

Christian Rosenkreutz originated from a German noble family. His parents – after becoming very poor – sent the child to a monastery, when he was five years old. The young man grew quickly, he learned Latin and Greek then set out to visit the Holy Sepulchre. At the vicinity of Damascus, he became seriously ill and the Arab wise men healed him. As a result, he learned Arabic and then he also learned the Arabic 'mysterious' sciences. Later he went to Egypt, where he got acquainted with the ancient Christian teachings. Furthermore, from there he travelled to Spain through North Africa. According to the legend, he found St John's lost book, which then he hid in the palace of Lordat in France. Upon his return, his fellow scientists excluded him, therefore he gathered seven friends and disciples around him, with whom in 1407 he founded the Rosicrucian Order. Although in relation with his life and with his mere existence, numerous scientific theories have been brought to daylight, the foundation of the Rosicrucian Order interwove with his name.

The symbol of the Order was the dark cross and the light coloured rose. The cross symbolised sacrifice and hardship, while the light coloured rose symbolised delectation and reward. According to the rules of the Order, its members, without exceptions had to be physicians and committed bachelors. All of them took an oath not to disclose the secret of the society to anyone – with the only exception that each of them had to find a successor before they die. However, the recruitment to the Rosicrucian Order had strict rituals. They did not disclose the secrets to the candidate immediately. The main master first tried to 'figure out' the person's aptitude with questions. Nevertheless, several generations of secret members replaced each other, until the beginning of the 17th century, when the growing religious freedom made it possible to expand the membership rapidly.

Christian allegedly spent his old age as a hermit in a cave and lived 106 years. Even in his seclusion he led a lively intellectual life, this is 'testified' by a set of amazing, incomprehensible signs, drawings and scrolls. Although to this day no one has been able to decipher his 'recipes', people believe that the master found the secret of the Philosopher's Stone, with which not only gold can be produced. The Rosicrucians in fact believe that with the help of the Philosopher's Stone any disease disappears and human life can also be extended.

Being aware of this, we can declare that Rosicrucianism maybe evolved out of an alchemical approach, as a result of Christian Rosenkreutz's influence. Its origin can be dated around 1614-1616 when three books were published, which were created by the occult brotherhood. The supposed author is Johann Valentin Andreae. The first work is *Fama Fraternitatis* (The Fame of the Brotherhood of Rosicrucianism). In this, Christian Rosenkreutz meets the wise men of Demcar. The second book is *Confessio Fraternatitis* (The Confession of the Brotherhood of RC) flashes details of Rosenkreutz's life and encourages to join. The third one *Chymische Hochzeit Christiani Rosencreutz* (The *Chymical Wedding of Christian Rosenkreutz)***,** in which the participant discovers the secret books of Wisdom.

Many scientists claim that the Rosicrucian Order is a direct branch of the Knights Templar Mystery and they took over the guarding of the Grail after the fall of the Templars. According to Andreas Libevius, the rose and the cross were created in relation to Luther's seal, which depicts a cross growing out from a heart in the middle of 5 rose petals. The rose refers to the chalice of Grail, which collects the blood, and the five petals of the rose symbolise the five holy wounds of Jesus. The centre of the rose is the symbol of Jesus' Sacred Heart and of love. The cross is the symbol of victory over death, turning toward the spirit and also the symbol of the four elements.

According to scientists, the Rosicrucians have showed up throughout the centuries under different forms and names, but always with considerable political influence. Nowadays there are several branches of the Rosicrucian Order, such as the Egyptian Rose Cross and the Golden Rose Cross. The strongest Rosicrucian movement is in the US, where the Rosicrucian principles closely mix up with the country's history, with the principles of freedom and independence. Several US presidents were also members of the Society, such as Abraham Lincoln. In Europe, these societies operate mainly in the Netherlands and England. In Hungary the first Hungarian Rosicrucian lodge was established in 1769 in Presov.

Famous Rosicrucians:
16-17th century:
Paracelsus
Nostradamus
Francis Bacon
Johann Valentin Andreae
Robert Fludd
Angelus Silesius
Jakob Böhme
Comenius
Henricus Madathanus Theosophus

Rosicrucians in Hungary in the 18th century
The Count of Saint-Germain
Sándor Báróczi
György Bessenyei

In the 20th century, Rudolf Steiner dealt extensively with Rosicrucianism in many of his presentations and books.

'Fortune favours the bold.' (Virgil)

WHEEL OF FORTUNE

István Széchenyi and Alexander the Great

The Interpretation of the Picture

The card Wheel of Fortune or Wheel of Destiny has many known variations, since the illustration has countless forms of visualisation. Generally, a blind and capricious Goddess spins the wheel of fate, to which people are handcuffed.

Their fate moves on with the wheel, because power and wealth are perishable and people cannot control their own fate. In Love Tarot, a Wheel of Fortune mandala can be seen on the card indicating that people possess free will. Here, too, the Goddess Fortuna stands in front of the wheel, on the wheel of fortune itself however there are three female figures, the Moirai, who represent memory, intelligence and divination. Since only these make it possible to understand past, present and future. Although the wheel seems to be motionless, it rotates counterclockwise. The wheel on this card is the symbol of birth and death, but can be interpreted as a symbol of karma and it also symbolises the chakras.

People have been intrigued about the topic of fate and destiny for thousands of years. Some say our fate is foreordained and no matter what we do, destiny will fulfil it. Others say we control our own destiny, there is however a guiding thread, but basically it all depends on our decisions.

I think that regarding the question of fate, as in all things, you have to find the balance. One has to accept that fate exists, everyone has a pre-determined path direction. Since it is not a coincidence that you were born precisely into that family, precisely in that location and precisely into that life situation. These showed you something, as you showed to those who have been around you since childhood. Later you got out into the world and kept changing constantly. Your teachers, friends, colleagues, relationships have shaped you. Everyone has 'added' something to you, and you also have given something out of yourself to them. Obviously, your abilities and desires determined where your path should lead. However, if you really think about it, all depended on your own decisions, because probably there was not only a single option in front of you.

Instead of philosophising, probably it would be sufficient simply to admit that fate exists, there are things we cannot avoid (e.g. our parents, our birth), but if we are mature enough, we can shape our destiny consciously, through our decisions, our moods and acts. This is why I have made some small changes on this card.

Number: X
Letter: J
Main element: Water
Astrology: Virgo, Capricorn Scorpio, Mars, Jupiter and Mercury
Meditation: cyclic meditation

Important Symbols Appear on the Card

The Moirai, also known as the Fates are part of a triad and according to mythology, each of them had a separate task. Clotho spins the Thread of Life, Lachesis measures its length and Atropos finally cuts the thread. Separately, neither of them could carry out their task. Namely: the thread could be spun without end, but without a goal it would not make any sense. If there is no spinning, there is no thread either, the length of which could be measured. If there is no thread, there is nothing to cut. Thus the three parts personify one and the same thing: Life.

The stationary shaft symbolises stability while the rotating wheel refers to the process of time, the successive cycles of years. Night is followed by day, day is followed by night, they alternate the same way as the seasons do. Although the processes recur, the wheel always moves forward.

The wheel i.e. the circle is an ancient and archetypal form that appears already while young children are learning to draw. This universal cosmic symbol refers to the eternal cycle and the different time cycles among others. The Wheel of Fortune card is a warning regarding the twists and turns of Fate. It has its ups and downs, always turns and is always on the move. It also refers to the reincarnation cycle, moreover to the changes that are due in everyday life. The embodiment of harmony is nothing but the perfect circle. Nowadays the wheel is used to depict the chakras i.e. energy centres, although they were originally portrayed with discs rather than wheels.

The Wheel of Fortune is usually an eight-spoked wheel thus is in connection with the eight cardinal directions of outer space and with the eight petals of the lotus.

Number ten is the Master number of the created world, the symbol of infinity and the completeness of the universe.

The Cards Meaning in a Spread, if you Picked This

Archetype: Fortuna's favourite

Negative pole: the eternal loser

Psychological Interpretation: once you understand fate, you can look differently at your path, your fate and destiny.

Spiritual Interpretation: You need to understand the laws of the Wheel of Fate, so you can finally dismount. If we take into account all the good and the bad that have been 'given' to us we are lucky because we can decide our own life's quality. Furthermore, it is up to us how we manage our innate abilities, our inner knowledge and experiences throughout our life.

General Interpretation

The term *luck* can be used in a variety of senses, but we usually call someone lucky if something good happens to a person in spite of what they reckoned, and if they do not suffer from that bad thing, which they expected. If you feel that nothing goes the way you want, remember that you yourself give rise to everything in your life, whether you believe in it or not.

Everyone has different dreams about what they want to achieve in their life. For instance, it is conceivable that you would like to change something about yourself, you want to live your life differently. Maybe you have even taken a few steps to do this, but maybe something is just taking shape in you and you have no idea how to begin. Maybe you would like to communicate a lot better, to surround yourself with better relationships, become healthier or simply just to earn more money. You can achieve all this and even more, if you can transform and regulate the forms of your behaviour and the processes taking place in your mind. I know it is much easier to give up citing the current fashionable expression: *aaaaah, fate definitely wanted it to be this way*, but I believe that fate has nothing to do with it. Fate can bring you together with the right people for you, but if you do not pay attention and you are not present in your own life, you can miss them easily.

Researchers have proven that there are some important habits that determine how lucky you can be, because most of the events that occur in your life are completely under your control. For instance, check out what is good in a situation, so you will attract even more good things to yourself. Visualise it, see realistically what you desire as many times as you can and thus it is more likely to happen. A big part of luck depends on seizing the opportunity, do not worry, be glad of opportunities. This card means that you are going to be fortunate in whatever you desire, everything seems to be successful and nothing can stop you. The laws of luck are serving you.

Reversed Interpretation

What was once up, it has to go down as well. It is time to slow down, unwind, the Wheel of Fortune will turn again, just wait until the time for action comes again.

Love Interpretation

'Laugh on Friday cry on Sunday', that is you have good and bad times – emotional fluctuation is now inevitable. If it stands together with the Empress, the Star and the Sun, you are going to achieve your desires soon, a happy period is going to begin in your life. Your loved one wants to share his or her life with you. But if you also picked out the Lovers, the Fool or the Moon card, your life is still going to be characterised by uncertainty. You have to learn to express your feelings in a more proper way.

Material Interpretation

Favourable situations are going to arise, and thanks to your spiritual strength and decisions, you are to achieve what you have been fighting for. Success is coming gradually, therefore be glad of 'everyday' successes too!

Work

You can count on professional success. It is a good time to sign contracts. However, if the Fool or the Lovers card stands beside the Wheel of Fortune, it indicates that although you work a lot, success will not be equivalent with your work. Do not give up, although things are moving forward slowly, your situation is going to become more balanced. Pay attention to details! (Number 10 refers to October or to the changes that are due within 10 months, always take this into account!)

The Question of Study

Minor results, small successes can be expected.

Health Interpretation

Only the fear of changes hinders you. If you dissolve this fear, nothing will stand in the way of your healing process. If you are healthy, pay attention, because your current intensive lifestyle can easily make you sick. The key word is change, alteration! (The Hermit and the 13th card together with the Wheel of Fortune warn of bone problems.)

Family Interpretation

Your relationships can consolidate, become tighter only if you find the proper way to express your feelings. This card brings stability and positive emotions.

Task

Good and bad are not preordained in our lives. Behind our acts, there lies our own will or the lack of it. We can neither avoid our fate, nor the tasks of our life, still we can do a lot in order to shape certain events of our lives. We can shift the events to our advantage or disadvantage. The movement of the Wheel of Fate enables you to feel high or down. At the same time, it encourages you to be the master of your own fate, exercise your free will more consciously.

The Message of the Card

This card indicates fateful changes in life, it shows gains and development. Your life is set in motion, changes can be expected. However, in reversed situation it indicates an unexpected misfortune caused by an external force.

Emotions: creativity, success or failure
Stage of life: progression, regression, restarting, self-realisation

Personalities illustrated on the card are István Széchenyi and Alexander the Great

István Széchenyi, The Greatest Hungarian (1791-1860)

He was the initiator of the reform movement in the 1820s, an excellent writer and a statesman, a member of an aristocratic landowner family. In accordance with his father's will, he was already a soldier at the age of 17. He took part in the battles against Napoleon, where he stood out thanks to his courage and audacity. He travelled a lot and while traveling he became aware that his country had been underdeveloped. He found that his historical name had been also associated with serious responsibility, thus he decided to promote his country's fate all through his life. On his return he became the initiator of reforms and the most important figure of the reform era.

It is almost impossible to enumerate all the things he did for the Hungarian nation during his life. He established the Hungarian Academy of Sciences, contributed to the steam navigation on the Duna (Danube) and Tisza, helped the construction of the Lánchíd (Chain Bridge), supported the construction of the railway network and supported the idea to unify Buda and Pest as Budapest. He was given the position of Minister of Transport and Public Works in the Batthyány government formed in April 1848.

However, he was not able to bear the tensions between Vienna and the independent Hungarian government. He resigned from his post and on 5 September 1848, he went to the mental institution of Döbling upon the advice of his doctor, Almási Balogh Pál. In Döbling he soon regained his spiritual creative power and shortly he started to follow the national and European political events and affairs with keen interest. However, the series of harassments and searches in his house again consumed Szechenyi's strength. Only his death stopped the persecutions, when he committed suicide.

He was not lucky in love affairs either: sinful passion and self-denial, fight and painful resignation accompanied him through his life. Although he loved and was loved in return, he had to wait decades for real happiness.

His first true love was his brother, Paul's wife, for which he was soon discredited as well. Therefore, he wished to forget this sorrow of hopeless love, this love experienced as sin – the memory of which accompanied him throughout his life and never let him rest. So, he followed Countess Hunyady Gabriella who his contemporaries referred to as 'the diabolical beauty' all the way to Italy. However, the Countess was also married, thus she kept rejecting the man's passionate approach.

After the rejections, Széchenyi came to an important decision: ending his former bachelor life and getting married. His choice fell on his first love, Caroline's sister, the beautiful Selina Meade, whom he eventually could not marry, because Selina's guardian refused his marriage proposal. The old rumour and probably also Caroline contributed to this.

His next love was another married lady, the wife of Károly Zichy Jr., born Countess Crescence Seilern, one of the most flourishing phenomena of the Viennese society. Széchenyi had known the famous beauty for some years already, but he began to adore her only in the late summer of 1824. From then on Crescence's life intertwined with the life of the 'Greatest Hungarian'. First she honourably withstood István Széchenyi's continuous love siege because being the mother of 14 children, she could not believe that young Széchenyi would choose her. Thus, for a while she had been just his inspiration, his 'Beatrice', at the beginning of the man's public career. To convince her about his seriousness, Széchenyi even sent his works on reform to Crescence, who also learned Hungarian for the sake of the man. She did not yet understand his 1828 work *Lovakrul* (About Horses), but two years later she encouraged her love to implement his plans, which he had written in the *Hitel* (Credit) and recommended to her barely veiling, and which she read and returned with her detailed notes. Following their wedding in 1836, she stood beside him as a faithful companion through the struggles and trials, until the tragic end in Döbling.

István Széchenyi has been deservedly honoured even to this day. Besides performing his political and patriotic deeds, he lived his daily life, he loved, protected, feared for and accepted his love even with fourteen children. In addition to their two own sons, Széchenyi raised Crescence's seven children as his own and also the seven children of her former deceased husband, Count Zichy from his previous marriages. Last but not least he maintained a very good relationship with the Zichy children, who considered him as their father.

Alexander the Great (356–323 BC)

Alexander the Great is one of the most famous historical figures from antiquity. He was the king of Macedonia, the ruler of the Hellenic world, the conqueror of Persia, one of the greatest generals of antiquity. What we know about Alexander the Great is based primarily on the writings of four men who lived nearly five centuries later. Not even the *Ephemeride*, Alexander's royal journal can be regarded reliable because winners like to write from their own point of view and thereby reshape history. The Alexander novel, which is often referred to as a reliable source, is nothing more than the product of imagination and has only little to do with reality. Therefore, I am telling stories for you about the warrior king, based on the writings of the two most reliable authors, that is with the help of Flavius Arrianus and Plutarch.

I am not writing about him exclusively as a great and benevolent conqueror. I am mentioning his faults as well. For example, that out of paranoia, he massacred his friends and often sent most members of his troops into senseless death. Although his brain was amazingly sharp, Alexander was also a big and fortunate gambler. However, it is indisputable that he was the first ruler who united the whole world. He was in the right place at the right time: he wanted to conquer the world and the world was ready to be conquered.

His teacher, Aristotle, who was the wisest scholar of his time, had a great impact on his life. He became an excellent military leader thanks to his fearsome tactical sense, reckless courage and ingenious, calmly considered strategies. It was not books that taught him the most important fighting techniques, but he learned them during crusades, fighting along with his father. His political cleverness was perfected in the royal court full of scheming courtiers, therefore it is no wonder that he was able to react extremely quickly to unexpected and dangerous situations. Although we will never know the truth, it appears that he was responsible for his own father's, Phillip's death as well, whom he killed on a summer night, together with his mother, the fearsome Olympias. (By the way, the beautiful queen, who was a member of a snake-worshiping cult, considered Zeus himself to be Alexander's real father.). According to other sources, the father's killer was her former lover, Pausanias who probably stabbed Phillip out of jealousy. In the Macedonian royal court, as a matter of fact, homosexuality was equally accepted and widespread as polygamy.

Thus we can state that in 336 BC, it was not a simple boy from an ordinary family who occupied the throne of Macedonia, but a fascinating yet fundamentally unpredictable young man, whom his mother raised as the son of Zeus. After his accession to the throne, he needed money because his father in his final years had led Macedonia into financial bankruptcy. He decided that if he was going to start a crusade anyway, he might as well kill two birds with one stone: to show the world and the people of the Greek cities under Persian rule, what a real liberator is like. We can say that he was driven by two goals: upload the Macedonian treasury with the gold of the Persians and liberate the cities under the rule of the Persians. During his long conquering crusades, he always had Homer's heroic poem, the Iliad with him. As he was passionately fond of the glorious past of the Hellenes, he even crossed the Hellespontus in the same direction as the ancient Greeks had done when they were heading to Troy. Thus he faced Darius III, the Persian king for the first time, who had no idea how dangerous opponent the young Hellenistic ruler would be.

The young warlord managed to defeat the Persian king in the first battle, who later was forced to flee twice. Although the Persian army outnumbered the Macedonian troops five to one, Darius' courage swayed against Alexander's audacity and his battle-hardened men. Losing the bloody battle of Issus, the

Persian monarch left his mother, wife and even children behind and fled in panic. Namely, according to ancient Persian customs the family accompanied the ruler to see how he gains an overwhelming victory. They did not expect defeat.

Later when Darius wanted to ransom his family, Alexander the Great, as a tough Emperor, charged him in a humiliating letter not to flee further, but stand up to fight with him instead.

King Alexander's message to Darius:

"In the future, whenever you communicate with me, call me king of Asia; do not write to me as if you were equal, whatever you used to have is my possession from now on. If not, I shall deal with you as a wrongdoer. If you wish to lay claim to the title of king, then stand your ground and fight for it; do not take to flight, as I shall pursue you wherever you may be."

After all this, it became apparent to Darius, that only the death of one of them would put an end to the fight between them. Although the political situation of the 4th century BC forced them to fight against each other till death, it is doubtless, that apart from the letter, they behaved with each other as gentlemen and did not conceal that they were impressed by the other's strategy. It was also clear to them that the winner would shape history.

The fact that he got his opponent's mother, wife, two daughters and the six-year-old heir to the throne into his hands, was a reward for Alexander the Great. The soldiers guarded the hostages carefully, Alexander himself treated them kindly. Two years later, when Darius learned that his wife had died in childbirth, before the final battle he sent a secret message to Alexander, in which he pleaded for his family to be released and betrothed one of his daughters with a dowry of total 30,000 talents. One might think that the Persian king was naïve, because he probably knew that Alexander the Great himself had got his wife pregnant. But he was not. He loved his wife with all his heart.

Similar to Alexander, Darius had come to the throne in stormy conditions and had the reputation of a fearsome warrior. However, cruelty was far from him. As a Persian ruler, he did not want to change the religion of the conquered people. All he insisted on was taxes and required that his subjects would bow down to the ground before their ruler, the Persian king. (It pained the Hellenes to perform this bowing and so did the Spartans). Alexander the Great and Darius faced each other in three battles over a period of nearly four years. Although they were both excellent warlords, the coolness and audacity of the twenty years younger Alexander the Great terrified Darius. So he met his doom.

After another triumph over the Persian monarch thanks to his excellent tactical senses, the broken Darius fled to the mountains to carry on a partisan battle, while Alexander the Great was marching in his much-loved Hellenic empire as a true warlord: a liberator.

Despite all this, he respected his enemy, an evidence of which is the fact, that when his soldier found the treacherously murdered Darius, Alexander immediately rushed there and had him taken back to the Persian capital. And then, to show that only a king can kill another king, he arrested the assassin and according to ancient Persian customs, he cut off his nose and ears before beheading him.

Alexander the Great was completely enchanted by the Persian culture and tradition system. He had taken up several Persian customs, passionately plunged into drinking and other delights. The greatest leader of all times had three Asian wives, two children that we know of, his soldiers fathered about a hundred-two hundred thousand children to the local people's women. These are not small numbers at all.

Alexander, like his father, had several mistresses at the same time. Two people played a prominent role in his life: his childhood friend, Hephaestion, who was his first love and Rhoxana, the beautiful Persian princess, who was his wife. She already fascinated him with her beauty on their first meeting, which naturally triggered great jealousy out of Hephaestion, although there was no real reason for this. In fact, Hephaestion remained Alexander the Great's sole supporter, confidant and lover until the end of his life. A very strong and deep alliance tied them together.

After the death of Hephaestion, Alexander was inconsolable, writhing on the ground with grief and then he had the doctor executed because he could not help his lover suffering from fever. While organising his friend's funeral with great care, (maybe it has been the world's most expensive funeral), his anger did not subside. He became irritable, suspicious and unhappy. He could feel that he was going to die soon, but he did not mind that at all. This tragedy perhaps foreshadowed his own doom, in the following years the ruler drank a lot and became wilder, while his health condition was rapidly deteriorating.

A few months later, he summoned his confidants and told them that his life was coming to an end. He talked about Rhoxana and the baby, which she carried in her womb. He told them that if the child was a boy, he would be rightfully entitled to claim the throne. However, the king was very well aware of the fact that the Greeks would not like to see a semi-foreign monarch on the throne. He also knew that his chieftains would fight over the realm which would fall apart because of them, so all he said with a sigh was: 'they should suffer their own fate'. Then, just eight months later he followed his lover to the grave, keeping the promise made to him: he would not survive the loss of his first love.

In connection with his death, from ancient descriptions for a long time some scientists concluded that the monarch had died from poisoning or from malaria aggravated by pneumonia. It is certain that the constant physical strain, the lecherous lifestyle and excessive alcohol consumption did enormous damage to his body and therefore, liver cirrhosis cannot be excluded either. Today's historians believe that in addition to his lifestyle, malaria killed the conqueror.

I have read that two weeks after his death, Egyptian embalmers arrived in Babylon, where the monarch's body was found in perfect condition, despite the hot summer. Even the colour of his face was as if he were still alive. This was considered as a heavenly sign referring to the almighty personality of Alexander. According to modern scientific views, the king was probably still alive in a kind of final coma. This state however was not known at the time, so the embalmers began to work immediately. If this is true, perhaps it is also conceivable that they exterminated the world's greatest warlord.

Alexander the Great was not mistaken, a fight for supremacy started already at his deathbed. Although the chieftains finally agreed and divided the empire, riots broke out soon. Meanwhile Rhoxana gave birth to a son, who was named Alexander IV. For the sake of peace, the leaders regarded the child as king, but ruled without him. A few years later, they poisoned him along with her mother, so he never actually ruled, the world's greatest empire simply crumbled.

The tomb of Alexander the Great later became a place of pilgrimage. Julius Caesar, Octavian, Hadrian and a dozen other monarchs went there and paid tribute to him. For nearly a century and a half, the monarch's body embalmed in honey and placed in golden coffin rested undisturbed and then, in spite of 1600 years searching, the corpse of the ancient world's conqueror completely disappeared and to this day has still missing.

A lively debate has been going on about Alexander the Great's political and historical role. Was he a wise visionary or just a ruthless, reckless conqueror? It is indisputable that following the footsteps of his father, Philip II, he conquered all Asia Minor and Persia in just 12 years. He covered a larger area than the Roman Empire did in thousand years. He did not reign with violence: he allowed the conquered kingdoms' rulers to keep their power and they would constantly provide him warriors in return. His short but successful reign meant the beginning of a new era in ancient history and culture i.e. Hellenism. Furthermore, he was the most famous military leader in world history up to Napoleon's age, who also fought in the first lines of battles, surrounded by his loyal bodyguards. His life is strongly linked to the history of Macedonia and its rise. Although his empire collapsed at the time of his death, Alexander's personality has become an immortal legend.

'There are only two mistakes one can make along the road to truth; not going all the way, and not starting.' (Buddha)

JUSTICE

King Mátyás and Archbishop János Vitéz

The Interpretation of the Picture

There are many kinds of truth/justice:

Legal truth is when we give everyone what is rightfully theirs. Historical truth is all the events that have happened. Mathematical truth is the law of ratios and proportion. Philosophic truth is the conscious reflection of reality. Logical truth is the law of evidence, namely, that everything is equal to itself, everything has a proper reason. There is also the principle of contradiction: meaning that something cannot exist and not exist simultaneously.

Justice is a classical virtue. The card depicts a serious woman holding a sword and scales. This card is a symbol of weighting the Soul, thus it is also related to Karma. The weighting of the Soul is incorporated into the Christian mythology and art also, through the depiction of the Last Judgment. At the same time, we can find related representations in Eastern art as well: for instance, according to Indian beliefs, after every earthly life the soul is judged in the afterlife and the individual receives the reward in Paradise or gets punishment in Hell, before (s)he re-enters the wheel of fate and is reborn. Many people relate the proverb, *As you sow, so shall you reap,* to the card and refer to Raphael's painting as well, which proclaims the virtues of truth, 'Iustitia suum cuique tribuit' – i.e. Justice renders everyone their due.

Number: XI
Letter: H
Main element: Water
Astrology: Cancer, Libra, Scorpio, Sagittarius, Mars, Venus
Meditation: Balance Meditation

Important Symbols Appear on the Card

The dress of Goddess Iustitia is red, indicating God Mars, while the indigo blue robe refers to Venus. Thus the duality of male and female energy is present on the card. A veil covers Iustitia's eyes, which emphasises that Justice is blind and that the Goddess judges ignoring prestige, performance and other visible factors. She focuses inward, that is how she maintains the Harmony of Order.

Her scale pans symbolise the beginning and the end, time and space, the sword indicates straightness and worldly power, with which Lady Justice is able to strike and separate bad from good. The scales also indicate the heaviness of the question. The woman's posture is straight, cannot be thrown off balance, also she sits opposite us.

In Christian numerology, 11 was the number of martyrdom, however, it is interesting that the medieval numerologists seeking secret meaning of numbers believed that every number had positive and negative implications. Except for the number 11: caught between the figures 10 and 12, 11 itself was pure evil and represented the sinners.

In modern numerology, 11 is considered to be the main master number, because it is a two-digit number that consists of identical numbers, thus its meaning is also doubled. As a matter of fact, according to present-day numerologists, 11 represents balance. This number refers to the link between male and female equality, indicates the balance between work and fun but also the mental and spiritual balance. Number 11 is the gamblers' favourite too.

The Goddess resembles a little to The High Priestess, because the number of Justice is the number of the High Priestess as well (1 + 1 = 2). In fact, Iustitia's straight posture suggests that there is no earthly power that could ever throw her off balance. So, this Arcana points to equality and balance in all aspects and creates stability.

The card's meaning in a spread, if you picked this

Archetype: The Judge

Negative pole: The hypocrite and/or dishonest person

Psychological Interpretation: This is the moment of truth. You get answers and feedback. As a result, you are going to change your lifestyle consciously, based on your own decision.

Spiritual Interpretation

The world is exactly as much as you perceive it. Everything you perceive is completely unique. The card shows how sincere and honest you are and how pleased you are with yourself.

General Interpretation

The processes taking place within you determine what happens to you, what you see and hear from the information and situations around you. You shape your present, nothing happens independently from you. Everything is influenced by your beliefs, misconceptions, your thoughts and choices. You need to become aware of the responsibility to control your words, thoughts and your attention because the power surrounding you and coming alive within you is enormous and intelligent.

Reversed Interpretation

Do not think that you can be only an observer of life just because you simply slide into a situation, into a world and then everything goes as it is written in the book of life. Most of the time this is not like that. Free choice, free will can be a sensational tool in your hands (and in the hands of others too), but if you make bad decisions, listen to bad advisors, this may turn against you. Most people were taught that one must accept the situation or sufferings that fate reserves for them. Now is the time to develop, influence and control your own reality, be the 'skipper of your own ship'. Seek Balance!

Love Interpretation

Now everything is going to turn out. If you are tired of conflicts, it is time to make firm decisions. Although sometimes change can be painful, but do not forget, not even in difficult moments that if you take the right choices, you may have a brilliant future in front of you. Soon everything will be clear and balanced.

Material Interpretation

It is a great moment to start your plans and business deals, because this card refers to the beginning of the seven years of plenty, meaning that every plan of yours is going to be crowned with success. Do not expect undeserved revenue, you can receive only what you deserve.

Work

Sometimes events happen very fast and sometimes you feel like being stuck in one phase. Hang in, you still have some tests to overcome in order to ensure success. If you work more now, you are going to reach your goals and social recognition more easily.

The Question of Study

In case of legal studies, you can expect great successes. In all other cases, the success of your exams depends only on the energy you invest. Warning: In case of cheating there is a huge risk of being caught!

Health Interpretation

Here too, truth dominates. Now the effect of the past months and years reveals: if you have lived a healthy life and paid attention to yourself, you have no reason to complain. However, if you have not done everything for yourself, now it is time to change. Turn to a doctor, go for a check-up. Pay attention to hygiene, now the risk of infection is also higher. Start to meditate!

Family Interpretation

In every family related official case (concluding contracts, real estate transactions) you should consult an attorney for advice. Now you can enforce your rights.

Task

One of the most important tasks now is to follow your inner self with the utmost attention. After a while, you will notice that the spiritual empathy that will grow in you will be affecting every area of your life. Look for answers, observe and try to figure out who you really are, where your life is heading to, how you experience love and your relationships. Sometimes this is certainly a mystery, but you are a part of this mystery and everything is possible in your life if you do your best to achieve it.

The Message of the Card

This card is the card of the inner self, the conscience. So far, you have done a lot of things in order to comply with the external world. You have to restore the balance, you have to follow your inner voice. You have to learn the laws of life better, because not knowing the law cannot be an excuse in the Court of life. This way you can avoid the penalties for breaking them.

Emotions: duality, justice, tranquillity, tact, incorruptibility, honesty and balance

Stage of life: A mature age: you have found your place in the world, the fruits of all your labour have ripened. You have raised your children, you are socially appreciated, something is still missing. You need you to dissolve dissatisfaction and the feeling of guilt in yourself, only then can you set new goals and achieve new wishes.

Personalities illustrated on the card are King Mátyás and Archbishop János Vitéz

King Mátyás the Just (1443–1490)

King Mátyás was one of the greatest Hungarian rulers. In Hungarian folklore he has survived as 'King Mátyás the Just', many legends tell how he wandered the countryside in disguise and how he defended the innocent against their afflicting masters.

He gained rich experience in social and political life already as a child. Under the instruction of the most educated man in the country, János Vitez, Bishop of Oradea, he acquired the humanistic general knowledge of his time. In addition to Hungarian, he spoke Latin, Czech and German. He became an interpreter at his father's important political meetings.

He was only 11 years old when his father knighted him in Beograd (Nándorfehérvár) with the Transylvanian voivode's sword. His father's premature death ruined him, when his brother was executed, he was imprisoned by King László V captivity, who first took the young boy to Vienna and then to Prague. In the autumn of 1457, László died of plague, thus the following year, on 24th January, Mátyás – with the help of the gentry classes who had supported his father – was elected king and Mihály Szilágyi was appointed to be the governor. This was an extraordinary thing actually, because Mátyás Corvinus had no family relationship with any royal families, more than that, he did not originate from any royal dynasties, neither from the paternal nor the maternal side. The fact that he could take the throne of Hungary, was due, above all, to his father, János Hunyadi's exceptional military and political career. And also to the fact that after László died without a successor, the enthronement of a country governing, authority-practicing nobleman seemed the most logical solution to eliminate internal divisions. The ascension of Mátyás to the throne was therefore unprecedented in the history of medieval Hungary. As he did not have royal roots, the situation soon led to problems.

A lot was expected from the young monarch: the aristocrats would have liked him to be obedient and meek; the gentry expected his support against the landowners and the cities wished he would overcome external looters and prevent inflation. Moreover, the pope wanted to see the 'man of God' in him, who then wipes out the rest of the heretics and Muslims. Mátyás Hunyadi, however, soon proved to everyone that it was not his father's merit that made him worthy of the kingship, but his own abilities. He wanted unrestricted royal power and took the country into his own strong hands. From 1471 onwards, Mátyás sought to govern independently of the orders. He convoked the National Assembly less and less frequently. He entrusted his officials with the governance of the state, he governed with regulation rather than legislation. It was then that János Vitéz and Janus Pannonius conspired against him because they feared for the country, but Mátyás quickly disciplined them.

The history of the country and Mátyás could have developed differently if the young king had married Anna, the daughter of palatine László Garai, as agreed in Szeged in 1458. Since Anna Garai was closely related to three royal houses, the Piasts, the Luxembourgs and the Habsburgs, which would have meant a significant surplus of legitimacy for Mátyás (and his son, if he had one). Life however intervened.

We know three wives of Mátyás. For political reasons, at the age of 12, he had to marry Elizabeth of Celje, this would have sealed the cessation of rivalry between the Celjes and the Hunyadis, but the marriage only existed on paper. The young couple did not know each other, they did not even meet. The actual marriage was therefore cancelled. His second wife was Catherine of Poděbrady, the daughter of the Czech king. This was a real, but still a political marriage that lasted only a brief year, until the death of Catherine.

After the death of his second wife, in the neighbouring countries, the marriage proposals of the young king were often refused. However, after his successful warfare against the Czechs and the German emperor Frederick III enhanced his appreciation, the now-powerful king intervened in inner Italian conflicts, the result of which was his third marriage, the matrimony of Naples.

In 1476, he married Beatrice of Aragon, daughter of the King of Naples, but their marriage was overshadowed by the fact that they never had a child.

According to the rumours of that time, the reason for this was Beatrice's past: the Queen allegedly lived a very active love life in her adolescence and this could have caused her infertility. By 1480 it had already become clear that she was completely incapable of giving birth to a child, thus from then on, out of jealousy she did her best to prevent the accession of Mátyás' illegitimate son, János Corvin to the throne. Because she herself wanted to reign as a queen after the death of Mátyás.

Namely, in 1473 (before his marriage to Queen Beatrice), Mátyás had a son with Borbála Edelpeck, a common girl, daughter of a citizen from Poroszló. János Corvin (the first name János was given in honour of his grandfather) was a bit limp, but relatively handsome boy. His father had him raised by Italian humanists so he acquired high education. (Since Mátyás was an active, vigorous monarch, it is likely that the girl from Poroszló was not his only concubine.)

In his last years of life, not caring about his wife's protests, King Màtyàs tried to ensure the throne for his illegitimate son, János Corvin. As we all know, the attempt was unsuccessful, the prince never came to the throne of Hungary. Although he was engaged to the Duke of Milan's sister, Bianca Maria Sforza, while his father was still alive, they never married. In 1490 Corvin was defeated in the struggle for the throne, partly because the majority of the barons whom his father raised, did not support him. In his last years of life, Corvin referred to himself as the prince of Liptov, his son Christopher born from Beatrix Frangepán would have inherited this, but he died as a child in 1505, a year after his father and the Hunyadi dynasty died out with him.

János Vitéz (1408-1472)

The reason he is present on this card as well is because Matthias should have taken his wise observations into account and so the country could have defended itself more effectively against the Ottoman Turks.

Read the High Priest card!

'We can spend our lives letting the world tell us who we are. Sane or insane. Saints or sex addicts. Heroes or victims. Letting history tell us how good or bad we are. Letting our past decide our future. Or we can decide for ourselves.'
(Chuck Palahniuk)

The Hanged Man

Count Gyula Andrássy and Judas

The Interpretation of the Picture

On this card a young man can be seen, upside down, hanged from his left foot. His right leg crosses the other one from behind, at the level of the knee. He keeps his head completely straight, staring ahead, his arms are folded behind his back. The character faces exactly the card's beholder, not turning away in either direction. The man's face is relaxed and satisfied, not tortured. He hangs down from a cross beam, which is fastened between two bald trees, they frame the card. His gaze is calm and does not reflect any fear at all. Coins fall out of his pockets. This card is one of the most special cards in tarot decks. Each author has a different theory about it, but they all agree – including me – that the Hanged Man indicates the possible great awakening. It reminds most tarot masters of the dying and resurrecting God's topic.

The Hanged Man signifies broken life, uncertainty, sacrifice, repentance and abandonment, but if it appears reversed then it indicates lack of sacrifice, recklessness and the negative attitude toward necessary sacrifice. The card of the Hanged Man prevents our most desired plans to be achieved and suggests that for the time being we shall give up on achieving our goals. While this card has several meanings, it is certain that it predicts a stagnant period.

Number: XII
Letter: L
Main element: Water
Astrology: Uranus, Saturn, Jupiter, Aries, Libra, Pisces
Meditation: Release

Important Symbols Appear on the Card

In old decks, this card appears as the Thief and as the Traitor too, because the hanged man used to be identified with Judas, the primal, original traitor and the money purses or the coins falling out of his pocket refer to the thirty silver coins. Similar to Oswald Wirth's drawing, the logs that support the Hanged

Man's gallows show stumps with twelve lopped branches, six on each side. Love tarot follows the traditional way of depiction.

The shape of the gallows is similar to the Hebrew letter tau, which belongs to the card named World. This suggests that people sacrifice themselves on the level of everyday experience, in which they started their spiritual development. However, the rope, which the individual hangs from, is not tight, this shows that if you release the role of the victim, you will no longer be influenced by earthly things, because heaven will transmit good through your foot and gives you strength to stand on your foot again.

The coins falling out of his pocket indicate that man prioritises worldly riches or on the contrary, the coins symbolise the spiritual richness that can be obtained only by sacrifice.

The card's meaning in a spread, if you picked this

Archetype: The Victim, the Martyr

Negative pole: The tyrant, the oppressor

Psychological Interpretation

The Hanged Man hanging from the gallows upside down indicates that the truth seeker should stand on his/her head in a psychological sense. During this period, you have to offer sacrifice, sacrifice yourself in order to rediscover something hidden or lost in your own depths.

Spiritual Interpretation

The card suggests that the spirit is able to rule over matter. The Hanged Man card points to the possibility of your spiritual uprise. If you ascend, you will be able to understand and control your life, rather than exploiting it.

General Interpretation

Accept that you must bring sacrifice to attract exactly those things into your life that you would like to possess. You still depend very much on your past and on the person to whom you wanted to belong. You must practice releasing things to draw those new energies into your life, by which you can be elevated to a completely different level. In order to do this, you have to let those things go that you do not need any more. You need to dismiss the relationship, in which you have been suffering for a long time.

Be careful, think thoroughly about what is really making you suffer! Because it is conceivable that the relationship only needs a renewal, in this case, you have to let the past go that burdens the relationship. The process may take a long time, even if it seems that this is only a temporary condition. Evaluate yourself and now release everything that hinders you.

Interpretation of the Reversed Card

You want the change, but you are still holding on to the past. You are not ready to completely dismiss it and to let things follow their own course. Perhaps you wish to slow down the events that are inevitable. You are floundering between the past and the future, you are stuck in holding on to your old self-image and afraid to let it go. No one can decide for you, you should know how long you want to stay in this state. Analyse and decide!

Love Interpretation

You feel vulnerable because you depend on your loved one. In order to meet their expectations, you are willing to sacrifice yourself, forgetting about your own desires. Emotionally you are extremely sensitive and fragile. This is the best moment to face the situation and start walking on the path towards change. Many hardships await you, you will need a lot of patience, but it is worth it. As you progress, you will gain new relationships and connections. They will love you and you will be successful. To achieve this, you will require constant perseverance. If you are not involved in a relationship, the card refers to the fact you are longing for an unattainable love.

Material Interpretation

You are constantly surrounded by unexpected expenses and problems and your plans face obstacles. This is because now you have to pay the tuition fees. You have to make compromises and sacrifice in order to be successful. Be patient, the situation will soon be solved.

Work

If you are looking for a new job, do not expect any changes now. The Hanged Man is the card of patience, which also warns that you should search elsewhere and differently. If you want to be successful, you must switch viewpoints. Think about the relationship with your boss too!

The Question of Study

This card suggests that you are to give up your plans of study (or you are thinking whether to start it at all) and you are procrastinating. Do not be vague and do not give up, if you hang in there, the later results will confirm your decision of learning. In this case too, the key word is patience.

Health Interpretation

The Hanged Man does not indicate quick recovery. It draws your attention to the fact that your disease has other causes, you should reconsider them with 'renewed' eyes. It would be worthwhile to consult several specialists, you will probably need a different or complementary therapy. Pay attention to your blood pressure, the card may warn of cardiovascular diseases.

Family Interpretation

It is better not to plan anything in the short term, because events are occurring very slowly around you. It is not advisable to start real estate investments or purchases, because you may be conned. Be very careful in legal affairs!

Task

You are stuck but with a deep analysis, you can change your life and your worldview. It is conceivable that you are forced to live a passive lifestyle due to an illness, because you need to think through your present life, your goals and desires. Just be patient, look deep inside yourself, the current 'blockage/stagnation' is not a coincidence. You do not need to do anything, for the change it is enough for you to recognise and see your current situation clearly.

The Message of the Card

You must learn to see everything from a new point of view, you need to break through the old behavioural patterns. This is the card of the Test. From a negative aspect the Hanged Man is the weak idealist who lives in his own dream world, from a positive point of view it refers to standing firm in trying and encouraging situations, for which courage, strength and faith in spiritual values are indispensable.

Emotions: numbness, release, surrender, devotion, extroversion, inspiration, constraint detention, deep insight, twists and turns.
Stage of life: the end of a stalling situation or a relationship.

Personalities illustrated on the card are Count Gyula Andrássy and Judas

Count Gyula Andrássy, 'The handsome hanged man' (1823-1890)

The Andrássy family was one of those old Hungarian count families, who trace back their origins to the ancient Hungarians who came from Asia. According to the legend, one member of this old Székely family cut a foreign warrior's head in two in a duel, during the feast of St Stephen's coronation. Therefore, from the king he received a coat of arms and the adjective 'strong' as a reward. Two years later, the king made the brave knight the voivode of Transylvania. Because of the incomplete information and documents, it is difficult to follow the history and rise of the family, but here and there their names appear in the chronicles.

It is not a coincidence that Count Andrássy appears on the card, he was Hungary's aristocrat with considerable estates, a founding member and president of several associations, a generous patron of the arts and a renowned art collector. In the second half of the 19th century, count Andrássy was the most prominent and significant Hungarian political personality. Due to the role he played in the War of Independence, he was 'in effigy' (figuratively) hanged in 1851. The death warrant was signed by the Emperor Franz Joseph, whom later the Count crowned as deputy Palatine (8th of June 1867). Since the sentence could not be carried out due to the absence of Count Andrássy, it could only be done symbolically.

Thus the executioner hung a black plate on the gallows, with the name of the convicted written in chalk. It did not take much time for the news to reach Paris and the handsome young man, Gyula Andrássy was soon called by the ladies (who competed for his favours) in the Parisian salons, just as *Le beau pendu de 1848* that is 'the handsome hanged man of 1848'.

The charming Count was never idle: after 1852 he took up military studies (attended the Saint-Cyriel military school) and vowed to retake the confiscated estates with weapons. Meanwhile, he was staying in London, Paris, Brussels and Geneva alternately. In 1854, at Franz Joseph's wedding, Andrássy's mother begged for amnesty for her son, but the request was rejected.

At the end of 1855 in Paris, the count met Countess Catherine Kendeffy, a woman originating from an ancient Transylvanian aristocratic family. The encounter quickly became love, which is not surprising, since Catherine Kendeffy later was considered one of the most beautiful and the most fashionable ladies. Andrássy decided quickly: in a few months, in Paris, he took his chosen one to the altar. Out of their marriage three children were born: Theodore, Helena and Gyula, the third one later became a renowned politician, one of the most influential Hungarian thinkers of the first three decades of the twentieth century.

In June 1857, Gyula Andrássy requested amnesty for himself. This was granted, he returned home and took the loyalty oath for Franz Joseph. On his return a new era began in his life: he became a parliamentarian and joined the Submission Party led by Ferenc Deák. Along with Ferenc Deak, he established the Compromise, in which Queen Elizabeth also played a major role. Having endeavoured a great deal for the reconciliation between the Austrians and the Hungarians, on 17th of February 1867, Franz Joseph appointed him as Prime Minister. So it happened that the handsome hanged man crowned Franz Joseph king on 8th of June 1867, who had sentenced him to death on the gallows. At the ceremony Gyula Andrássy filled the deputy Palatine position, therefore he put the crown on the monarch's head, together with archbishop János Simon. With this deed, Gyula Andrássy, who had been symbolically hanged in 1851, permanently reached a compromise with the oppressor of the Hungarian freedom in 1867.

He was not driven by agreement: he became aware of the old truth of the Reform era; Hungary, being wedged among the great expanding nations, needed the monarchy. Besides, he also stated that the Habsburg monarchy could regain its superpower status only by compromising with Hungary. Andrássy's star was rising: in 1871, he became the Minister of Foreign Affairs of the monarchy and even after his resignation in 1879, he did not completely retire from politics.

The meeting of Queen Elizabeth and Count Andrássy was a historical and crucial love encounter, which sealed not only their life, but also the fate of the Hungarian nation. Sissy was 28 years old, while Andrássy 42. It could be read everywhere that their love was purely platonic, for they could never really be alone in sweet two. However, on 22nd of April 1868 Marie Valerie the 'Hungarian child' was born who became Sissy's favourite. This proved the 'love' between the emperor and empress although, according to the Andrássy followers, this confirmed the secret relationship between Andrássy and the empress. Nobody has evidence for or against, but it is a fact that the sick Sissy flourished into Europe's most beautiful lady.

Andrássy's granddaughter, the wife of Mihály Károlyi, in her memoirs refers to an old vineyardist from the vicinity of the Tokaj estate, who says that sometimes the count had visited his vineyard house accompanied by a beautiful veiled lady, whom he thought to have recognised as the queen. One thing is certain: Sissy's attitude, willpower, sense of beauty and her legendary grace totally enchanted Gyula Andrássy too and enabled the 'Sissy cult' and their legendary romantic love to survive vividly to this day. In love tarot the cards of the Empress (III) and Lovers (VI) are also connected to them.

Judas

The Judas story seems to be a simple one. He is the traitor, he renders Jesus to his enemies. Jesus is crucified, Judas, when the burden of his own action weighs upon him, commits suicide. However, the question arises: why did Judas betray his master? After all, he was one of the few chosen ones, who belonged to Jesus Christ's direct, innermost circle of disciples. He was fascinated by the teachings and miracles of Jesus. He was a smart, receptive and creative man, in whom many kinds of desires, ideas, plans and passion dwelt. He was an apostle, Jesus anointed him, gave him a part of his own power and mission. Judas taught, healed and belonged to the most distinguished ones among the apostles. He handled the common funds, thus the ones who turned to Jesus also approached him with respect and love, since he was the donator. People appreciated Judas for understanding them.

Seemingly, Judas had everything – and still he betrayed the Messiah. Thus perhaps he was more and more convinced that, although Jesus may be the great teacher, the master with miracle power, maybe even the Messiah, but he is simply not competent in certain things. So he observed the deeds of Jesus with growing incomprehension and the other Apostles with growing jealousy. He was looking for signs, became suspicious and impatient. He waited for the Lord to express his messianic power – to convince the high priests, elders and all the people. He wanted the Romans to leave, and Israel to be finally free. Perhaps this is why he finally decided to take control of the events and betray Jesus in order to make him take action. But when he realised where all this had led, he returned the 30 silver coins to the priests and hanged himself. A lot of theories have been published regarding this, I have outlined the one I consider the most acceptable one.

A little more curiosity:

In Washington, on 6th of April 2006, before Palm Sunday The National Geographic Society revealed a leather-bound, 26-page Coptic language codex, which bears the title The Gospel of Judas. This codex, which is also called Tchacos codex, was found by ordinary people in the Egyptian Al-Minya in a cave, in 1970. First it was brought to Europe, then to the USA. It was put on the market, but it could not be sold. Thus for 16 years, it was kept in a bank safe. Finally, in 2000, an antiquities dealer, Frieda Nussberger-Tchacos, bought it. She gave it for restoration and translation to the Maecenas Foundation for Ancient Art in Basel. Upon completion of the work the codex was returned to Egypt and the valuable artefact was exhibited in the Coptic Museum in Cairo.

The media describes the content of the document in a nutshell, according to which Jesus himself persuaded Judas to betray him, because that was the only way he could fulfil his mission. Judas was not therefore a greedy traitor who denied everything he learned from Jesus in three years, but rather the only one who really understood Jesus, his favourite disciple. The hero, who undertook the most difficult mission for Jesus, betrayed him at his request, so that Jesus could be executed and could get rid of his body and his soul would be free…

The Gospel of Judas is a so-called Gnostic document, which was a very fashionable school of thought at the time. The Gnosis represents higher knowledge, secret education, world vision which may be acquired from masters through secret initiation. The Gnosis was characterised by regarding the world's spiritual existence as real and the material to be deteriorated and inferior. According to Gnosticism, the material world was not created by the real God, but by an inferior deity. In the world, the true reality is what is not visible, the sphere of spirits, and above all, there is the ultimate perfect spirit. Man himself is also a higher spiritual creature, however, his spirit is locked in the prison of his body and only the enlightenment, the Gnostic knowledge and initiation empower it to recognise real truth. In this book, Jesus passes on a secret teaching to Judas about the world, the creation of man, the angels and about the heavenly realms, and then he says: 'You will be the thirteenth and the next generations are going to curse you, but you will come to rule over them'.

The revealing of these teachings is the content of the Gospel of Judas. According to the records, Jesus considered only Judas sensible enough to talk to him openly about all these. Today the whole text is already on the Internet.

The view of the world, of man, of redemption and of Jesus, which evolves from the surviving Gnostic documents, differs from the biblical teachings in all-important points.

'Death is not the end. Death can never be the end. Death is the road. Life is the traveller. The soul is the guide. When the traveller is tired and exhausted, the guide instructs the traveller to take either a short or a long rest, and then again, the traveller's journey begins.' (Sri Chinmoy)

THE UNNAMED ARCANUM

(DEATH, THE GRIM REAPER)

Count Lajos Batthyány and Pilate

The Interpretation of the Picture

CLOSURE AND NEW BEGINNING. This card has the unluckiest number, which is why the creators of old tarot cards did not name it. They were afraid that they would summon the grim reaper into their lives. I did not name it either, which is why the bottom of the card is still blank.

The card, however, is not exclusively the symbol of death, because at the same time it symbolises transformation and change. Instead of the usual skeleton, in Love tarot this card depicts Hades, whose identity has been somewhat close to me since my childhood. The first time I dreamt of him was when my mother died and the second time was two years later when my father died. Interestingly, he also appeared when my grandfather left. Since he has appeared in my life so often, I have read a lot about him, then I have put him on the Unnamed card, regardless of the fact that he is a bit out of line.

Hades on the card (just as in my dreams too) does not seem dangerous, yet he demands respect and he is serious. He is a conservative creature in a man's body, standing above all and his every action and motivation is awfully logical. He is the Lord of life and death, able to resurrect and destroy people. He is immortal, his exact age is unknown. The skeleton and the scythe are also important elements of the card, according to some myths, Hades cuts the thread of life with the scythe.

Number: XIII
Letter: M
Main element: Air
Astrology: Scorpio, Taurus, Capricorn, Aquarius, Saturn
Meditation: release, power transfer

Important Symbols Appear on the Card

Hades: according to the Greek mythology, he is the God of the Underworld, the Lord of the Dead. His parents are none other than Cronus and Rhea, Hades therefore is the brother of Zeus and Poseidon. He received the name Hades due to the 'invisible' helmet that the Cyclops had made for the Lord of the Dead. The helmet made its wearer invisible, so, similarly to death, he can be everywhere and also pop up unexpectedly out of nowhere.

According to the myth, Zeus, Poseidon and Hades divided the world among themselves by drawing lots. This is how Hades received the underworld. He is often mentioned as 'the richest' God, because he is the god of the treasures below the earth and of the undiscovered mines, as well. The realm of Hades cannot be visited by mortals, because if a mortal gets down to the realm of the dead, they will not come back alive. Therefore, the Lord of the Dead was not aware of what exactly was happening on the surface of the earth or on Mount Olympus. (In fact, mortals ventured down to the underworld only if they wanted to get back their passed-away relatives. But only Orpheus succeeded in doing so once, who touched the soul of Hades by his heart-breaking song. Others turn up in the underworld to defeat monsters, such as Hercules, who chained Cerberus.)

People were afraid of Hades: they did not even like to pronounce his name, because they were concerned they might draw the god's attention upon themselves. That is why he was the only god to whom they did not consecrate great sanctuaries or keep great celebrations. If however they brought sacrifice to honour the God, by all means they killed only black animals, especially black sheep and bull, the blood of which they collected in a bowl. When people were praying to Hades, they were turning their palms toward the ground and hitting it, that is how they were begging to the God. A lot of work has been written in connection with Hades, so now I am not going to get into more details.

The skeleton as a symbol: the skeleton, since the late Middle Ages, has clearly become the symbol of personified death.

Skull: the symbol indicating death or transience, the reminder of our own mortality. In Christianity, the skull shown with the crossed leg bones at the base of the cross refers to Golgotha (the 'mountain of skulls') and emphasises the relationship of the Fall and redemption. Combined with other symbols, we obtain a new meaning. For instance, the snake coming out of the skull symbolises the knowledge that survives death.

The Sword: occupies a prominent place among the symbols associated with the esoteric tradition. It symbolises struggle, fight, power, strength, justice, courage and protection, dignity and virtue. In the East, man's soul was depicted as a sword, while the woman's usually as a mirror. The sword as metaphysical symbol represents discernment, intellect, the power of spiritual development, the necessary strength to eliminate obstacles. In Buddhism the sword is one of the most sacred symbols, the sword of wisdom (Khadga) cuts the knot of incompetence.

The card's meaning in a spread, if you picked this

Archetype: Death and Rebirth
Negative pole: the Evil

Psychological Interpretation

The card represents transformation and metamorphosis. It refers to something that is dying in you, so you are going to be able to lock down your past. (Depending on the cards standing next to it, it indicates your own death or the death of a loved one.)

Spiritual Interpretation

'Die before you die.' This card represents important changes in your spiritual life as well: something inferior is dying in you, so you can be reborn on a higher spiritual level. Remember, as long as you have the fear of death or the fear of complete release in you, you cannot live your life to the fullest. Every affection, every 'NO' prevents you to become part of the natural flow of life.

General Interpretation

The transformation process is bringing you the power of revival and indicates that it is time to move on. You have to close the old in order to clear the way for the new. This whole thing may seem like a mysterious process which is painful, but in the end, you can feel that every cell inside your body and your entire being is nearly reborn. The same applies to your love relationship and also your attitude toward it. In any case, radical changes are taking place in this area too. There are two possible ways: the relationship is either permanently ending, so that later you can reach full completion in a new relationship or it is getting transformed and renewed. Many things are changing around you right now, but do not forget that change is life itself. Despite its ominous appearance, this card promises a new and more beautiful life, the key to which is change itself.

Reversed Interpretation

This card indicates inactivity, stagnation, complications; it suggests that what you are doing is halted. Rebellion and fight can be expected in your life whether from your side or from your partner's. The crisis is continuing, constant battles, endless fights 'can be seen on the horizon'. You have to rearrange your strengths and you have to decide whether you really want this relationship. Maybe you just have to stop, rest for a while, to see everything more clearly. It is no coincidence that the folk wisdom says: "I will sleep on it." It is worth listening to it. Although now you are tired to initiate the change and the future is late, you can be sure that a new beginning is on the horizon. (Sometimes it may also indicate that, although you are very enthusiastic about your new love relationship, something keeps delaying it.)

Love Interpretation

Something is ending and something new is beginning. The whole card's theme swirls around this. That is why sometimes you may feel very abandoned and at other times you can dive into completely new, deeper feelings. If you are able to finally close the gates linking to the past, you can be reborn in a new/renewed love relationship.

The cards standing nearby indicate whether the closure is final or rather is about lifting the affair up to a whole new level. Whatever the case is, the most important thing right now is to look back on your love disappointments, learn the lesson and try to create relations, in which trust comes first. If the card refers to the closure of your love, no matter how much you fight against it, your love is going to end within three months. If you are not ending it despite the signals, destiny will do it for you. This stage of life is very hard, but hang in there, everything happens for your own good, to serve your benefit.

Material Interpretation

The card refers to changes in this field too. If you have had little money so far, that is about to change. If you have not had any reasons to complain, you should economise because your expenses can increase unexpectedly.

Work

Despite your heroic efforts and sleepless nights, you may feel that you are much further away from achieving your goals then you were previously. This card refers to taking a serious decision, in terms of work it also indicates the conclusion of a period. If you do not have a job, you are going to find a new one soon, but if you have one now you may want to start looking for a new job because you are going to lose this present one within three months. Again the adjacent cards indicate, whether the position change is happening within the workplace or you must say goodbye to the workplace itself. In both cases, the transition is going to be difficult, be prepared!

The Question of Study

The card shows the risk of failing. Prepare more thoroughly for your exams. However, upon completion of the studies it may also mean that it is time to leave the schoolroom and plunge yourself into real life.

Health Interpretation

Do not panic, normally the Unnamed Arcanum does not indicate physical death, but you must take into account the adjacent cards or pick another one over it! In case of illness it also suggests that it is time to let the diseases go. Forgiving and release are of high importance.

Family Interpretation

The card refers to change in this area too and once again the adjacent cards show the character of the card. Someone is definitely going to leave the family, but it does not necessarily mean that death will come for him/her. Perhaps someone from your family is not talking to you for a long time due to a fierce quarrel, maybe someone is starting their own family or even moving abroad.

Task

Accept the changes and renew yourself! Apply new methods, shut down everything that hinders you. If you do so, everything will succeed just as you want!

The Message of the Card

This card continues the story of the Hanged Man whose sacrifice has been accepted and he is no longer the same man. His old self is dead, giving place to a completely new self, which is entirely different from the previous self. Egotism ceases because the possibility of rebirth lays in death. Now is the moment to get rid of the burden and the start on a new road.

Emotions: death and rebirth, transformation, external changes, passing, renewal
Stage of life: parting, saying goodbye, rebirth

Personalities illustrated on the card are Count Lajos Batthyány and Pilate

Count Lajos Batthyány (1807–1849)

Nobleman, politician, Hungarian Prime Minister (1848)

He was a prominent figure in the Hungarian Reform Era, the Prime Minister of the first independent, responsible Hungarian government and a martyr of the post-independence war retaliation.

The First Prime Minister of Hungary was born into a prestigious, wealthy magnate family. Shortly after the birth of Lajos, his mother, Barbara Skerlecz of gentry origin, separated from her husband and moved to Vienna along with her two little children. In 1812, after the death of his father, the five-year-old Lajos inherited a huge fortune. However, the widow got hold of his inheritance for her lavish luxurious life and sent her son to a Viennese boarding school, so he entered the military career at an early age.

He studied law at the Academy of Zagreb, and in 1831 Lajos Batthyány took over the estate of Ikervár. He started to modernise his demesne, while he was getting more and more involved in political life. About the count's public, social appearances and his Parliamentary declarations we can read in his work titled *Journal*.

In 1834, in Bratislava he married the 18-year-old Antonia Zichy. It was love at first sight, which lasted until their death and did not cease to exist, not even for a minute. (About their love I have already written for you on the Strength card.)

Széchenyi was planning to attract the young Batthyány beside him, who was appointed Prime Minister by the monarch, Ferdinand V on 17th of March 1848.

After this, Batthyány established the National Guard, and undertook a huge role in the creation of the independent Hungarian military force. From December 1848, the imperial army attacked, Pest-Buda was in their hands, the government fled to Debrecen, the count organised the country's defence from here. After the ally troops collected victories in every battlefield, Lajos Kossuth conferred the power to Artur Görgey, who surrendered at Világos on 13th of July, 1849. This capitulation was followed by severe retaliation, imperial armies invaded Hungary. Batthyány was also arrested and sentenced to death (gallows).

Wanting to escape the humiliating method of execution, Batthyány tried to commit suicide, with the dagger smuggled to the prison by his wife, Antonia, but he did not succeed. Finally, a year later, on 6th of October, 1849 he was executed by bullets. His last words were, "Long live the homeland!" Today at the place of his execution there stands the Batthyány Eternal Flame.

According to the Habsburg legend, Sissy once said to the decorative Antonia Zichy, Batthyány's wife: "Believe me, if we had the power, my husband and I would be the first ones to resurrect Lajos Batthyány and the martyrs of Arad." However, Antonia Zichy never forgot the Habsburg atrocity and that she desperately requested amnesty for her husband, but in vain… so later the Austrian secret police named her 'the most enraged patriot Lady'.

I have to mention Batthyány's outstanding friendship with Franz Liszt. Destiny let them meet, heading to Pest from Vienna, Liszt first met the count in Bratislava, on 18th of December 1839. That day a true friendship began. Lajos Batthyány aimed at listening to all of Liszt's concerts in Hungary. Franz Liszt was in Bad Eilsen when the news reached him that the thirteen senior army officers and his beloved Lajos Batthyány had been executed at Arad. So, he composed a heart-breaking bereavement music, the *Funerailles* 1849. With this, he wanted to commemorate Lajos Batthyány, the martyrs of Arad and the heroes of the War of Independence. Franz Liszt referred to this funeral music exclusively as Hungarian work. It is important to clarify this because many people understand that by this funeral music, he commemorated his esteemed colleague, Chopin, who also deceased in October 1849. But with the *Funerailles* Liszt bids farewell to his friend, Lajos Batthyány. The executed prime minister's secret resting place was in the Franciscan church's crypt in Budapest, for decades. After his death, Liszt also wanted to rest there.

Pilate

We all know the saying: "I got involved in the case, like Pilate in the Apostle's Creed…" Many people defend themselves in such manner in the crossfire of justified or unfounded accusations. The phrase of biblical origin is used as if to say: "I am just doing my job, I am just a simple clerk, I do not even have the right to decide."

To this day, no one has known anything certain about Pilate's birth and death, about the previous period of his life, but his name is known throughout the world and will always be. Emperor Tiberius entrusted Pontius Pilate the governance of Judea in 26 AD. About preceding events nothing was recorded by historical science. We do not even know the proconsul's first name. From his nickname, 'Pilatus' many people believed that among his ancestors there might have been a freed slave (freed slaves were called *pilateatus* i.e. the 'one with the red cap'), or he could have been the son of an officer who had been rewarded with an ornate spear (pilum).

We know nothing of his personal life either. One sentence of the evangelist Matthew mentions that he was married. In a later (secular) scripture we find out the name of his wife: Claudia Procula. We can rightly suppose that Pilate belonged to the knightly order, because if we compare his life to the career of other knights, we may think that he probably did some military service before his arrival to Judea.

Pilate was endowed with a double rank: the procurator – a clerk mainly dealing with financial issues – and the Prefect – political and military leader – to govern Judea. He was a plenipotentiary ruler over the life and death of his subjects (the *ius gladii*, the right of the sword), he could strike coins, but he had to respect the rights of the neighbouring kings who were appointed by Rome. For example, Herod Antipas, Galilee's tetrarch (governor) and the Roman governor of Syria, who was not above him politically, but had some control over his work. His headquarter was not in Jerusalem, but in the city of Caesarea on the West Coast, where mainly Greeks lived. A few years ago, at the excavations there a stone was unearthed with his name engraved.

When Jesus was dragged in front of him, in spite of his toughness Pilate could see that he was an innocent person. He even claimed this four times. The quotations are from the King James Version of the Bible.

Pilate:

"Art thou the King of the Jews?"

"My kingdom is not of this world," Christ answered, but he did not deny that he was a king.

Pilate assumed that the statement of the accusers was not true, he understood that Jesus did not strive for earthly power. Besides, Jesus' gentleness and pure gaze also convinced him about his innocence. Matthew also noted that Pilate's wife came to her husband with the details of a dream which was about Jesus and she begged for Jesus' life. But Pilate wanted to get rid of the responsibility of taking the decision, this is why he sent Jesus to Herod, who was staying in Jerusalem. Herod wanted to see a miracle from Jesus, but as no miracles happened, he joined his soldiers and mocked Jesus. Jesus did not say a word. The prisoner was returned to Pilate, it was up to him what to do. The city was preparing for a great feast, the risk of a possible rebellion was high, so there was an excellent opportunity to leave the decision to the public, since each year on the occasion of Passover a prisoner was released. The proconsul offered this opportunity: to choose between Barabbas, the robber-murderer and Jesus. The people shouted the name of Barabbas in unison.

After this, Pilate ordered Jesus to be whipped. From contemporary descriptions we know this barbaric way: with a whip prepared with sharp pieces of bone and metal. So the cruel Roman soldiers beat the prisoner, who was tied to a post; until he collapsed unconscious. Then they twisted some thorns to a crown, put it on his head and gave him a purple robe. They went up to him one by one and said, "Hail, King of the Jews!" then smacked his face. Pilate appeared again in front of the building: "Behold, I bring him forth to you, that ye may know that I find no fault in him." Jesus then came out, wearing the crown of thorns and the purple robe. Pilate spoke again: "Behold the man!" (This scene can be seen in Dürer's graphic, as he presents him to the people: Ecce Homo 'Behold the man'!) As soon as the high priests and the servants saw Jesus they cried out, "Crucify him, crucify him!" Pilate said to them, "Take ye him, and crucify him: for I find no fault in him."

It is interesting that Pilate, who had so often opposed the will of the Jews, this time he carefully manoeuvred against the public mood. It is also true that

Pilate was mainly preoccupied with his own career and a rebellion breaking out in Judea due to a bad decision would certainly have put an end to it. So why would the death of a simple preacher have counted to him? However, it seems that Pilate considered important not to be held responsible for the killing of Jesus. He sent for water and washed his hands; because he knew the Jewish customs and knew that in this way one can be cleansed from his sins. Then he declared: "I am innocent of the blood of this just person." However, this issue has triggered debates of an incredible intensity: were Pilate's hands really clean?

The fact is that a series of legends about Pilate emerged in a short time. Tertullian, a historian writing in Latin, reduced Pilate's role in the death of Jesus to a minimum. This had understandable reasons: with the spread of Christianity, it was important that Christians would not hold a Roman proconsul responsible for killing Christ. In his writings Pilate is almost a Christian. (This takes an interesting form in the Ethiopian Coptic tradition, where, from the 5th century onwards, Pilate is regarded as one of the most important saints. Many apocryphal gospels (e.g. Gospel of Gamaliel) commemorate his martyrdom and his wife, Procula, was named saint by the Greek Church).

In 1959 (according to other sources in 1961), Italian archaeologists unearthed the remains of a Roman theatre in Caesarea. Among the ruins an 80×60 cm milestone was found, on which a Latin inscription snippet with Pilate's name could be read, so it is certain that he existed and was a real historical person. However, there is not too much information about the real Pilate, the truth is somewhere between the two extremes of legends. Pilate probably was not particularly an outstandingly talented politician or military leader. He lived in difficult period in a difficult area, where he was less able to stand his ground. He was a cunning, violent man who took care of his career tremendously, but also paid attention to the legal forms.

'According to some people he died in the Gallic Vienne, to where he was allegedly banished, according to other sources after his suicide the demons took his body from Rome to Vienne, and threw it into the Rhone. However, the water ejected the corps so it cast him out on the shore. Then they carried him further and threw him into Lake Geneva. But the dead man did not find peace there either. The coast dwellers fished his body out and hid it in a well in the mountains. This fountain is still bubbling from the diabolical spell.'

‘Our happiness depends on ourselves and not just a little, and our unhappiness is often caused by our own faults rather than by the wickedness of others.’
(Ferenc Deák)

Temperance

Ferenc Deák and Saint Stephen

The Interpretation of the Picture

This card is one of the best ones in tarot, which embodies the classical virtue of self-restraint, self-control. At the same time this is the card of Time too.

Usually, a female figure appears on these tarot cards. She is the Angel of Temperance, who pours water from a silver pitcher (Moon-subconscious) into a gold one (Sun-consciousness). The water is the water of life itself. Her dress is usually silvery, blue and red. However, according to another approach, the liquid pouring from one pitcher into the other is the symbol the effect of one mind on the other. That is telepathy and the power from spiritual healers. Because the reality of the universe consists of oscillations, a series of vibrations, and these vibrations can be moderated and adapted by the human mind.

Since everything is bipolar, I have decided that the Magician and the High Priestess both should be present on this card as spiritual Teachers. One of them holds the silver pitcher, while the other of them holds the golden one (obviously silver is the female quality). Behind them in the background there is a row of disciples who are smaller than the Teachers, and the water, i.e. the Knowledge forming the sign of the infinity flows directly toward them. The gown of the Magician symbolises the Fire element while the dress of the High Priestess refers to the Water element in a kind of spiritual concordance. They are both mature, self-conscious and beautiful. They are masters who already know the secrets of spirituality and love, and they can transmit this knowledge to people. With one foot, they stand on the ground and the other foot in the water. This also indicates the conscious and the unconscious.

Number: XIV
Letter: N
Main element: Earth
Astrology: Scorpio, Aquarius, Capricorn, Sagittarius, Sun, Moon and Saturn
Meditation: Harmony meditation

Important Symbols Appear on the Card

Water: Water means life. We drink it, cook with it, swim in it, it occupies a special place in our lives. If our body did not get water, life would end. The 'journey' of water is similar to the 'journey' of the soul: water is liquid, then it evaporates and thereby its form also changes, although it is still water, it is not the same as it was. The knowledge, the information is retained in it, whether we evaporate it or freeze it.

The sign of infinity: infinity symbolises unlimited time and space for ordinary people. In infinity, our world's polarity and duality appear. Infinity always appears in the tangible, in the finite (finite lines also consist of infinite number of points, plains of an infinite number of lines) and in the infinite we find the finite as Yin is always in the Yang and Yang also is in Yin, because the two cannot exist without each other. For example, if you love someone infinitely, you are able to hug the whole world, that is why true love feels so good, because you date infinity, you meet the feeling of unity.

The sign of infinity is the numeral *8* lying on its side. The right side of the numeral rotates clockwise, this is the Yang pole, while the left side rotates opposite to it, this is the Yin pole.

Red: Red can be the sign of both life and death; in both cases it can be associated with blood. It is the symbol of sexuality, the colour of libido. In prehistoric times, a red colour powder was scattered next to the dead during funeral ceremonies. An ancient superstition had that red protects against demons and dangers. The Egyptians painted their trees, their cattle, their assets in red in order to protect them from fire and other damage, but they also used it for ensuring fertility. The Jews painted their doorjambs with the sacrificial lamb's blood in order to protect their houses from the exterminating angel of the ten plagues. In Greece, the dead were covered with a red shroud and thereby were symbolically inaugurated to victims to be able to make peace with the ruler of the underworld and get down into his realm. In antiquity, red was the expression of affection, love and passion. In Rome, brides wear a bright red veil, this is the *flammeum*. Red colour also symbolises strength, fire and it is a symbol of power too. In Jewish and Christian tradition, it is the colour of seriousness and majesty. In the New Testament, it is the colour of sin, propitiation, penance and sacrifice. Red symbolises the alchemists' furnace, as well as the third degree of the 'Great Work'. Its negative meaning is connected to the stigmatisation of bodily passions, scarlet is the colour of the 'great harlot of Babylon'. As the colour of the red-light houses, it indicates harlotry.

Blue: This is the colour of the sky, the colour of the sea and the symbol of intangibility, infinity and transcendence. It is the expression of intellect, reflection, relief which may also be attributed to imagination and the surreal world. Blue is the expression of the superhuman, heavenly power referring to celestial gods, in this sense it is the opposite of the earthly passions symbolised by red. In Christian symbolism, it is the colour of angels and Virgin Mary. Being the colour of worldly rulers, it indicates the celestial origin of their power. While the blinding blue sky of daytime has masculine connotation, the dark blue of the night refers to the feminine principle.

The card's meaning in a spread, if you picked this:

Archetype: Harmony
Negative pole: Chaos

Psychological Interpretation

You can consider yourself lucky. Through your calm behaviour and carefully planned actions you are capable to develop a harmonious relationship with everyone. Soon, you are going to start a new activity, you are going to work in a new place or live in a new environment/atmosphere. Retreat to a place where you can calmly think about your future.

Spiritual Interpretation

If you listen to your inner voice and your wisdom, and if you are able to give truly yourself accepting every part and manifestation of you, you will be able to trust yourself, your inner strength, and keep the internal harmony and 'walk' the golden middle path.

General Interpretation

Temperance means that we must be able to consume everything with moderation and we must want and do something to a sufficient extent. Thus, in every sense it is mainly about finding the golden middle way. It indicates that a more thoughtful stage of life is coming with more serious tasks.

Interpretation of the Reversed Card

The card in reversed position refers to strife, hostility, impatience, or maybe infertility. Indifference and frostiness are surrounding you, your friends are becoming estranged from you, maybe someone, whom you trusted, is betraying you. In order to step out of this situation, once again you need to re-evaluate your life and your relationships. Only then are you going to be able to step on the right path.

Love Interpretation

You are going to discover new emotions in yourself, you are going to tie new relationships and these are making your life richer. In addition to harmony, now you are getting to know such happiness which you have always dreamt of. In your love relationship, qualitative improvement can be expected, especially peace, love, understanding, affection and harmony are going to dominate.

Material Interpretation

You have to examine your financial matters. There is no harm in paying attention now, even if thanks to your confidence you are concluding advantageous contracts and your financial situation is going to stabilise. According to the card, it is a favourable period for investment and new beginnings, but it also warns you to be discreet and pay attention to balance. The Temperance card guarantees the improvement of your financial situation.

Work

If you have a job, then you can expect a promotion, a more serious task or even a salary raise. However, in case you do not have a job, the card draws your attention not to settle for casual work, but begin to search more intensively, because within three months you are going to find the right job. If you have worked very hard, the appearance of the card indicates that this difficult period will end soon. Your career is moving forward nicely.

The Question of Study

The work you have invested so far is paying off now and thanks to your diligence, you are going to achieve results, which you have been longing for a long time.

Health Interpretation

Avoid intemperate, excessive eating and drinking. The key of recovery is water in any form, and meditation.

Family Interpretation

In your family life, improvement can be expected, your relationships are going to become more harmonious. Be careful not to judge other people's actions and if your advice is needed, think twice about what you are going to say. Make sure that you spend proper quality time with your friends and family, otherwise they may feel that you neglect them.

Task

Make peace with your past. Shut down your present stage of life, to be able to live a happy and full life from now on. The appearance of this card warns you to review the situation carefully and rather than listening to the advice of others, listen to your own intuition.

The Message of the Card

Be careful not to exaggerate! Try to find the golden middle path. Look inside yourself, turn inward! Love yourself and live in a balanced way, in accordance with your environment!

Emotions: Harmony, balance, evenness, soberness and peace of mind.
Stage of life: Now you are able to find the real middle way between your desires and opportunities.

Personalities illustrated on the card are Ferenc Deák and Saint Stephen

Ferenc Deák 'The Wise Man of the Hungarian Nation' (1803-1876)

Ferenc Deák was one of the greatest politicians of the 19th century Hungarian history, his name is associated with the Compromise. Today one has to search intently for such a politician and scholar of law, whom almost everyone likes and respects. Ferenc Deák was such a man, who was not accidentally called the wise man of the Hungarian Nation by his contemporaries: his friendly personality coupled with a unique moral purity and exceptional political sense of reality.

His life developed in an unconventional way. His mother, Elizabeth Sibrik died while she was giving birth to him and thus his father gave the few-days-old baby into the care of his relatives in Zalatárnok. After his father's death, his siblings took the 5-year-old boy to them. The brotherly love accompanied Ferenc Deák throughout his life. His brother and sisters raised and taught him and smoothed the path for him for the rest of his life. Deák studied law, and then concluding his studies with exams, he became a prosecutor, a notary and a deputy sub-prefect in Zala county. From 1833, as a member of the Bratislava parliament, his outstanding law knowledge, determination, excellent speaking skills, political maturity and moral attitude soon raised him among the reformer leaders. In the 1840s because of the disputes in the county offices and his shattered health, he retired to his rural manor, nonetheless he supported the movement of the defence unit and mediated the debate between István Széchenyi and Kossuth. In order to unite the liberal camp, in 1847 he finalised the Manifesto of the Opposition, which was the evolving program of the Opposition Party.

The 1848 revolution pulled him out of his rural life: he accepted the position offered to him in the first responsible Hungarian government and he became the Minister of Justice. He tried to temper Kossuth as well, worked out a bill regarding the further development of the abolition of serfdom and discussed in the matter of peace in Innsbruck and Vienna. When in September 1848, the attacks of Jellačić made the government resign, Deák also quit his position and continued to work as a Member of Parliament. He was a member of the peace delegation, which prince Windischgrätz welcomed on 3th of January 1849 in Bicske. The mission failed, Deák could not follow Kossuth to Debrecen, so he returned to his estate in Kehida, Zala. Here, he survived the downfall of the war of independence, the first hard years of oppression, proclaiming the passive resistance against tyranny through his personal example.

From 1854 onwards, for most of the year, his Budapest apartment in the hotel named 'Restaurant for the English Queen' became the meeting place for those who expected him to control the resistance. The wait-and-see tactic pursued by Deák finally bore fruit. He also realised that the best possible option is the compromise with Vienna. He was the representative of Hungary during the negotiations leading to the Compromise of 1867. He was started to be called as the wise man of the Hungarian Nation.

In the new system of the Austro-Hungarian Monarchy, he did not undertake any official mandates, but rather watched the developments from the background. Ferenc Deák was a lovable man with a rational and jovial whose personality made it possible for him to make contact with a whole range of writers. With Vörösmarty he became best friends for life, moreover he was very close to János Arany, Zsigmond Kemény and Pál Gyulai as well.

Although he never married nor established a family of his own, still he adopted Vörösmarty's orphans and loved them as his children. His specific philosophy about marriage is probably due to his early love – the Inkey girl originating from a Transdanubian noble family – who turned him down, this disappointment had deeply affected him. According to the anecdotes, he talked about marriage and love vitriolically, doubtfully, almost dismissively. He illustrated marriage as a problem, as an issue, he commented women's loyalty, their behaviour in terms of love and marriage pejoratively.

Ferenc Deák appears on the Temperance card because he was a conceptual reformer and a masterful tactician. He barely had personal ambitions while moral values moved him in his political career. He was known to be a tough debate partner who did not forget the correct proportions. He politicised in a balanced manner, calmly, utterly insisting on constitutionality and defended the interests of the nation.

Saint Stephen

The Founder of the Hungarian State (975-1038)

St Stephen was the first Christian ruler of Hungary, the founder of the Hungarian state, who single-handedly succeeded in the enormous work of uniting the state, organising the church and legislating.

Less than half a century before his accession to the throne (1000), the Hungarian cavalry were fatally threatening the West and Christianity, moving forward all the way to the Lech field next to Augsburg. However, Hungary redesigned by constitution and expansion, culture and history-shaping power starting from Stephen, became the outpost of the Christian West against the advancing Mongol and Ottoman Turkish danger, and, over the centuries, it served as a defence wall against the barbarism of Asian invaders. From political, religious and social point of view, he was the one who actually created Hungary, he appointed and assured the path to the future for the Hungarian nation.

His diplomatic and political sense, with which in practice he could often achieve conflicting goals, made him the greatest statesman of his age and the whole Hungarian history. This is precisely why he also appears on the Temperance card.

Stephen, originally named Vajk, was the only son of Prince Géza (reigned 971-997). Immediately after his father's death, he found himself confronting his uncle, the pagan Koppány. According to the ancient custom of seniority, his uncle – as the eldest male member of the family – claimed Sarolt, the widow of Prince Géza, to be his wife and wanted to gain the main power too. Since he did not get either of these, his armies clashed with Stephen's knights near Veszprém in 998. The battle – with German support – was won by the Christian monarch. The battle has been countless times written about and sung of. The rebellious Koppány's body was cut into four and the pieces had were hung on four of the most important castle rooks as a clear message to those who might consider to defy the will of Stephen. After the defeat of Koppány, the young monarch completed the construction of the abbey of Pannonhalma and turned to Rome for the crown. Soon, in the year 1000, at Christmas he was crowned in Esztergom, thus – in legal sense – the Christian Kingdom of Hungary was established. However, the royal title itself did not provide the actual main power, for that the new monarch had to engage in battles for several decades, against the chieftains who became independent after the conquest.

In parallel with his struggles to unify the homeland, Stephen laid the foundations of the Christian state, in which his main helper was the Church. In the territory of Hungary, 10 bishoprics and two archdioceses were established, through which the country formed an independent church district and thus was able to become independent from the German-Roman Empire. Stephen also established laws for the young Christian kingdom: with his two Codes – one of them created at the beginning of his reign and the other one at the end – forced his subjects to convert, exercise the Christian religion and respect private property, and by this he facilitated the spread of settled life form.

While he expected his subjects to bear the costs of keeping the churches function and supporting the priests ('ten villages should build one temple'), the ruler also spent considerable sums on constructions. His name is associated for example with the founding of the monastery of Pécsvárad and the nunnery of Veszprémvölgy, moreover he built guesthouses for Hungarian travellers on the pilgrimage road leading to Jerusalem.

At the beginning of his reign, Stephen's foreign policy was determined by the alliance with the Holy Roman Empire. The support he received against

Koppány, maybe the crown itself, and his marriage to Gizella, the daughter of the Quarrelsome Henry, Duke of Bavaria could be acknowledged to this. However, later he became a strong handed, serious statesman who held the interests of his nation to be most important.

The great ruler has been considered to be the supreme symbol of the Hungarian nation, whom since 1083 – thanks to the also canonised King László I – we have honoured among the Hungarian saints. The most important Hungarian national holiday is linked to his name (20th of August). His reign meant the most important four decades in Hungarian history, which paved the future of a whole nation.

'Everyone sees what you appear to be, few experience what you really are.' (Machiavelli)

THE DEVIL

Haynau and Queen (Bloody) Mary I

The Interpretation of the Picture

This page is often called the Black Magician as well, which indicates the creative force and intelligence used in achieving selfish goals and greedy desires. Usually we refer to it as the negative counterpart of the High Priest. This is the card of temptation, negative power, passion, habit, addiction and material success. That is why the card is dominated by a handsome, pleasing and well-dressed man, who can possibly be recognised because of the colours only by those who can see, not just look. Because temptation (especially in terms of love) never comes in the original (evil) form. The devil also has his own place in the system of things, we must not look down on his abilities, with which he ensnares people. His whole figure is surrounded by fire (which also refers to passion), the Ouroboros snake biting its own tail appears in the background. The latter reminds us of the cycle of things, transformation. The tempter's eyes are expressively suggestive and strongly indicate the negative pole too.

Nonetheless the Devil card does not have an entirely ominous connotation. Because, whether we want it or not, the Devil too has a place in the world's system. If we think about it in terms of an obstacle, a pitfall, taboo or mental fear, these include the fact that by defeating them, good will arise. Thus, the evil power illustrated by the card also suggests that we must reconcile with our own negative side, we have to overcome it and must transform it into good force.

Number: XV
Letter: Sz
Main element: Air
Astrology: Mars, Saturn, Venus, Sagittarius, Gemini, Libra
Meditation: Leaving imprints behind you, putting-down-the-burden meditation

Important Symbols Appear on the Card

***The Devil*:** The Bad present in the world is a concept, the origin and the meaning of which are theologically explained by all religions. 'The concept of the devil begins with Christianity' – writes Röhrich Lutz, then immediately he adds also that the real era of believing in the devil is the late Middle Ages. The early art of Christianity had not yet depicted the devil. Images about the forces of evil, for the first time, came forth in medieval religious art (especially in Benedictine monasteries). In the imagination of monastic orders who feared the devil, it first appeared as an attacking, prosecuting, harassing, scary monster. Its tempting function developed a little later, in the 13th century.

However, according to the traditional profane folk belief, every disease, epidemic, natural disaster and trouble are caused by demons. There are specific disease demons (for example from the Hungarian folk culture: Spell (headache, fever), St Anthony's fire (erysipelas, rash, fever), Fright (psychological illness), Evil Lizard – 'theria' (diphtheria, sore throat), Heck (malignant tumours, 'to heck with it!' 'what the heck!'). Cosmic meteorological phenomena also have their Demons: the 'great evil Dragon' hides in storm, the names and characteristics of various winds refer to demons hiding in them (Wind, Whirlwind, Nemere). Various natural spirits can also be manifestations of the universal Bad (e.g. little forest elf, wild old man, wild girl, fairy lady, water fairy, etc.), the demons who overthrow the cosmic order and eat celestial bodies ('march-wulf' belief circle – markolab), and men who became demons (e.g. the werewolf myth). The so-called pseudo mythical figures living in the human world, but having supernatural characteristics, (e.g. witch, scientist miller/driver, garabonciás, Baba Yaga), can also have scary demonic qualities as they can cause a wide variety of troubles arising in everyday life (economic damages, evil spells, diseases, etc.). The seductive, dangerous female demons (e.g. fair lady, water fairy, mermaid etc.) also belong here.

***The snake* as a universal symbol**: the coiled shape of the slippery skinned, limbless, periodically shedding animal often carries conflicting meanings. It can be a solar symbol (symbolises the Sun's rays) or it may be a lunar symbol (if its molting shows the periodic renewal of the Moon). As a phallic symbol it refers to male and female traits. Its spiral or circular representations indicate the cyclical time and the changing fate as well. Its hiding way of life, winter hibernation and its crawling into ground cavities may embody the underworld as well. Due to the renewal of its skin, many times it is also the symbol of immortality and rebirth. The coiled body can also evoke the brain convolution, therefore it can symbolise logic, wisdom and the gift of divination too.

The serpent's shape is a complex symbol in the Judeo-Christian tradition also. For example, in the Garden of Eden a snake coiled around the Tree of

Knowledge, which represents the tempting Evil, Satan. However, in the story of Moses, the stick changing into a snake has a positive connotation because it demonstrates God's presence. The bronze serpent of Moses, which he set on a pole in the desert following the Lord's advice, is a doctor of wounds, i.e. a life-giving animal. In the New Testament, in the Gospel of John, it is a prefigure of the crucified saviour: 'As Moses lifted up the serpent in the wilderness, even so must the Son of Man be lifted up so that whoever believes in Him shall have eternal life.' The snake has a positive meaning in the words of Jesus also, when he says: "Be gentle as a dove and wise as a serpent." By this Jesus means that with the help of the Holy Spirit (dove) you can remain untainted and you will spread the word of God instinctively (like a snake). However, in the art of the Reformed Church the serpent is usually the symbol of temptation.

***Ouroboros Snake*:** The snake biting its own tail. It indicates eternity, as well as the eternal cycle and continuous renewal. This embodies eternal return in the form of an animal and suggests that at every ending there is a new beginning.

The possible meanings of the card in a display, if you picked this:

Archetype: the Tempter
Negative pole: the Liberator

Psychological Interpretation

This card refers to subordination and oppression. You should be freed from these. This card could mean deep fears and even a relationship which you are unable to get out of, because you depend on the other. You have developed serious bonds, there is a lot of responsibility on you.

Spiritual Interpretation

The Devil symbolises the person who is able to influence and control you and refers to those temptations which you are incapable to withstand. Find a kinesiologist, who can help you reveal the causes of the situation through dissolution and, if you become emotionally balanced again, it will be easier for you to make the decisions you need to live your life the way you want.

General Interpretation

Everyone has an obsession, a passion and a mania. Yours are now even more prominent. You are becoming almost obsessed with sensuality, you do not have your sexual energies under control. Right now, you may attract relationships in your life that are brittle on the long run, but you may feel that everything is going on the best way and you have found the one you were looking for. Be careful because this is a false and erroneous feeling, it can be deceiving, it is conceivable that everything looks so beautiful, that you are capable to stick to it compulsively, no matter what. For those, who live in a relationship, a third party may appear, who is promising hotter passion. You are in a difficult situation, because the temptation is big. This passion cannot be suppressed, like many other things that the mind comprehends, but if you want, you can get rid of its coercive effects and with that power you can create the infinite beauty and miracle.

Interpretation of the reversed card:

You are letting your passions and fears go, you are getting rid of an addiction. Now you have the power to release constraints, to break away from the indoctrinated way of thinking, principles and ideas, and to become free. Now you already know what passion is, you cannot tell about it, but experience it. You have already indulged, have accomplished the ups and downs of crying, anger, joy, dancing, sexuality and you are able to keep your instincts in balance. You have learned that the power of making your own decision is a miracle that gives you freedom which is born out of freedom.

Love Interpretation

You need to reassess passion and love. You need to become aware of the darker side of yourself, you have to face the fears, the temptations and the suppressions. If you have picked this card, you must pay attention to balance, because during this period you tend to possess things powerfully and to be immoderately greedy. Moreover, your attractiveness is increasing, thus you are exposed to even greater temptations. If you are single, an irresistible person is coming into your life, of whom your friends are saying that (s)he is unscrupulously abusing you. Notice and end this, if you do not want the sorrow of love. If you live in a relationship, you and your partner are going to be exposed to temptations.

Material Interpretation

In this period money is just flowing to you. Be careful not to get into businesses out of which you can hardly get out on the long run!

Work

You are going to be exposed to temptations in this area too. If you use the secrets that you hear, you can conclude advantageous deals, you can even change your position. Beware, even bribery can be included.

The Question of Study

You can get over any exams, you are going to pass any exams. Even if you did not learn enough. Even if you cheat, you cannot be caught.

Health Interpretation

Something may come to the surface, which you have not known. You need to dissolve the blocks of fear, jealousy and envy. If you have eating disorders or alcohol problems, do something about it as soon as possible and seek professional help.

Family Interpretation

Your family relationships are also transforming, everything is going to be revealed. You can place your life on new foundations and/or make a long-delayed decision. Be careful not to make the decision out of impulse, count to 100, before you say something that you might regret later.

Task

You have to get to know yourself and the darker side of life. You have to stop looking for a scapegoat always. You have to realise that you form your own life. You must come to terms with your own weaknesses, gullibility and suppressions. Note that not everything is the way or is right as you think, see or feel it.

The Message of the Card

Surely you remember the greatest, most powerful, most demonic thriller of all times: *The Devil's Advocate.* In fact, the essence lies in this film. Every day we meet the dangers, the enticement, the temptations of Satan. Many times we sin, each day of the week. These are small sins, but they are enough to make Satan laugh and tell us perfectly calm: "Oh, please call me Dad! Let us be on good terms, and sin every day. Of course, I will give you wealth, glamour and fame in exchange, just be mine! Vanity is definitely my favourite sin." And he starts laughing immediately. And thought-provoking questions with the thought-provoking answers are coming. Of course, the answers are for you to know. You have to choose between Good and Bad. This is reality. This is your life, your decision. You decide what you believe in and how you live. It depends on you, whether you are accepting the enormous opportunities being offered or are rather waiting and working diligently for success, while you are drawing strength from the opportunities offered by the devil.

Emotions: sensuality, sexuality, creative energy

Stage of life: Now you can finally be the Master of your life, if you can face your own weaknesses and temptations.

Persons illustrated on the card are Haynau and Bloody Mary I

Haynau the 'Hyena of Brescia' 1786-1853

Baron Julius Jacob von Haynau was an Austrian general, the Elector of Hesse, the illegitimate son of William II. His name is associated with the counter-revolutionary terror after the 1848-49 Revolution and War of Independence.

Haynau was an experienced military officer, whose military career began in 1801 in the Austrian army. He took part in the Napoleonic wars, where he felt a fanatical hatred towards the revolutionaries. He did not even attempt to control his early notorious brutality and violence. He retired in 1847, but he returned for the armed struggle against the 1848 revolution. First he fought in Italy, where he was named the 'Hyena of Brescia' as the result of his brutality against the Italian freedom fighters. As in Brescia he executed the hospitalised revolutionists and he whipped some of the women in public. The international public opinion was outraged, but his commander, field marshal Radetzky thanked him for the decisive action in a congratulatory letter.

Haynau was quite an autonomous and nervous kind of man, who did not have a good reputation in the Austrian army either. According to his friend, Marshal Schönhals, "he could not control himself and constantly got involved in a whole series of disagreements... Haynau was an excellent superior, but a bad subordinate; he was born to give orders, not to obey." Unfortunately for the Hungarian nation, after the independence war was crushed, Franz Joseph needed exactly a man like him. Thus Haynau, as the omnipotent commander of Hungary, led the crusade of revenge against the Hungarian freedom heroes, soon the young monarch granted him a free hand for the executions also.

Since Haynau considered himself the saviour of the empire, he desired to use the most extreme means of retaliation, in order to turn the Hungarians away from further disobedience. Therefore, on 6 October, 1849, he began the physical annihilation of the elite of the independence war. This day, Haynau executed the martyrs of Arad and in Pest he killed Count Lajos Batthyány, the president of the first independent Hungarian Government ('the Ministry').

(Since then, Hungarians do not clink glasses with beer because after the execution at Arad, Haynau and his people did this to toast for the Austrian victory.). In 1849-50 at least 130 people were executed, hundreds more were imprisoned and about 40-50 thousand soldiers were enlisted in the imperial army as punishment. The retaliation did not spare the civilian population either. Village priests, clerks, teachers fell victim to claiming the regulations of the revolutionary government; others were sentenced to death for participating in popular uprisings or for hiding weapons.

On 26 October 1849 – as the result of the international outcry – Vienna was forced to stop the executions, thus in 1850 Haynau was dismissed and even honoured with a significant amount of state bonds for his bloody services. Despite this, his 'activities' have been in great silence ever since. Marshal Karl von Schönhals, the 'good friend and comrade in arms' simply states in his widely published book that 'he was not the law, but merely its arm.'

It is a fact, that Haynau's particular cruelty became uncomfortable for the Austrian court too, because after the Compromise, the assessment of Franz Josef raised difficult questions in Hungary. Historians and official circles mainly tried to hide the ruler's personal involvement in the retribution and attributed the young emperor's 'aberration' to the influence of his bad advisors (primarily Prime Minister Schwarzenberg and the emperor's mother, Archduchess Sophie)

About the death of Haynau there is a legend, which fits horror movies, the bloodthirsty 'monster' was allegedly alive on the autopsy table. What is more, as the aftermath of a head injury, Haynau regularly lost consciousness, however many people did not know this, so when Haynau collapsed during a celebration in a Viennese restaurant, everyone thought he was dead. Only on the autopsy table, when the skull was opened, the brain turned out to be still throbbing; so one of the doctors freed him from torment with a long knife. However, this is only a legend, because in fact many people remember Haynau's frequent migraines, but also the brain and pulmonary haemorrhage could be distinguished from apparent death even in contemporary medical science. The true diagnosis of Haynau's death was 'acute pulmonary and brain haemorrhage.' The legend could have formed due to the date of his death: 15 March 1853, it was the Hungarian Revolution's fifth anniversary. 'God's hand struck the sinner' – stated the Hungarian nation unanimously and contentedly.

(Bloody) Queen Mary I (1516-1558)

Posterity knows Queen Mary I just as Bloody Mary. Mary Tudor is a tragic figure in history, who experienced a lot of disaster in her life and who is still acknowledged as one of the most ruthless English monarchs. Nonetheless when she was little, she was a real, nice, genuine princess, who turned into a stonehearted person due to the people she loved. During her reign an unprecedented persecution began, because the queen certainly was not in possession of the means, with which she would rule correctly. She failed as a queen, as a wife and as a mother too and precisely these three areas were the most important for her. Probably no one will ever wash off her the name Bloody Mary, even though she was the world's most unhappy wife and queen.

Mary Tudor came to the throne of England after the death of her brother Edward VI. She was a devout Catholic since birth, who governed with the desperate aim to restore Catholicism in the country. Therefore, she executed crowds of Protestants and other heretics. She was not picky: commoners as well as prominent people of the court had to die. (Among them was the Archbishop of Canterbury as well, Thomas Cranmer.) During the time of her reign, England began to decline and people were terrified. However, the Queen was not dark spirited, she sincerely believed that once the Catholic religion could be restored, order would be also restored in the country. She was tremendously wrong.

The eldest daughter of Henry VIII was born into her father's first marriage with the Spanish Catherine of Aragon. Her life could not have begun any better: her mother loved her, her father loved her to the point of adoration and lavished magnificent gifts upon her. At the age of nine she already had a separate royal household, she spent her childhood in idyllic circumstances and grew up with the assurance that she was one of the most important princesses in Europe. However, Henry VIII obsessively longed for a male successor and later, knowing that his wife had several miscarriages, decided to look for a new woman. His choice fell on one of the queen's ladies-in-waiting, the young, beautiful and sexually very attractive Anne Boleyn. Thus he pushed away his six years older wife and as the lady-in-waiting was unwilling to favour the desire-driven Henry until he would marry her, he decided to end the marriage. The Pope, however, did not support the divorce, Henry failed to convince him with the argument he invented, namely the incestuous nature of the matrimony. Since the Queen refused to divorce, (insisted that, although for a short time she had been the wife of Arthur, Henry's brother, the marriage was never consummated), the king himself broke up the marriage. All this had serious consequences for the Church and for England: Henry ended the deals with Rome and declared his daughter to be an illegitimate child.

In 1533 he married Anne Boleyn, but she also gave the obstinate monarch a girl child. Three years later, he got bored of Anna too, so he captured her with outrageous accusations as an excuse and executed her and then married again. When his third wife, Jane Seymour gave birth to the long-awaited son, he declared both daughters bastard and ruled them out of the inheritance.

Thus 'Lady Mary', by the birth of Elizabeth had been degraded to the rank of lady-in-waiting for her sister, she was torn away from her mother and was not even allowed to attend her mother's funeral. The lonely girl, in life threatening danger finally signed the document about her own illegitimate origin, but refused to deny the Catholic faith. Years later, her father relented a little toward her and at the end of his life he made his two daughters heiresses again.

The nine-year-old Edward VI succeeded to the throne after Henry VIII, but six years later he died of tuberculosis. Before his death, Edward – ignoring his both sisters – named Lady Jane Grey as his successor, however the poor girl ruled only nine days before being thrown down from the throne and then executed. Thus on 1st October, 1553, the crown landed directly on the head of Mary, so she became the first British Queen regnant.

The 37-year-old new queen considered the dissemination of her own faith as the most important task: so she immediately withdrew the regulations of her predecessors and once again made Catholicism the state religion. With a huge swing, she also began to search for a husband. At all costs she sought to avoid the throne getting back to her Protestant sister after her death, so she quickly wanted to give birth to her own children. So, her choice finally fell on the son of the Holy Roman Emperor Charles V, the 26-year-old Spanish Prince Philip, with whom she fell in love immediately. The marriage took place two days after their first personal encounter, in the summer of 1554.

However, the British were angered by the fact that Mary once again put the focus on the Catholic religion, and triggered an even stronger aversion by choosing the heir of the Spanish Empire. Because along with the husband, Spanish Inquisitors also arrived, who immediately set about to weed out heresy. Instantly, bloody confrontations began: the Protestants grabbed weapons against the Catholics. Elizabeth's name was stitched on their flags, so Henry's other daughter became more popular, while Mary was watching the situation in amazement. This is when she committed the fatal error: ignoring the riots, she carried out her stubborn plan in the holy conviction that she was doing God's will. From this day on Mary earned the nickname, by which she is known even today. The erupted riots were crushed and 'Bloody Mary' introduced the heresy laws, according to which everyone, who denied the Catholic faith, ended on the pyre.

Therefore, England was wrapped in a deathly silence, lit only by the fire of the pyres, nearly 300 000 people were sent to death on account of heresy – so the Queen's reign of terror began. Although she decided to lead the people back to the path of the one true faith, the people were divided and began to refer to the victims of the Protestant persecution as martyrs.

Mary's love life did not develop well either. Although she fell in love with her charming and handsome husband, the man was not attracted to the older woman. Actually, he had other plans: he sought to set the British on his side against the French. Behind her back he referred to the queen only as a poorly dressed, elderly woman, but for Mary he was the prince of her dreams until the end of her life. They did not have any children, because the lonely queen, desperately longing for a child, showed the symptoms of pregnancy only on a spiritual basis, for ten months in both cases.

On the second occasion, Philip's patience was at the end, besides he became more and more disgusted with his wife, who he considered unkempt and unambitious. Therefore, he announced that his duties call him to the Low Countries. While he was amusing himself with pretty whores in Amsterdam, Mary was fiddling with the rosary and writing him daily. Philip later returned to her, but only because he needed the support of his wife in the war he carried against the French. The Queen bloomed again and in spite of the bitter protest of the Parliament in June 1557 she declared war against France. After this, Philip went away again and Mary's body again produced the pregnancy symptoms, but she did not have a baby.

While her health was rapidly worsening, the Queen did not realise that England was slowly falling apart due to the Catholic religion. The people got tired of the burnings, taxes and indemnity. Furthermore Mary's foreign policy also failed: she lost the city of Calais, the last English estate in France. (From then on, the proud British royal families could not wear the King/Queen of France title.) Losing this city, which was under British rule for two centuries, was one of the greatest failures of the Queen. The seriously ill woman retired to her bedroom after this and named Elizabeth as her successor, so her husband could no longer have an influence on the British government. She secretly hoped that her sister would convert to Catholicism, but Elizabeth remained a Protestant and as we all know, later she became the founder of the British world power position. The decision might have been extremely difficult for Mary, since her sister took away her father and seduced her husband and, in addition, Elizabeth's mother was not even of royal blood. Still this seemed to be the most logical decision for the sick woman, since she wanted to protect the English crown from Phillip, at any price. At the end of her reign, the subjects hated her and were afraid of her, because death by burning still waited for several heretics. The Queen, who was probably suffering from cervical cancer, spent the last hours crying and lamenting, mourning over the desired child, who existed only in her imagination. The day of her death, 17 November 1158, was celebrated even centuries later.

A little more curiosity: the first Bloody Mary cocktail was mixed in 1933. The drink was 'born' in New York, according to tradition, the creator was an innkeeper of French origin. Its present form was probably named after Mary I. The main ingredients are: vodka, tomato juice, Tabasco and Worcester sauce. The cocktail's birth name is Red Snapper.

'Words and paper did not seem real enough to me. To put my fantasies on solid footing, something more was needed. I had to achieve a kind of representation in stone of my innermost thoughts and of the knowledge I had acquired. Put another way, I had to make a confession of faith in stone. That was the beginning of the tower, the house I built for myself at Bollingen.' **(Jung)**

THE TOWER

Elisabeth Báthory, and Nimrod with his wife Semiramis

The Interpretation of the Picture

In this card, we see a huge tower collapsing in flames, usually we connect this with the tower of Babel. This page shows destruction, yet it has more than one interpretation. It could also mean an external intervention (usually intervention from God or the spiritual world), in case you have been receiving warning signs for a long time, but still have not done anything about it. Therefore, the secondary interpretation of the card is that if you move in time, even if the situation collapses, you can rise above it. If not, you may fall down. This is why a few people fallout from the tower, while one or two rise instead. The card points to these two possibilities. At the same time, the Tower is not entirely a negative card. In general, it indicates unforeseen events, unbalanced stability, lost friendships and divorce. However, it refers also to a new start and rebuilding as well. In 1922 – when he was well over forty – Jung bought a piece of land next to Lake Zurich, close to Bollingen. And he began to build a tower on it. Many years passed until the tower gained its final shape that can be seen even today. Jung's Tower included the profound mystery of existence and at the same time it was the representation of the secret and spirit itself.

Number: XVI
Letter: Ayin
Main element: Earth
Astrology: Venus, Jupiter, Mars, Sagittarius, Aries, Scorpio, Taurus
Meditation: Internal self-surrender meditation

Important Symbols Appear on the Card

Tower: In sacral architecture, besides temples and sanctuaries, towers indicated the stages of rising from the earthly towards the divine (e.g., Mesopotamian tower temples, ziggurats, Christian church bell towers, Islamic mosque minarets, Chinese-Japanese Buddhist pagodas). This tall building therefore is an edifice connecting Earth with Heaven, the world axis which, similarly to ladder, ensures the connection between Heaven and Earth. In most tarot decks, in the Tower card people fall down from a lightning struck tower, which symbolises destruction and decline. In Christian tradition, Watchtowers represent alertness, Lighthouses guide with the light of faith, provide guidance and guide the souls to the Heavenly Port.

The card's meaning in a spread, if you picked this

Archetype: Collapse, Transformation
Negative pole: Rebuilding

Psychological Interpretation

Life sometimes closes doors, because it is time to move forward. This is a good thing, because often you will just not move forward unless the circumstances force you. If you experience some 'hard' times, remind yourself that no goal can be achieved without pain. Because sometimes progress itself involves pain. Do not forget what this pain teaches you.

Spiritual Interpretation

Everything in life is just temporary. As good things do not last forever, neither do those times when things turn for the worse. Every moment is a new beginning and a new ending as well. You always get a second chance. You only have to seize it and make the best out of it

General Interpretation

A sudden change is taking place in your life, you see your situation more clearly than ever before. The card indicates surprising and unexpected events in your life, that can change your life or your point of view. An old situation is suddenly coming to an end, maybe you are getting out of an old relationship. At the same time, this card may indicate wonderful, unexpected events: a new baby or that you will soon find the love of your life. However, be careful, because now an accident is possible, due to which you must re-evaluate everything. One thing is certain: you are at a major turning point in your life, after this you are not going be the same person as before. Do not plan anything, examine your goals too and if you see that it is time to make a change, do not hesitate, make the necessary steps to avoid any external factors force you to act. (The cards adjacent to the Tower show you always the current message).

Reversed Interpretation

Perhaps you feel that life is not fair to you, the circumstances are conspiring against you and nothing is going the way it should. You are trying to shape your life considering the circumstances, but you always bump into obstacles, nothing works out. You always end up with people who are not real friends and who do not stand by you when you are in trouble. You feel that you will always be alone. You are not naive or stupid, still fate always throws these kinds of situations and people in your way. However, this is going to end soon and you can leave this chaos behind. To do so, you must learn to handle problems instead of quitting and escaping from them. There are and always will be obstacles. The feeling of success comes only from overcoming the obstacles with our own strength. It takes great courage and persistence, but later it will become easier.

Love Interpretation

This card can be scary because it indicates changes, over which you do not have any power. You may experience some difficult moments, but do not worry, everything is going to be alright soon.

Material Interpretation

Your financial situation is not too good right now, you feel everything is crumbling around you. However, after the big losses, constant revenues are coming, which are going to restore the financial balance.

Work

Change is inevitable in this area too. You are going to lose your stability, you are going to quit or you are going to be fired. Although it seems that you have lost everything, in the long run you will realise that this had to happen. Be patient and receptive, the future promises a lot, because if you pass the test, your chances will significantly improve

The Question of study

This card indicates setback, refers to failure. The situation is not hopeless, you just have to decide what you truly desire and must build upon that.

Health Interpretation

If you have not done it already, now you definitely need to change your lifestyle. The card draws your attention to detoxification, fasting and radical dietary changes. Pay attention, because now the risk of accidents relating to exercise and sport increases. Those who complain the most, reach the least. Do not worry, but see where you need to fix the way you live. Change, move forward and never look back.

Family Interpretation

The card suggests that you must say goodbye to someone. Do not take things too personally, even if they appear to be personal. The change is now inevitable. Those old structures that have prevented your development must crumble now, so that new, more stable ones could be built instead.

Task

Be positive, even if you are surrounded by negative people. Smile even if others try to bring you down. The task for you now is not to lose enthusiasm and focus. Do not let the bitterness of others change you! Do not change anything just to impress someone! If you change, do it in order to be a better person and to create a better future. Remember: people will always talk about you no matter what you do or how good you are doing it. Do not worry about what other people think! If you believe in something, fight for it!

The Message of the Card

Examine your earlier failures and find out what you did wrong or how the trouble could have been avoided in those given circumstances. Think about what kind of necessary steps you have not taken, what you have not paid enough attention to and what the consequences of all this have been. If you realise these, you will no longer make the same mistakes one after the other, and it will become clear to you that you can give yourself just as much, or even much more than anyone else from your environment. Do not forget that no one can love you as much as you love yourself.

Emotions: profound transformation, trauma, healing, spiritual renewal, self-knowledge

Stage of life: Intensive transformation process, the old dies to make way for the new.

Personalities illustrated on the card are Elisabeth Báthory and Nimrod with his wife Semiramis

Elisabeth Báthory (1561-1614)

Many people think that Elizabeth Báthory was only a victim of political games and power struggles. Yet she entered history as the Blood Countess and as an insane serial killer. Her creepy story has been adapted by many: historians, writers, poets, playwrights, composers, painters and filmmakers. They have all tried to describe and illustrate the unimaginable.

Strange tales were spreading about the Countess, according to which she was dealing with occult sciences and torturing servants. Legend has it that mostly women fell victim to the cruelty of the Countess: she humiliated them, bathed in their spilled blood, tore off the flesh of the victims with her teeth and then killed them. Moreover, in the surroundings of her Csejte Castle, young girls disappeared regularly and found dead by exsanguination. Because Elizabeth allegedly believed that from their blood her skin will remain young and beautiful. Thus it is no wonder that she stepped into the public consciousness as 'the one who bathed in the blood of virgin girls', 'sadistic and lesbian', 'Vampire Queen'. According to folklore, once she hit her favourite maid so hard that the girl's blood dribbled down onto her hands – from then on, she bathed in the blood of virgin girls. Her guilt was not questioned for four hundred years, but modern researches question this legend. Today's opinion is that Elizabeth may have been the victim of a show trial which aimed to obtain her vast estates. Nevertheless, the Countess has still been listed in the Guinness Book of Records as the bloodiest killer of mankind. Therefore, the question rightfully arises: whether she was really an extremely vain and cruel chatelaine bathing in blood. I have read a great deal about the contemporary political situation, here are the putative and/or actual facts.

Elizabeth Báthory was highly cultivated, she spoke Hungarian, Greek, German and Latin. Thanks to her promising beauty and prestigious family, ambitious candidates surrounded her. She finally married at the age of 14 with the also wealthy, valiant hero, Count Ferenc Nádasdy. By this marriage, he acquired an even greater authority (he used the name Báthory Nádasdy). In this period marriages were concluded out of political considerations, not out of love.

The personality of these two 'agreed' on one thing: both of them had sadistic inclinations. Nádasdy was referred to as the black captain, because if someone upset him, this person could have expected brutal beating and whiplashing due to his violent temper. Being drunk he did not even spare his wife and raped her, who presumably for this reason had several miscarriages.

The presumably false witnesses claimed that Elizabeth knew no boundaries either as far as cruelty was concerned. Her behaviour was explained with the fact that within her family there had been plenty of examples of insanity (although we have no evidence), and the disadvantages of inmarriage were mentioned. (Elizabeth's mother and father were relatives).

The fact is that the Countess was tortured by epileptic seizures from infancy, she was also predisposed to stroke and due to her uncontrollable temper tantrums, she thoroughly frightened her environment. However, this would not make a person an insane murderer. Her strange behaviour was topped by the fact that she was raised as a spoiled girl, so she accepted no criticism nor reprove from any of her educators. She became an arrogant woman, conceited with her own beauty. Furthermore, she was also perceptive to the ruthless and barbaric customs of her time, so she considered public executions as a form of entertainment. Since her husband often went in military expedition, Elizabeth lived in solitude and it did not take long when spirituality attracted her attention. Soon she coloured her life with occult practices, for which she even hired a few like-minded servants. She experimented, produced different medications and herbal concoctions. According to remaining documents, already Elizabeth as a young girl acquired knowledge relating to healing, known in the manor houses and among people, and she consciously conducted organised, therapeutic activity during the time of her marriage and widowhood also. On all her estates, she had physicians, 'grassy women', but also her escort included healers who she took with her during the journeys and, if it was necessary, she could use their knowledge for the sake of people.

Due to the medical methods and prevalent diseases – infections, gangrene – of the time, it was a common practice that, in order to ensure the survival of the patient, a body part had to be amputated. Such interventions were not pain-free, that is why roaring, crying and screaming often could be heard the leaking out of the castle. Maybe this is why suspicion arouse in common people's mind that in the Báthory castle people were tortured and murdered. It did not take long and the story later won its present mythical form. Whereas the truth could have been just the opposite as well: Elizabeth Báthory maybe was not a bloodthirsty killer, but a generous person, a healer who just wanted to help others.

The number of her subsequent victims is estimated to be six hundred. However, in this regard technical issues arise. Having so many victims is almost impossible, the infamous bathing in blood is questionable due to the quick coagulation of human blood.

Her persecution began in October 1610, when in the provable absence of the Lady, in the course of a single week eight girls from Csejte died under epidemic-suspicious circumstances. The old woman and the servant who had been nursing the sick – probably terrified of the already started interrogations – hid the deaths from the Lady and they even kept not buried corpses in different places. These 'evidences' however came handy for the Palatine, who did everything to begrime the Báthory family's reputation and make them scape-goats by scare-mongering, false testimonies obtained by torture. Nobody recognised that testimony of the nearly three hundred witness was full of contradictions.

After reading the testimonies, we realise that most of these people had never been near any scenes of the alleged crimes and had acquired their knowledge related to her courtyard's crimes from the scuttlebutt, scare stories scattered across the country for years. Very different testimonies were born about the number of victims too. The Palatine however classified the events as being caught in the act and arrested the Countess. The Báthory family did everything to save her life and the honour of the Báthory name, but their huge estates were confiscated (though Elizabeth never made a statement and no sentence was brought against her), the freedom of the chatelaine was taken away and she was walled her up in the bedroom of Csejte. Her guilt has never been proven, the refuting documents have never been thoroughly investigated. After four years the deranged woman finally died in captivity.

Was Elizabeth Báthory guilty? I think that despite all the new aspects and new arguments, we can only guess. We can vote on any reviews of any historians, rely on our literary knowledge or trust our own imagination. Perhaps the most exciting thing is not to decide what really happened in Elizabeth Báthory's court, but the way this story has travelled around the world. The way the legend of the vain Hungarian countess took its flight, who did not end the lives of 600 girls for the joy of torture, but for virgin blood to preserve her fresh, youthful beauty.

What is more, in foreign works the former chatelaine of Csejte appears to us already as the female Dracula who did not abstain from lesbian orgies either. Even more interesting is the total rehabilitation namely that in our century we finally get to the concept of the victim, the woman who is unable to defend herself alone.

The story thus has undergone a variety of cultural and scientific ways of approach, interpretation of different ages and of different nations having different traditions. It is totally our decision what kind of Báthory image we accept, but it is certain that Countess Elizabeth Báthory will forever remain the cruel chatelaine bathing in blood. This is why she appears in the Tower card.

Nimrod, the grandson of Ham and his wife Semiramis

Since the card is also linked with the tower of Babel, that is why Nimrod and his wife appear in the card of the Tower. Probably everyone knows the story of the Tower of Babel, the confusion of tongues, i.e. the confusion of Babel. Still I am quickly summarising it: according to the Bible, after the Flood, people came from the East, who decided that their city would have the tallest tower 'whose top may reach unto heaven'. Because they did not want to lose each other, like their predecessors after the Flood. Moreover, they thought that with the help of this tower they would be able to walk from one star to the other.

Until the building of the Tower of Babel, one tongue was spoken all over the world. However, because they dared to hurl defiance at him, Yahweh (God of Israel) punished the inhabitants of Shinar, by confusing their tongues. From then on, people did not understand each other, and gave up the construction. They scattered throughout the world, founded different nations and they lived separate lives. This is the story of the Tower of Babel, which is nothing more than a symbol of human haughtiness and greed according to the Book of Genesis… but whose name is all this associated with, in the first place?

According to the Bible, the first city-states were founded by Nimrod along the rivers Tigris and Euphrates (Babel, Erech, Accad, Calneh, Nineveh). The man was a talented hunter who provided protection for his people against the proliferated wild animals. He bordered the cities with high stonewalls, he gradually changed governance into despotism, because he saw no other way to turn people away from God. So, this man was Nimrod, the one who 'raised all the people against God'. The construction of the Tower of Babel, which in the Bible has become the symbol of the evil empire is linked to his name.

The deed of Nimrod was condemned by the Book of Genesis, because it wished to achieve goals contrary to the will of God. Two statements face each other: God promised the Messiah for humanity and 'Be fruitful, and multiply, and replenish the earth, and subdue it'. In contrast, Nimrod propagated self-redemption – 'let us make us a name' – and preached the unitary, settled way of life as opposed to the migration of people.

Nimrod – and especially his wife, Semiramis –are also considered to be the founders of religion in the history of religion. According to several Christian religion researchers, Babel (Babylon) is also the symbol of various religious cults, including idolatry because in this place the cult of fallen angels and demons was born. The ancient historian Herodotus also mentions that Babylon was the initial source of idolatry.

Nimrod's wife was Semiramis, who, after the death of Nimrod, gave birth to a child. She claimed that the little one was born without her even been touched by the man and that Nimrod himself had incarnated in the boy, named Tammuz. From then on, people began to worship Tammuz as the Sun God, thus the two of them were depicted as the modern Virgin Mary and Jesus (i.e. as today's baby Jesus in the manger). Therefore, the sun cult also stems from Nimrod.

According to the story, Nimrod acquired astronomical knowledge by observing the movements of the Sun, the Earth and Venus, through which knowledge he could predict specific events, such as solar and lunar eclipses, and from these observations (by developing occult religion) he could extort absolute power over the people living in the city-states he had founded. Thanks to this, he could keep people surrounding him completely intimidated.

Once Nimrod realised the value of the knowledge in his possession, he explained the solar and lunar eclipses to his people with the arrival of the Ouroboros snake-god. He made them believe that they will see the power of the serpent god, because when it comes, he will devour the Sun which gives fertility, life and light. Thus the snake swallowing the end of its tail has become the symbol of the occult belief related to Sun worship. Since Nimrod also knew (thanks to his astronomical knowledge) that these phenomena would end by themselves, so he stood in front of the people as the saviour Sun God. He claimed unlimited obedience and child sacrifices and he promised his believers and worshippers to liberate them from this evil serpent-god and give them fertility and blessing.

After this, Nimrod had statues carved for himself and his wife, which people had to worship in the same way as Nimrod. (Nimrod's statue was a figure with a bullhead and human body and a solar disc between its horns.) He was thus the first ruler who started deliberately to distort the image of God in people to his own image. Naturally, from Babylon to the present day, the science of divine origin has been passed on along with the astronomical knowledge, mathematics, geometry, and the science of symbols which are mainly cultivated by modern Kabbalah and Freemasonry.

'Thou hast no taste, no colour, no door, canst not be defined, art relished while ever mysterious. Not necessary to life, but rather life itself.'(Saint-Exupéry)

THE STAR

King Saint Ladislaus I and King David

The Interpretation of the Picture

This card is the symbol of harmony and creative forces. A young naked woman pours water from a pitcher on the ground, this symbolises the source of inspiration received from above. The beautiful woman in the card is naked, but it does not create the impression of lust in us, but the feeling of purity. She is the one who brings the world to new life with the water of Life. The traditional interpretation regards the Star as one of the three protective cards that promises a joyful success. We know three divine virtues, these are Faith, Hope and Love.

The ability to find the key of harmony is there in everyone. Harmony, however, manifests itself differently for everyone. Of course, there are 'basic components' the infinite combinations of which could lead to harmony, but you have to figure out which one is yours. If you work on yourself, on your self-awareness, those opportunities that come into your life, will carry you forward on your path. In order to achieve harmony, it is essential to see opportunity in everything! The opportunity is to polish your mind. However, for this you usually need very hard cathartic experience, which even makes the ego tremble.

Number: XVII
Letter: P
Main element: Air
Astrology: Mercury, Venus, Capricorn, Virgo, Aquarius, Gemini
Meditation: Harmony meditation

Important Symbols Appear on the Card

Star of David

The Star of David appears on the pitchers, which are two isosceles triangles turned into each other, facing each other. It symbolises unity and harmony. The upper triangle symbolises the cosmos from above and it widens downward to the earth. The lower triangle comes from the direction of the microcosm and it further widens 'pointing' toward the macrocosm. Thus these two triangles intertwine into each other, so harmony develops in the middle, which is the energy of the Heavens and the Earth, reminding us of the principle 'as above, so below'.

The star

Seven small and one big star shine above the woman, this refers to the direction of the upper forces, pointing the way to be followed. In the background there is a tree and a bird sitting on it. This is the symbol of the soul which is able to ascend to a higher level.

The water of Life

Countless tales talk about the water of life, which ensures long lasting life and eternal health for its consumer. Many poor lads and princes set out in order to find it and thus achieve the much-desired immortality or eternal youth. Water is the most important medicine! Please pay attention on how much you drink of it, because your health may depend on it! I will write about water programming in the meditation section.

The card's meaning in a spread, if you picked this:

Archetype: Hope, Wisdom
Negative pole: Hopelessness, loss of Reality

Psychological Interpretation

You know that happiness does not come only from the achievement of goals, but rather from the journey in achieving them. You are on the road, and at the same time you are the journey yourself.

Spiritual Interpretation

In everyone's case, it is a matter of maturity, when they really start to deal with self-knowledge and spirituality. You have reached that level of development, where you can turn inward and deal not just with the material world. Now the point in your life has come when you have to get rid of the innerved bad habits, your spacious comfort zone and your current way of thinking inside the box.

General Interpretation

Do you start your day with a smile or rather wish to be a person who is always cheerful, smiling and happy? For this, nothing else is necessary, but positive thinking, because this produces positive energy, which creates positive reality for you. It is time again to meditate, to be in love, listen to beautiful music, laugh and smile a lot! Meanwhile, be more specific in terms of your desires, for which you would even be capable to bring smaller sacrifices.

Reversed Interpretation

Your relationships are remaining superficial, you are isolating yourself. However, this situation is not going to last long, because thanks to a friend your emotional life is about to be renewed. From this you are going to feel more confident again.

Love Interpretation

This card promises luck, nice hopes and success. Your relationship is developing as you would like it, you can reach your goals and enjoy a carefree life. If we talk about a relationship already fulfilled, the next period promises happiness. If your love is still in its initial stage, feel free to hope for the long advance, because the relationship is developing in the best possible way. You are finally receiving the love you wanted for so long.

Material Interpretation

Your all business deals are developing luckily, you may expect great financial benefits. Now it is time for charity, do not forget to donate!

Work

If you are in the phase of looking for a job or changing your job, now you will have great success only if you are willing to bring some sacrifice. Be helpful, considerate, kind and thanks to your good nature you can count on joyful news.

The Question of study

Study diligently and meanwhile help your companions who turn to you as well! Success is not going to lag behind, now you can easily reach your set goals.

Health Interpretation

Physically and mentally you are getting into a good shape, so you can mobilise more energy in achieving your goals. Nevertheless, expressly pay attention to cleanness and take enough time to rest!

Family Interpretation

Your friendships are developing perfectly, you are turning more and more towards your family and holding onto your home even more. Do not delay anything!

Task

If you are an artist, now it is the time for an exhibition or to look up a publisher with your work which you have created through hard work. Focus on your creations, your invested energies are soon going to pay off.

The Message of the Card

You are planning or beginning things extending into the distant future and the positive development of which you can rightly hope for. This is an excellent opportunity to enjoy your creativity.

Emotions: radiation, clairvoyance, creativity, confidence, hope, visionary power, astrology, divination
Stage of life: realisation of plans

King Saint Ladislaus I and King David are in the card

King Saint Ladislaus I, the Knight King (1046-1095)

King Saint Ladislaus was born in Poland. His grandfather, the pagan Vazul was blinded on the orders of King Stephen. Ironically, although he and his family had to flee the country to avoid the wrath of Stephen, it was Ladislaus who continued the great state founder king's lifetime work.

King Ladislaus came to the throne in 1077. During his reign (1077-1095) he made peace and order through laws, in a country troubled by throne feud and external attacks. These laws are still the most stringent ones of the Hungarian legal system. He created three codes of law (the first one was released in 1077), the most important issue among these was the protection of private property. Despite the extremely strict laws his memory is kept by dozens of legends (*Gesta Ladislai Regis*) and murals (Gelence and Székelyderzs).

St. Ladislaus is the Hungarian Knight King and the defender of the weak. He owes this name to the fact that in 1091, when he was fighting in Croatia, the Cumans invaded the country, ravaged it and plundered it. Upon the news of the destruction, the king returned home with a huge, strong army and then chased the Cumans who were loaded with booty and defeated them. Even after his death people still believed that the holy king would 'come out' from his grave if a danger threatened the Hungarians and would help his people to victory. The legend comes from the old Székelys who told that in the summer of 1354, when they were fighting a life and death battle with the Tartars, "some big knight was in front of them sitting on a tall steed, with a golden crown on his head, holding a battle axe with which he destroyed all of them with massive strikes and cuts." (*Anonymus minorita chronica*) This knight was the one who decided the battle in favour of the Hungarians. After the battle – according to the legend – King Ladislaus' embalmed body was found sweaty in Oradea. (Janus Pannonius also mentions this in his poem entitled *Farewell to Várad*).

King Ladislaus got married twice. His first wife, whose name we do not know, probably was a Hungarian aristocratic girl. His daughter, born from this marriage, married the Russian Prince Yaroslav. After his first wife's death, Adelheid became his wife, the daughter of Rudolf of Rheinfelden, a German counter-king. They had a daughter, named Irene, who married the Greek Emperor John. Therefore, thanks to his conscious policies he became related with almost all of the neighbouring dynasties, including the two most powerful Greek and German imperial ones.

Saint Ladislaus of the Árpád House was very educated: he stood out among his contemporaries not only with his physical strength, his tall figure, but also with his knowledge, artistic sense and spiritual goodness. His name is associated with endless rows of miracles and myths. In Hungary we can find springs bearing the name Saint Ladislaus, which supposedly the noble king created with his battle axe for his thirsty soldiers. He was the one who stopped the plague by using a concoction and ended the famine. Furthermore, on the request of King Ladislaus King Stephen, Prince Imre and Bishop Gellért were canonised.

First he was buried in Somogyvár and then in the church of Oradea, which he had founded together with the bishopric. After his death, he was also canonised. The cult of St Ladislaus was formed by the other Knight King, Louis the Great.

In conclusion, St Ladislaus was a real Hungarian Knight King, a manly, courageous warrior, heroic yet gentle and protective. He defended women and was merciful with those in distress and with the sick. That is why I put him in the Love Tarot's The Star card.

King David

David's figure in the Old Testament is outstanding as a king as well as a man. Born in Bethlehem, the prophet Samuel already appointed him, in his childhood, to be the future king of Israel. At first, he appeared as Saul's armour-bearer, who was also able to dispel the king's bad mood or his depressed state by playing the harp. He won King Saul's benevolence and the Jewish people's trust by defeating the Philistine giant. According to the Jewish religion, the Messiah will be the descendant of David, and Christians trace back Jesus' genealogy to him, through Joseph and Mary. His name is linked to the so-called Star of David. This symbol has been connected with him based on Jewish mystical texts since the 14th century. Its 12 sides represent the 12 tribes of Israel, its seven parts refer to the seven days of creation. It is an accessory of the Israeli flag and a generally known Jewish religious symbol.

The Story of David and Goliath

Perhaps no story illustrates the optimistic approach of the Bible so vividly, as the Old Testament story of David and Goliath. We are around some time 1000 BC. The armies of Israel and the Philistines are camping in the valley of Sochoh in order to engage in a battle. As the two camps are preparing for the fight, a huge man comes out from the Philistine army, with the following words: "Why are ye come out to set your battle in array? Am not I a Philistine, and ye servants to Saul? Choose you a man for you, and let him come down to me. If he be able to fight with me, and to kill me, then will we be your servants: but if I prevail against him, and kill him, then shall ye be our servants, and serve us. I defy the armies of Israel this day; give me a man, that we may fight together." (1Sam 17,8–10; King James Version (KJV). Everyone is scared, the Israeli army's demoralisation is at its highest.

Goliath repeats the speech for forty days, each morning and evening. Obviously, because he has an audience. The king promises that whoever defeats

Goliath, he gives his daughter to him as well as wealth and exempts his household from all services. Still no one volunteers. However, one day David appears in the camp. The shepherd boy of Bethlehem, was sent by his father to the battlefield in order to bring news of his brothers serving in the army. When he hears what happened, David decides that he will challenge the battle-hardened giant. His brothers mock him and do everything to dissuade him, but to no avail. His trust in God's help, national pride and the image of the reward are such motivating powers that not even the king could dissuade him about his undertaking which seemed to be impossible. So he goes to the nearby stream, picks up five stones and calls Goliath out to duel. The end of the story is well known: the shepherd boy whirls his slingshot and hits the giant's forehead so hard that he drops dead on to the ground.

'You never know what will happen when things suddenly change. Yet do we know what will happen if they remain unchanged?' (E. Canetti)

THE MOON

Flóra Sass and Virgin Mary

The Interpretation of the Picture

The Moon is the planet of the night; it symbolises the beauty and the light in the dark infinity. However, the Moon is also the symbol of the female principle, devotion, fertility, cyclicality and variability of nature. Since it is a female symbol, the card itself is feminine. The Moon is the lover of the night, the mistress of the deep waters of the unconscious. The menstrual cycle, the ebb and tide, the accelerating and decelerating alternation of life are also associated with the Moon. In most of the old decks, the Moon is threatening and nightmarish, in my deck however it is a more complicated, variously interpretable feminine type of card. Just like the Moon itself, the card is also strongly related to dreams, imagination and fantasy.

Number: XVIII
Letter: C
Main element: Water
Astrology: Mercury, Moon, Venus, Aquarius, Cancer, Pisces
Meditation: devotion-meditation, bonding-meditation

Important Symbols Appear on the Card

The card refers to the three levels of human existence. The Water is the unconscious mind and the dark past, the Earth is the material world and the conscious mind, the Moon illuminating the sky symbolises the higher order of the soul. Generally, in the cards a road appears leading away from the water, two dogs bark at the Moon and a crab crawls out. The two dogs are the symbols of good and bad, the crab symbolises that whoever embarks on this road, cannot turn back… no matter what kind of threat one may feel. However, in this card beside the Moon, the Moon Goddess herself appears, she is on horseback in a windswept veil, with a crescent shaped tiara on her head, shedding light on mortals. Her dress is silvery. The path leads in the middle of the tower ruins, which indicates overcoming unconscious fears.

The card's meaning in a spread, if you picked this

Archetype: The child growing in the womb, the Night
Negative pole: The distorted mirror image of reality, the realm of illusion

Psychological Interpretation

Self-confidence and self-criticism are coming to the fore, now you must dissolve the deep-rooted emotional and reaction patterns. It is important to really look within yourself. The card warns not to deceive yourself, avoid the trap of your illusions.

Spiritual Interpretation

The Moon is related to the cosmic law (karma) and to higher destiny. It encourages you to break through your mist wall and look at what is behind it. Sometimes the Moon happens to play a false joke on you. So be vigilant and cautious!

General Interpretation

It is time for you to really confront yourself, deeply and honestly. Accept, recognise, become aware of the instincts working in you and slowly change, slowly transform. Now the struggle with yourself, and the appropriate control of your desires and tempers are coming to the fore.

Reversed Interpretation

You may pile up mistakes if you are not conscious. You feel very lonely, you are facing a sad and lone period. Doubts are overwhelming you, listlessness and melancholy are becoming your companion for a long time. Start working on problems, because if you do not, unpleasant feelings can make you act desperately, even commit suicide. If you cannot get out of this situation on your own for a long time, ask for help!!!!

Love Interpretation

You should not decide hastily, because you cannot see clearly. Keep stalling! Do not change anything, but rather listen and wait, even if you feel offended or disappointed. If the card gets next to the Magician, the Empress, the Sun, the

Judgment and the World you may feel relieved because in the long run, it promises happiness. However, if it is picked out along with the Hanged man, the Unnamed Card and the Tower, you need to get ready for disputes, while the sense of abandonment is going to strengthens. You have to admit that it is not right, if you are looking for the answers and the solutions only in others and outside. Now it is definitely worth to turn inward, to search within yourself.

Material Interpretation

In terms of finance, the Moon card is a pretty uncertain one. No matter how impatient you are, you still have to wait. Cut down on some unnecessary expenses, for the moment lower your expectations. If now you are able to keep all expenses under control, you can be sure about your positive future.

Work

You need to rearrange your schedule and must be more careful about your communication. Now you must not make any changes!

The Question of study

Although the results cannot be seen yet, the future will bring great success. Be patient and persevering!

Health Interpretation

Now emotions, tenderness and forgiveness are coming to the fore, you must work on these. The Moon promises wise and loving relationships. Although the healing process is slowing down, with a little lifestyle change it can be accelerated. Drink plenty of water and avoid alcohol!

Family Interpretation

This is a period of ordering your emotions. It is time to fix your relationships, because your female, receptive energy helps a lot in this. Common activities, relaxation or working together with your partner are worth to be put forth in the next period.

Task

The Moon encourages you to turn inward and face yourself. Look in the mirror of the shadow within you and see what is beyond it. There you will find the answer to what prevents you from making your life more rich and productive.

The Message of the Card

What is not yours will be lost. Who is not yours, shall depart. The Moon directs your path towards new realisations, brings ancient wisdom and helps in your development. It teaches you how to shape your environment so that your goals would be achieved in everyday life and you find the golden middle way.

Emotions : intuition, imagination, opening up, acceptance, devotion, attachment, panic, fear, lack of self-confidence, lack of self-criticism, despair, disappointment, sensitivity
Stage of life: stalling, slow decisions, self-knowledge coming to the front

Persons illustrated in the card are Flóra Sass and Virgin Mary

Flóra Sass (Lady Florence Baker), *Daughter of the Moon* (1841-1916)

Flóra Sass was a charmingly beautiful Hungarian woman explorer, who, in the second part of the nineteenth century, travelled all across Africa, together with her husband Samuel White Baker. She kept a diary about their adventurous journeys, which was discovered only a hundred years later in an attic, in the bottom of an old, dusty chest. In her writings (though not meant for the public) she talks interestingly about the colonisation of the black continent and about the everyday life of a world which is less known to us or maybe even unknown.

About Flóra's childhood we do not know much, perhaps it was an even more adventurous and difficult period than when she was in Africa. Until the age of 7 she lived with her Székely family in Transylvania. However, in the autumn of 1848 the girl's parents and brother were massacred by insurgent Romanian peasants. Flóra was saved by the family's Romanian servant, who stated that she was her child. After a long escape, an Armenian family took her in, and from them she got the family name Finnian too. As her stepfather Finnian was Major in General Bem's army, after the fall of the freedom war the little girl had to flee again. Her new family started off to Turkey. However, in the city of Vidin, due to the confusion, little Flóra vanished, thus unfortunately we know nothing about the next decade of her life.

Samuel White Baker, who was a scion of a rich Londoner family, disembarked at the town of Vidin with a friend in January 1859. They looked around and reached the illegal slave market of the city as well. There the man saw the beautiful Flóra Sass, he immediately paid the ransom for her, took her home and then after a while he married her.

Shortly afterwards, Samuel led an expedition to Africa, where he sought to explore the source of the Nile and here he was already accompanied by Flóra as well. During their journey they encountered a lot of hardship. They often had to deal with their rebellious people and wild natives. Flóra Sass, however, did not turn into a vulnerable gentlewoman: thanks to her aplomb and persevering power she repeatedly won both her husband and the companion's recognition. After this, she was named the daughter of the Moon. I chose her because of this.

Their journey was successful. They discovered the second source of the Nile which they named Albert-lake. They also discovered a waterfall, which is located before the Lake Albert on the Nile. They named it Murchison Falls. The journey homeward was not easy either, but what gave them strength was the knowledge that they had made it into the history books. They were not disappointed: in London, people had been expecting the successful married couple with joy. Flóra also got acquainted with everyone and was respected by everyone, though the queen did not receive her for a long time, because for a while, she had lived in 'concubinage' with her husband.

Until the end her life, Flóra lived with her husband in complete peace and quiet in Devonshire, southern England. Baker died in 1893, Flóra Sass followed him in 1916, the sarcophagus containing their ashes was placed in the church garden in Grimley, a hamlet near Worcester. Details about the diary of Flóra Sass were provided by Anne Baker in her book, Morning Star published in London, 1972. (In Hungarian – Anne Baker *Rabszolgák földjén.* A Hungarian woman among explorers and slaves 1870-1873, Budapest, 1987.)

Virgin Mary

The Gospel of James (Protoevangelium of James) does not belong to the canonical Gospels of the Church, it is an apocryphal Gospel. In this gospel we can find the life story of Mary, Jesus Christ's mother, the daughter of Joachim and Anna, from the very conception of her.

Joachim, Mary's father, was a very rich man, however he distributed a large part of his wealth among the people and offered the other part to the Lord for pardon of his sins. One day, someone told him that he had no right to offer a donation to the Lord, because he was the only one out of the twelve tribes of Israel who had no children. Hearing this, Joachim became very sad, but he remembered Abraham, to whom the Lord had given a child only at a very old age, namely Isaac, thus Joachim began to hope that maybe God would help him too. He fasted and prayed for forty days in the wilderness. He said he would take no food or drink until the Lord looked upon him. His wife, Anna did not know where her husband had gone, so she started crying because she thought she was a widow. She blamed her own infertility for her misfortune, so in the evening she went into the garden and sat down under a laurel tree to pray. She asked God to bless her womb, let her bear a child similarly to Abraham's wife, Sarah. Then an angel of the Lord came to Anna and said: "Anna, Anna, the Lord has heard your prayer, and you shall conceive, and shall bring forth; and your seed shall be spoken of in all the world." (Protoevangelium of James). Anna responded that if she was going to give birth, whether boy or girl, she would offer her child to the Lord, to serve Him throughout his/her life.

After nine months, Anna gave birth to a healthy girl, who was given the name Maria (Mary, Miriam). When the little girl turned one year old, Joachim organised a great feast, to which he invited the priests, the scribes, the council of the elders and all the people of Israel. Joachim brought his daughter to the priests and they blessed her. When Mary turned three, Joachim took her up to the Lord's temple to fulfil their promise according to which Mary would serve the Lord. The priest kissed the little girl and said a blessing for her and then sat her down on the third step of the altar. Mary danced gleefully, as if she had always wanted to be there.

At the age of twelve, however, the priests began to consult what to do about the adolescent girl in order not to 'stain' the sanctuary of the Lord. They agreed that they would pray and whatever the Lord said, they would do that. Soon the angel of the Lord appeared and said to Zacharias, the priest, "assemble the widowers of the people, and let them bring each his rod; and to whomsoever the Lord shall show a sign, his wife shall she be." So, many widowers gathered, including Joseph, the carpenter. When he received the rod, a dove came down from the tree and settled on his head. Then the priest said to Joseph, that the Lord had given a sign, he must keep the holy virgin for the Lord. Joseph was unwilling to accept this, he said he had children and he was old already, he would become ridiculous, if he took this virgin girl home. But the priest convinced him that he could not disagree with the will of God. Joseph therefore took Mary home to guard her.

Shortly thereafter, Mary was going to the river to fetch water, when a voice said to her: "*Hail, you who hast received grace; the Lord is with you; blessed are you among women!*" Mary looked around to see where the voice was coming from, but she went home, because she did not see anyone. At home, Gabriel, the angel of the Lord appeared to her and said: "Fear not, Mary; for you have found grace before the Lord of all, and you shall conceive, according to His word." And she hearing, reasoned with herself, saying: "Shall I conceive by the Lord, the living God? And shall I bring forth as every woman brings forth?" And the angel of the Lord said: "Not so, Mary; for the power of the Lord shall overshadow you: wherefore also that holy thing which shall be born of you shall be called the Son of the Most High. And you shall call His name Jesus, for He shall save His people from their sins." And Mary said: "Behold, the servant of the Lord before His face: let it be unto me according to your word."

After this, Mary visited her relative, Elizabeth. When Elizabeth saw her, she rejoiced and said: "Whence is this to me, that the mother of my Lord should come to me?" Mary did not even mention what the angel had announced to her. Elizabeth however, who was expecting to give birth to the later John the Baptist, had already known the news because the developing infant 'exulted' in her. So, then Mary remained with Elizabeth for three months. Mary was only sixteen years old and the child in her womb was growing day-by-day. She was very frightened of what people would think about her, so she went home to Joseph's house to hide from prying eyes. Joseph was returning home from a construction, when he saw Mary and he burst into tears and threw himself to the ground. He was in despair to think that somebody had abused the virgin entrusted to him. He was afraid that God would smite him for not looking after Mary appropriately.

Meanwhile, of course he was questioning Mary too. The young girl swore crying that she was certainly pure, no man touched her. Joseph was puzzled, but had no idea what to do, whom to believe. That night the angel of the Lord appeared to him in his dream and said, not be afraid because who Mary was expecting was from the Holy Spirit. The angel added that she would give birth to a son and name him Jesus, because he would liberate the people from their sins. Then Joseph woke up, thanked God and continued to take care of Mary.

One day, a visitor arrived at their house. When he saw the pregnant Mary, he immediately ran to the high priest and said that Joseph had tainted the virgin who was left in his care. Joseph and Mary were led away to be judged. So Mary said to the high priest: "As the Lord my God lives, I am pure before Him, and know not a man." Then the high priest decided to make them drink the so-called water of curse, which would kill them if they were guilty, but would not hurt the innocent. First, Joseph drank the water and then Mary did, but it did not harm either of them. They were proven innocent and set free. Mary and Joseph went home and waited the arrival of baby Jesus. The rest of the story is well-known. I chose her because the Moon refers to Virgin Mary in Christian art.

(By the way, Mary was a very beautiful woman both at a young age and in her older years. Lots of men wanted to marry her, but she never received any men's approach.)

'The two most important days in your life are the day you are born and the day you find out why.' (Mark Twain)

THE SUN

Saint Stephen and Saint Francis of Assisi

The Interpretation of the Picture

The Sun is the life-giving light, the representative of the highest divine principle and unity. It carries that white light within, in which every colour can be perceived. The Sun gives light, warmth and life itself on Earth. In each hierarchy, it occupies the first place – for example in astrology it is superior to all other symbols and powers. Should we want to translate its meaning to the level of Earthly analogies, the Sun would be the king, the ruler. Alchemists used the golden Sun as the embodiment of creative energy, a symbol of creation. While the Moon is passive, the symbol of water, female principle and of the unconscious, the Sun is active, the male principle, which symbolises fire and conscious.

Number: XIX
Letter: Q
Main element: Fire
Astrology: Sun, Saturn, Aquarius, Cancer, Pisces, Gemini, Leo
Meditation: Creative Force meditation

Important Symbols Appear on the Card:

The Sun: On the card we can see a Sun, the rays of which shine upon a young loving couple. Nature around them celebrates, as a new day dawns (at all levels). The page indicates an almost paradisiacal state, since it is the symbol of power, divinity, brilliance, wisdom, enlightenment, man/father. As the counterpart of the Moon, it is the symbol of life, death and rebirth.

Red rose: In the picture a red rose can be seen, the flower of which represents love, while its thorns symbolise death. Rose is basically a female symbol. The symbol of shyness, beauty, love, lust and the expression of life, completeness, also the symbol of blooming and devoted love. At the same time, it is a token of suffering. Furthermore, rose is the image of rebirth. For the Romans it also symbolised eternity. To the Indians it is the symbol of beauty, completed perfection, the soul and the heart.

The card's meaning in a spread, if you picked this:

Archetype: The Sun
Negative pole: the Night

Psychological Interpretation

The Sun gives energy to the higher intellectual contents, it sheds light on the truth. Now you can see clearly, whether you live your life according to your own free will or still let someone else control you. Here is your chance to expand the boundaries.

Spiritual Interpretation

I know a lot of mythological traditions, in which (as in the Book of Genesis) the night precedes the day. This is so because our ancestors considered darkness to be older, more primitive, through which only the light, i.e. the Sun can penetrate. In the tarot deck the Sun – following the Moon card – disperses the night, thus symbolising the birth too (the child about to come out from the womb). For the soul and the family too, now it is time for creating harmony and balance. Your perception is deepening, you are getting encouragement for more in-depth, clarifying conversations.

General Interpretation

Now you need to transform your emotional relationships, so they would really become viable. Finally, you can get out of mental constraints. It is time for different thinking and to be cleansed from old things also. It is also conceivable that in the forthcoming period, fate is simply forcing your real mission and predestined task on you. For the sake of a new and higher level of existence there is no other way, but what is really meant for you. The intuitions are coming gradually and through these feelings the 'instructions' are arriving. Even if your financial or emotional life is becoming questionable these days, in this period your dreams are also showing you how can you step on a road that is going to lead you to light and rebirth.

Reversed Interpretation

Night is a natural phenomenon with a peculiar sense. It is the opposite of light: it covers everything in murk. As light reveals the visible properties of things to us, night absorbs all that and it threatens to swallow you as well. It is not simply Nothing that is immersed in the night. Everything keeps existing at night, but they are so indeterminate, invisible and shapeless as the night itself. Or they are shadowy and ghostly; that is why darkness is so scaring. You may feel that the dangers lurking in the night threaten your existence both internally and externally. You lose the use of your senses, night inhibits your mobility, paralyzes your strengths and makes you lonely. Thereby you yourself can become shadow-like. Therefore, now be careful regarding your intuitions and do not make serious decisions. Even if you feel helpless because of insurmountable difficulties and problems, just keep coming and growing.

The task now is to reassess everything and also see things from a different angle. Think about the moonlit, magical night, flooded by mild, gentle light which is in contrast with the dark and scary night. Choose the moonlit night! This night does not absorb anything rather it bights up your nocturnal face. It alleviates, deadens every hard, sharp and flamboyant feature and highlights the essential, which is never seen by daylight. It brings out sounds that otherwise the daytime noise suppresses. It puts an end to the rush and roar of the day, bringing tranquillity and peace.

This seemingly difficult time has a great impact on your spiritual life. In the gentle glow of the spiritual night you can be exempted from the daily plodding and you can enter the deeper connections of your own being, life, the world and the other world freely, relaxedly and collectedly.

Love Interpretation

This is the time to be united in True Love. In your relationship you are surrounded by peace and harmony, however in this period sexual energies are also functioning with greater intensity. Now distance yourself a little from everyday worries, look at yourself and your relationship from outside and 'from above'. Whatever is happening, the solution now is pure emotion, the sincere expression and experience of desires. The Sun indicates happy marriage and joy.

Material Interpretation

After a long, difficult period now you can finally count on significant improvement. Pay attention and act prudently though, therefore your work is going to be recognised and also your financial situation is solidifying.

Work

Now you are getting a strong urge to your goals, with a lot of energy. The revival is relevant, because the power over your own destiny is strengthening. Now this period is proper for any changes and brave steps. The Sun is illuminating the way for you or the way out. If you are looking for a job, hand in an application to many places, your efforts are soon going to be crowned with success.

The Question of study

The Sun promises success. Successful entrance examination, successful exams. This however, cannot be associated with fraud. Fairness and diligence are the prerequisites for success.

Health Interpretation

In this period, you are getting an enormous power and inspiration in order to create unity, harmony and balance in your life. The Sun is the card of health itself.

Family Interpretation

Now you must have those talks, by which you can make order in your life and soul. Honesty is very important – if you dare to speak about things that have been so far hidden, swept under the carpet, the situations will become clear and you can reap the desired results. The Sun means peace, harmony and happiness. It is time for commitment and/or to start a family.

Task

You can now put in material form the lessons, which you learned in the past. Pay attention to your inner desires and needs, because if your desires are true and sincere, they will also show a true path. It is time to establish, to create something!

The Message of the Card

Whatever plan, desires you have cherished so far, now is the time for the big embarking, the big Start! Even if you are not immediately in the implementation phase, it is important to devise, reconsider the plan, to get acquainted with new features, new ideas, new views, the closure of the old, specific planning, preparation and departure.

Emotions: great joy of life, vitality, warmth, trust, optimism, creativity, wisdom, awareness
Stage of life: settling down, happy marriage, starting a family, new friends, reward.

Personalities illustrated on the card are Saint Stephen and Saint Francis of Assisi

Saint Stephen – the founder of the Hungarian state (975-1038)

St Stephen was the first Christian ruler of Hungary, the founder of the Hungarian state, who single-handedly succeeded in the enormous work of uniting the state, organising the church and legislating.

Less than half a century before his accession to the throne (1000), the Hungarian cavalry were fatally threatening the West and Christianity, moving forward all the way to the Lech field next to Augsburg. However, Hungary redesigned by constitution and expansion, culture and history-shaping power starting from Stephen, became the outpost of the Christian West against the advancing Mongol and Ottoman Turkish danger, and, over the centuries, it served as a defence wall against the barbarism of Asian invaders. From political, religious and social point of view, he was the one who actually created Hungary, he appointed and assured the path to the future for the Hungarian nation.

His diplomatic and political sense, with which in practice he could often achieve conflicting goals, made him the greatest statesman of his age and the whole Hungarian history. This is precisely why he also appears on the Temperance card.

Stephen, originally named Vajk, was the only son of Prince Géza (reigned 971-997). Immediately after his father's death, he found himself confronting his uncle, the pagan Koppány. According to the ancient custom of seniority, his uncle – as the eldest male member of the family – claimed Sarolt, the widow of Prince Géza, to be his wife and wanted to gain the main power too. Since he did not get either of these, his armies clashed with Stephen's knights near Veszprém in 998. The battle – with German support – was won by the Christian monarch. The battle has been countless times written about and sung of. The rebellious Koppány's body was cut into four and the pieces had were hung on four of the most important castle rooks as a clear message to those who might consider to defy the will of Stephen. After the defeat of Koppány, the young monarch completed the construction of the abbey of Pannonhalma and turned to Rome for the crown. Soon, in the year 1000, at Christmas he was crowned in Esztergom, thus – in legal sense – the Christian Kingdom of Hungary was established. However, the royal title itself did not provide the actual main power, for that the new monarch had to engage in battles for several decades, against the chieftains who became independent after the conquest.

In parallel with his struggles to unify the homeland, Stephen laid the foundations of the Christian state, in which his main helper was the Church. In the territory of Hungary, 10 bishoprics and two archdioceses were established, through which the country formed an independent church district and thus was able to become independent from the German-Roman Empire. Stephen also established laws for the young Christian kingdom: with his two Codes – one of them created at the beginning of his reign and the other one at the end – forced his subjects to convert, exercise the Christian religion and respect private property, and by this he facilitated the spread of settled life form.

While he expected his subjects to bear the costs of keeping the churches function and supporting the priests ('ten villages should build one temple'), the ruler also spent considerable sums on constructions. His name is associated for example with the founding of the monastery of Pécsvárad and the nunnery of Veszprémvölgy, moreover he built guesthouses for Hungarian travellers on the pilgrimage road leading to Jerusalem.

At the beginning of his reign, Stephen's foreign policy was determined by the alliance with the Holy Roman Empire. The support he received against Koppány, maybe the crown itself, and his marriage to Gizella, the daughter of the Quarrelsome Henry, Duke of Bavaria could be acknowledged to this.

However, later he became a strong handed, serious statesman who held the interests of his nation to be most important.

The great ruler has been considered to be the supreme symbol of the Hungarian nation, whom since 1083 – thanks to the also canonised King László I – we have honoured among the Hungarian saints. The most important Hungarian national holiday is linked to his name (20th of August). His reign meant the most important four decades in Hungarian history, which paved the future of a whole nation.

Saint Francis of Assisi (1182 – 1226)

St Francis of Assisi, 'God's pauper' is one of the best-known, most influential saints of Christianity, a great figure of the Catholic monastic renewal.

He was born in 1182, under the name of Francesco Bernardone, in Assisi, in an urban community organised upon a modern basis. His father was a wealthy cloth and linen merchant, who intended to share his career with his son. By nature, Francis was interested in people and animals. His behaviour was characterised by gentleness, generosity and gaiety. His hometown went to war with the city of Perugia in 1202, in which it was defeated; then Francis was jailed for one year. The imprisonment brought a huge change in the boy's life and a new man returned home from the war.

His fuller life opened up a series of profound spiritual experience for him. While praying in front of the cross in the San Damiano chapel, Christ said to him: 'Francis, go and repair my house which, as you can see, is falling into ruins.' After this, Francis renovated the chapel with his two hands, meanwhile realising the true meaning of Christ's message as well. Permanently breaking away from material goods, stripping down naked and giving back everything to his father, he left his rich and comfortable life as a penniless beggar. Although he suddenly found himself in the most difficult conditions, lacking food and warm clothing, he literally followed what was written in the Gospels. His example and perseverance launched a tremendous reform within Christianity. Setting an example, he gave hope to those poor people, who were excluded from the ecclesiastical world because of their situation.

A wonderful divine power emanated from Francis. He lived a very simple life just like the poorest people. He kept vigil and prayed, in deep trance on the verge of crying and catharsis frequently, many nights in a row. His sufferings were indescribable, his deprivations were constantly accompanied by with illnesses. Within a short time, many people began to follow his example. On his influence, voluntary poverty and the following of Christ were first fashionable and later evolved into a powerful religious movement.

Accepting every affliction, his first followers sought the life, which is clean, uncompromising and free from falsehood.

As it is characteristic of the lives of the greatest saints, Francis started a positive process in the world with almost every act. He even had a major impact on animals: the ferocious wolf of Gubbio was eating out of his hands and thousands of birds gathered to listen to his preaching. Meanwhile, robbers were converting, and people who had turned away from God suddenly began to live a saintly life after meeting him.

As the effect of Francis' influence three orders were also established, which were sanctified by the Pope himself. The first one was a male monastic order, the 'Lesser brothers'; the second order was the Franciscan nuns, the Poor Clares, that was named after St Claire, Francis' lifelong soul mate and helper; the third order was created for the ordained men and women, they were the tertiaries. All events of his life were special and fit for a novel, therefore his deeds inspired many great artists.

In 1224, at the Alverna or La Verna Mountains, after a long prayer, God revealed His love in the form of stigmata. He belonged to those special stigmatised people who wore all the scars of Christ on their bodies. Thanks to the delicious smelling wounds, his healing power multiplied. One of the most well-known descriptions of his life is the Fioretti and the Perugia legend collection.

(I warmly recommend you the *Brother Sun, Sister Moon* (*Fratello Sole, Sorella Luna*) movie, which is Franco Zeffirelli's wonderful creation based on the life events of St Francis of Assisi, or the *Canticle of the Sun* written by Francis.)

'Life is really simple, but we insist on making it complicated.'
(Confucius)

Judgment

Chief Álmos and Jesus

The Interpretation of the Picture

In the picture Archangel Michael can be seen with his huge wings in the sky, just as he is blowing a blast in his trumpet. His head is surrounded by a halo. Below him (facing us) there is a man and a woman with their hands raised in prayer. They are only half-visible, because the child in front of them, getting out of the water (with his back turned to us) looks at them. As we observe them, we get the feeling that the child teaches them. Just as a newborn child teaches his or her parents (and of course in the meantime he/she also learns from them). In the old cards originally, there could be seen people emerging from a tomb and the child rose out of a coffin. This version is far from me. Since water indicates purification and a gateway to the other world, here the child rises out of the water and the parents also stand in the water. This refers also to the fact that this is the card of rebirth and/or being blessed with a child.

Number: XX
Letter: R
Main elements: Earth and Fire
Astrology: Saturn, Mercury, Pisces, Aquarius, Virgo
Meditation: birth-meditation

Important Symbols Appear on the Card

Archangel Michael, the Protector: According to the Catholic tradition, Archangel Michael is one of the seven archangels. He is the great leader of the heavenly armies and a victorious fighter. His symbol is the mighty sword, with which he overcomes all evil. His will power is enormous, just like he himself. His loyalty to God is unwavering. Archangel Michael is a powerful guardian angel, who can answer our most important questions. His unlimited power allows him to be everywhere at the same time, yet we feel his presence to be personal and special. He was the angel who handcuffed the traitorous Lucifer and his followers and knocked them out of heaven. Archangel Michael is the one who, after our death (similarly to the Egyptian Anubis) measures our good and bad deeds committed during our earthly life on a scale. He opens the gates of Heaven wide in front of the good souls and he accompanies the bad ones into purgatory. Nevertheless, when the Last Judgment comes, the horn of Archangel Michael will be the one that shall resound on the horizon, alerting humanity that the Last Hour has come.

The child: the symbol of the future, creation and maturation and of course the milestone of patience as well. As a parent, one of the most important recognitions about a child's upbringing is nothing else than the fact, that the child teaches. If your thoughts and your actions are full of emails, text messages, reminders and a way too crowded agenda, with the arrival of a child all this will change. The most important thing, instead of completing every point of your full schedule will be the fact that you show your child the world, as you have forgotten to view it: with all its beauty. If you are conscious, then you will realise that the little one leaves time for everything: he/she is able to stop and talk to an elderly lady, look at snails, butterflies and beetles (and a lot of other things) for hours. For them, time does not exist, they live in the present, in the Now and do not understand why they cannot do everything now, get something now… or why you do not have time for this or that. Therefore, a child can teach you to live again in the present, to sit quietly and pay attention to each other, smile and enjoy it, to experience life around us. Beside them you will realise that if you stop to experience the simple, small pleasures of life, you really live. Because the child is the true expert among those who live a life full of joy. At the same time the child is a being who lacks the basic capabilities for physical subsistence. He needs us. We have a responsibility towards him.

I have to mention that in the parent-child relationship there are always twists and turns, in which only the presence of authentic parents can bring a solution. This is precisely why I planned a master-therapy training among the training sessions, in which the participants (parents and children separately and then jointly, of course) will discover their own life story. In these trainings we will discover the story about you, your roots, dreams, goals, failures and fears. In the meantime, you will realise that you do tell stories to your child not only in the evening, through bedtime stories: but you tell 'stories' through your presence, behaviour, your attitude towards yourself, the world and the people. Because setting and enforcing the rules and boundaries are all about you as well. With your actions you talk about what you believe in, what you fight for and what helps you get through difficult situations. Furthermore, behind your child's problems there lies the tale of his own life. Not only what has happened to him so far, but also what he wants, needs (desire for love, desire for acceptance, dreams, wishes, grievances, anxiety). Each child views and interprets the world in a unique, special way. If we allow his own story to unfold, then we can witness a huge transformation. (About the program you can read on the back of the book.)

The card's meaning in a spread, if you picked this

Archetype: Redemption, Purification, Transformation
Negative pole: Damnation
Psychological Interpretation:

Your secrets, feelings or experiences that have been so far deeply guarded, deeply buried are being revealed. It is time to look deep inside and close the past.

Spiritual Interpretation

Mortality and Immortality, the balance of the opposite forces of Nature.

General Interpretation

The focus is put on longing for higher things. In order to achieve this, you have to step on the path of solution and transformation without looking back, in the situations where old qualities are already gone. You must completely finish pointing fingers at others, because the solution lies in you and if you do not look inside yourself now, there will be no enlightenment.

Reversed Interpretation:

Deep sorrow is engulfing you and this has an impact on your environment also. You are unable to realise how much love is directed at you, because you feel that your relationships are superficial. It is time to face yourself, either in a mirror or during a meditation. Change is going to be created by you or others will generate it. In any case, the first version is more fortunate.

Love Interpretation

Fate is now proving that things can be different from what you previously believed, thought, learned, imagined and operated. If you feel fed up and it is all over, sit down for a moment and close your eyes. Then imagine: what would there be if you could do whatever you want? Afterwards open your eyes and realise: you can actually do that. A flow of emotions, feelings, spiritual information is taking place, now is worth talking about your ideas of the future. However, you should take a decision later.

Material Interpretation

Soon the difficult period is going to be over, then abundance will finally arrive.

Work

At last you are reaching the status, for which you have been struggling for a long time. Consequently, you can lay the foundations of a promising future.

The Question of study

Thanks to your preparedness and wise initiatives, you are reaching your much-envisioned goals. A good opportunity is arising in order for you to lay down the foundation for a promising future. Self-delusion is never a good advisor. Remember that only your enthusiasm and dedication can lead you onto the right path, where higher inspirations may come.

Health Interpretation

On emotional levels, a very profound cleaning process has already commenced, which is going to help to bring forth the deeply buried experiences, injuries, fears also, so they would be healed. So let them come forth, give them power, clean them! It is time to let go your grievances, to stop complaining and get rid of the deep-rooted illusion and pain.

Family Interpretation

Seek balance, strengthen the ability to love, understand and accept! Now you may find those boundaries or drawn limits from which it is time to get out and create others chosen by us. If your relationships are built on deep love and honesty, they are going to be more and more harmonious. If not, you definitely have to make a change, unless you want someone else make the change for you.

Task

It is time to quieten down, to turn inward and it is time for transformation. If there is a situation in your life, into which you would like to bring balance and harmony, then it is definitely time to make a change and to renew actively. It is worth to get rid of those material things or addictions that are related to a past life stage. It is time to finally trust yourself and your carefully considered/ taken decisions.

The Message of the Card

Now, the discovery of the internal content, the operations behind the visible are coming to the fore. The transformations taking place within you are raising you up to a clean, higher quality.

Emotions: anger, passion, purification, fervour, patience, desire to act, time, missed moments

Stage of life: Again, this card brings rearrangements and changes. Everything may become understandable; the understanding of the conclusions from the previous teachings is going on, if you dare to really look into yourself and make a decision.

Personalities illustrated on the card are Chief Álmos and Jesus

Chief Álmos

Chief Álmos (?895) is one of the leaders of the pre-Conquest Hungarians. He was the father of Chief Árpád and one of the leaders of the seven original settlers. Chief Álmos was something like a Moses for the Hungarians, who led them to the Promised Land, that is the Carpathian Basin. Similar to Moses, Álmos could not set foot in the promised land, thus his son, Árpád, had to finish the commenced work. His figure is also outstanding because ruler Álmos founded the first Hungarian dynasty, which was named Árpád house, after his son Árpád (also known as the Turul generation.).

Every nation's folklore has its own totem animals. The Hungarian belief's most influential character is the Turul bird. This bird appears to Emese the mother of chieftain Álmos and tells the woman that she will give birth to a son. And her son is not just anybody: because this boy will be a ruler and the fruit of his loin will be a series of glorious kings (who later will not reign on their own land). Upon hearing this, Emese bows deeply, slowly lifts her head and some strange, majestic feeling and tranquillity pervades her whole being. She understands that this is a reward, because her people endured all those years of tribulations with dignity and never left their God. As after the disintegration of King Attila's empire, serious years of hardships weighed upon the Hun and Hungarian people. It was already the time for redemption.

As Emese had seen in her dream, soon she gave birth to a son, whom she named Álmos. When Álmos grew into a tall and slender statured, mature young man, he became a wise and brave soldier. Soon he married the daughter of a noble leader. She bore him a son named Árpád, with whom he later started out to Pannonia. Since his homeland was unable to feed his people, he had to look for a new land. The seven chieftains unanimously chose Pannonia. (We call them The Seven Magyars). They preferred precisely this area because the leaders were convinced that Pannonia belonged to that King Attila from whom they derived their origin. With common decision they sealed a blood oath and elected Álmos as their leader. They vowed that they and their descendants would choose their ruler always from among the children of Álmos. Thus the first Hungarian dynasty, the Turul-House or House of Árpád was born.

At the same time, the founding of the Turul-house is lost in the mists of mythology. According to legends, ancient chronicles and oral tradition, the ruling house can be traced back until Nimrod (Ménróth, Nimrud) the post-Flood world's first king. Nimrod was a famous hunter and extraordinary physical strength was attributed to him. He started the construction of the Tower of Babel in Mesopotamia according to different medieval sources such as Flavius Josephus and Hungarian chronicles. The Bible does not associate Nimrod's name with the Tower, but it does not contradict the medieval sources. Nimrod is illustrated on the Tower card there you can read more about him.

Jesus

Check the Unnamed Arcanum's card

'He felt now that he was not simply close to her, but that he did not know where he ended and she began.' (Leo Tolstoy)

THE WORLD

Adam and Eve

The Interpretation of the Picture

This card is the card of superlatives (the best), meaning it takes everything. A real fortune card that enhances the impact of any adjacent card. It represents the world of the ultimate spiritual reality, at the same time it is the symbol of our everyday reality. The World Tree is displayed on this card along with the meditating/spectator Adam, and Eve who is dancing in front of him. The Eternal first Woman's nakedness is covered only with a veil and she is currently expecting a baby. She dances and through her dance she shows the joy, the harmony and the order of the universe.

The number belonging to the World is XXI, this number is precisely the opposite of 12, that belongs to the Hanged Man card. Therefore, if you take a really good look, you will notice that the dancing Eve's feet shape a cross, but as opposed to the Hanged Man who hangs upside down, the Woman rising from the matter dances the universal dance of motherhood. She is the mother, who will give birth to the child that will become the newborn child on the Fool card. The tarot begins with this again, meaning the timeless path of Wisdom, your new internal, developmental, initiatory path.

Number: XXI
Letter: T
Main elements: Earth and Air
Astrology: Saturn, Venus, Sun, Virgo
Meditation: Birth meditation

Important Symbols Appear on the Card:

The symbol of completeness and of whole (health) – meaning the World Tree: the world tree is the most basic systemising form in the ancient religion of Central Asian equestrian nations including the Huns and Magyars. The World Tree is very important in symbolism: it refers to life and death, eternal development and growth and thereby continuous renewal. We can find a lot of drawings on shaman drums, which are direct relatives of the Avar world tree. According to the shamanistic belief of Eastern nations, the universe consists of an underworld swarming with reptiles, toads and evil spirits, the middle world is a scene for the earthly life, and the upper world includes the double layered sky populated by charitable spirits. These three levels are connected by the wonderful world tree, the sky-high tree, the tree of life. Depth psychology interprets this root, trunk, crown triad as an expression of the id, ego and super-ego.

The Tree is generally the symbol of life force, life, regeneration, eternal existence, development, the Man and the Holy Knowledge. According to psychological approach, the tree is the mirror image of personality, the symbol of its evolution. The sky-high tree is also known as the 'spirit tree' in the folklore. It is rooted in the underworld, in the unconscious, in the ancient past, its trunk is the personal life path and the crown evokes the area of consciousness. Its branches usually go through the seven layers of the sky. It shows the development of personality, the 'here and now' status, the past, the future, social relationships and life path.

The World Tree is the symbol of time, life, the circle of the year and as such, it is the symbol of an important development, transformation (renewable life/life-and-death symbol). It symbolises the unification of Heaven and Earth (in Shamanism) – meaning the unification of God with the Goddess.

The mother: Women appear in every great religion. In some, they are goddesses, in others they are saints or sinners. In India, they are Parvati, Lakshmi and Saraswati. At the Greeks, they are Hera, Aphrodite, Demeter and Pallas Athene. In Egypt, there is Isis and Nephthys. In China there is Kwan-yin, in Rome they are Juno, Venus, Minerva, Ceres and Diana and in another religion, there is Astarte (Istar). There are likenesses of Isis where she holds the child Horus in her lap, just like in the Catholic faith the Virgin holds the Baby Jesus.

In several places, insiders mention an enormous creature, who is actually a huge angel to whom an enormous army of angels belong. Her work – her defensive, protective role – expands on the entire female gender. She is the Universal Mother. It is said that every woman in the world is under Her protection, especially in times of the greatest trial, when they carry out their most important task and they become mothers in reality.

In the past, some stories were told – especially among the peasantry – that some women saw the Universal Mother standing next to them in the difficult hours of childbirth. Others, however, did not see her, but felt the help they received from her and the force that emanated toward them from her. The Universal Mother, as the most dedicated defender of the female gender, works together with the Lords of Karma, to find a suitable birth for the huge mass of souls awaiting incarnation. However, she has another important mission as well: to alleviate the sufferings of the world and to comfort, encourage and help everyone who is in trouble, who suffers misfortune, who is in need and who is sick.

According to Jung, the Great Mother is the most fundamental archetype, who can be both good and a bad mother as well.

The parents: In order to have a happy, balanced relationship, it is important that the father-mother model should find its position within everyone. Later on, this gives us a huge advantage throughout parenthood, because as a mother or a father, without exception, everyone has to walk on the yellow stoned path, until – similarly to Dorothy – they recognise the inherent magical power, meaning the internal streams that connect man with nature. Being a parent is one of the most amazing experiences in the world, at the same time it is not easy, since it is difficult to constantly find the balance between the supporting and controlling behaviours in the current situation. Because the methods of education are not as important as what happens between the parent and the child's soul. However, in this regard no one can give you a sure recipe.

I raise my children consciously, therefore I try to leave my automatisms behind and see every situation with a fresh eye, as if they happened for the first time to me/us. So, even though I am an experienced parent, still I approach each situation creatively, more open-minded and I do not react to what I already know, but only at the present moment. I turn my attention to what is going on in my children's inner world and I do not focus on what I think of the given situation. In the evenings, I always make time to focus intensively on the little ones, to give my full attention to them. I do not apply educational strategies, but rather I am more consciously present. I make sure that both of my children have enough of my attention separately.

The card's meaning in a spread, if you picked this:

Archetype: the Universe, Paradise, the System, the Cycle
Negative pole: Hell, Chaos

Psychological Interpretation

It is natural to raise offsprings, it is in the natural order of things, it is an innate program in every person. Becoming a parent is one of the most decisive life experience. Both in individual life as well as in a relationship it is an all-shattering experience, since it is not only about a child coming into this world. Now you are confronting yourself, your boundaries and the multitude of conscious or unconscious mental factors that result from your individual life experiences, but are also related with the previous generations, with the life stories of your ancestors. This card indicates not necessarily the birth of a child, but rather the birth of anything else as well.

Spiritual Interpretation

You may find out how and where you should transform your destiny. You may look towards the future. The time has come to commit yourself on paths and missions of higher level. In the spiritual sense your knowledge is already clear. The four elemental challenges come to the fore: Knowing, Daring, Wanting, and Listening. This ends a learning process, a spiral, a circle and restarts a magical initiation process, already on a higher level.

General Interpretation

The World card means realisation, the reward of good deeds, success and happiness. Your efforts are now going to receive their worthy reward. If you have not done so already, then it is time to finish whatever does not grow harmony, prosperity and happiness in your life as well as within yourself

Reversed Interpretation:

Although you have done everything in order to achieve your goals, in the current stage all this is impossible, due to reasons that do not depend on you anymore. Do not worry, you will not suffer any losses just have to wait until everything goes back the way it was and during that time you are going to realise how important it is to fulfil your personal mission. If you have not done it already, you have to let go of everything that stands in the way of this.

Love Interpretation

In your relationship fulfilment, balance, harmony, order and agreement can be expected. The card promises reconciliation after break up and dissolution of inconsistencies. One may be prepared for conceiving a child within three months, because the next period is fertile.

Material Interpretation

The World is the card of great luck, thus financial growth is guaranteed. Put aside your doubts, walk with your eyes open, in order to recognise if fortune winks at you.

Work

If you are looking for a job, make sure you clarify what position you desire. In order to be successful, now dedication and the dissolution of internal contradictions are indispensable. Pay attention more consciously, because in this period you may get very clear information and inspirations. Productive, stabilising forces are flowing into your life, pay attention to your dreams, because they are showing the way. Soon you are going to receive the necessary guidance for the following period. You may become aware of where you should go on, how to act in the future.

The Question of study

If you have spent sufficient time and energy on your studies, the World card is bringing you now success and good grades. However, if you are currently thinking whether it would be worth to study again, feel free to dive in, this card promises great success.

Health Interpretation

The World card promises recovery in case of a serious disease as well. On mental level it is time for a complete transformation, now you are very deeply experiencing what it feels when everything is enlivened and moved by love. During meditation, wash everything within yourself, with the healing vital force of love.

Family Interpretation

This period is the spirit of love, fire, harmony and energy. The World as a fortune card is now giving you strength to any transformation and change you are making in your life so you may live in the spirit of love – with the people you love, in a state of love. This card also promises to be blessed with a baby, the gift of love can be expected to be a girl.

Task

This period is flooding you, emanating towards your strength and inspirations of purification. Half-solutions and superficial changes are not enough in this period. If you finally dare to open your eyes wide, you may become the master of knowledge, wisdom, which is controlling your own destiny.

The Message of the Card

It is worth thinking about how to create or shape your future. Being richer with the knowledge brought from high spheres, and possessing ideas received from above, you may go forward now more intuitively and easily. With your strength and knowledge, you know exactly how to rise above your own borders, how to break through your own limits and rise toward the light. In this, now you can help your mates, your friends and your family too.

Keywords: completion, cosmic union, liberation from under constraints, the closing of karma, found unity, happy ending, reaching the goal, intuition.

Stage of life: the World card shows the re-found unity, the experience of profound harmony and the joyful end of a development process.

Personalities Illustrated on the Card are Adam and Eve

Adam: see the Magician's card

Eve: see the High Priestess' card

‚You are a living magnet. What you attract into your life is in harmony with your dominant thoughts.' (Brian Tracy)

THE FOOL

Béla IV and Nehemiah

The Interpretation of the Picture

This card is one of the most important and most mysterious cards in the tarot deck, which is generally exempted from the rules and in a spread, it can occupy any other tarot card's position. I also have also received my most interesting visions from this card, thanks to the fact that this is the card of the beginning and the end.

Some people identify the fool with the Dreamer or the Visionary and believe, just like me, that his attention is directed to the things of the soul and therefore he cannot see the everyday happenings clearly.

If we look at the course of development of the Tarot, the Fool may represent a child in the mother's womb or a young boy who is simple, pure and innocent, which is why he cannot see the traps or challenges awaiting him in life.

Number: 0-XXII
Letter: S
Main elements: Fire and Air
Astrology: Moon, Sun, Uranus, Taurus, Cancer, Leo
Meditation: fresh start, beginning of a journey

Important Symbols Appear on the Card

In the picture we see a young boy who sets off on a journey to try his luck. On his shoulders there is a green robe, on his side the inevitable satchel or bundle, and a stick in his hand, which is similar to the magician's wand, but it is not the same. He still has a lot to learn in order to catch up with the Magician. A butterfly flies around him (the butterfly is the symbol of the soul, the psyche and of resurrection), the young man smiles happily upon the world, to nature, while at the same time his eyes are watchful and dreamy. The road leads him from the night into day (with one leg still here and with the other already there), this also shows the duality of his existence. At night, the bright Moon illuminates him, by day the sun shines down on him. The river, from which he steps out of, is the spring of the life-giving water, at the same time the dividing line between life and death. This is the spirit's path connecting this world with the afterlife and purification itself, because water can wash away every sin, every evil in the human existence. A crocodile crawls after him and although it does not reach him, this animal represents the unnoticed danger, for which he always has to look out. On land a wolf joins him, which also refers to dangers, but draws attention to adaptation and fidelity as well. Wolves are social animals, they are extremely adaptable and communicate well. They live in packs, which are controlled by an alpha male and an alpha female, which stay together until the end of their lives. Wolves are loyal, bold, family centred, at the same time humble, because they not only dominate but also serve. They economise their strength and starve as well if needed.

The card's meaning in a spread, if you picked this

Archetype: the child
Negative pole: the misunderstood genius balancing on the edge of insanity

Psychological Interpretation

This is the time for a full insight into the purifying processes taking place in your soul, for the liberation of the soul through bright, clear recognitions. Now your old desire, which is worth realising is going to show itself.

Spiritual Interpretation

Look deep inside yourself, feel and discover who you really are, your true self! See why you are unique, what valuable skills, talents, missions you brought with yourself when you were born. Because only you are able to operate all these and pass them on to the world.

General Interpretation

This card is the symbol of eternal start or fresh start. Still every road is open in front of you, even if you have no precise ideas about the future. This card means a finished developmental period, the beginning after a past life stage, now the unknown is attracting you and the desire is driving you towards the new. In this state, just pay attention to yourself, now you do not have to adapt or perform. This card indicates unutilised talent and latent abilities. You are going to have an experience that is leaving a deep impression on you and it is going to lead to the transformation of your being, to a new untrodden road. In a spread the card can represent a soon-to-be-born or minor child, work or a fresh start, the approaching of something new too.

Reversed Interpretation

You have lost yourself or your real goals. Difficult changes can be expected, you need to be prepared for everything. This card refers to a life situation, where you do not have the strength to execute your tasks. Everything is pointing to failure. It may indicate childlessness and the resultant fears and also draws the attention on parent-child relationship problems. You have to get out of this as soon as possible, because this is the first step to choose better partners, whether in business, friendship or love relationship.

Love Interpretation

In terms of relationship, it is time to renew your existing points of view. If you have been being surrounded by depressing forms of behaviour and relationships, heading for destruction then I have good news: the refreshing, revigorating stream has arrived and is opening new doors in front of you. The wheel of fate is restarting and pulling the water to your own mill. You need to become aware of the fact that every relationship is viable until you can develop in it through one another. If it only holds you back, retains you, if it is just an inhibitory factor in the flow of love and development, the time for a change has come.

Material Interpretation

You must learn that you need to deal with money smartly. Hang in there a little while longer, soon you are going to achieve your goals. Soon you can enjoy financial successes.

Work

Since the Fool's aim is to become independent, to be the master of himself, so now you have to stop for a while. You need to think your situation through and build new, more stable foundations. Do not confuse work with friendship. The card can also indicate working abroad, this can be found out more precisely through the adjacent cards.

The Question of study

If you are into serious study, then it is time to look for foreign schools or scholarships. If you take an exam, do it honestly and clearly, otherwise the risk of being caught is threatening. In case you are just starting to learn, look at the whole thing as a long-term process.

Health Interpretation

You know exactly what you should do to preserve or regain your health. Pay attention to what came to your mind first when you saw the Fool card, because the solution lies there. The first reaction is always the intuition which is wise and free of prejudice like the Fool card itself. Getting to know yourself and liberating yourself are essential to reach change, healing, new order at the level of the material.

Family Interpretation

You can count on your loved ones in the next period. They are going to help and understand you. Now it is all about how much you can do in the present for your future. The Fool card can mean moving, settling down abroad or may indicate the arrival of a new family member (child).

Task

Your task is working for the Future and sorting out the recalling words of the past. You have reached a serious crossroad, which is offering more opportunity for further advance in the progress you have made so far. Put down the burden you have been carrying, get rid of what has stood in the way of your own fulfilment, success, financial or emotional thrive!

The Message of the Card

A new chapter is beginning in your life, you only have to realise the opportunities that life has to offer to you. Walk with your eyes open, be proactive, put aside your old mentality. Watch life, the world more openly and more curiously, thus you may know areas, of which you thought to exist only in books or in movies.

Emotions: playfulness, vivacious carefreeness, openness, curiosity, spontaneity, craziness, directionality, defencelessness, independence, creativity, freedom
Stage of life: This is the period of starting over.

Why are precisely Béla IV and Nehemiah on the card? Personalities illustrated on the card

- Béla IV is one of the outstanding figures of the Hungarian history, the second founder of the state, the 'rebuilder' King
- Nehemiah, whose book in the Old Testament is in one of the most important books in the Bible. It is a memoir that notes the rebuilding of Jerusalem and the events up to around 450 BC.

Their stories:
Béla IV

Béla IV was a Hungarian King from the Árpád dynasty (1206–1270). He was the ruler of Hungary from 25th of September 1235, until his death. He was the brother of St Elizabeth, who can be seen on another card.

Immediately after his accession, he already triggered aversiveness by two great actions. One was about the repossession of the given away royal estates which also included the curtailment of the rights acquired during the reign of his father; his other action was settling the Cumans fleeing from the Tatars. These arrangements gave opportunity to continuous conflicts, especially because the Cumans did not stay in the designated areas, often wandered over the Hungarian estates where they caused serious damage and browbeat people.

The circumspect king, however, insisted on keeping the Cumans, he planned to strengthen the defence against the Tatars with them. He knew that together with the Cumans he was able to call forty thousand horsemen to battle and he was also aware of the fact that the Cumans were tough warriors. The lords, however, were angry with their king, they were not convinced by his tactics, therefore at the first opportunity they killed Kötöny the Cumanian monarch. Thereby, in the most critical moment, the country lost the help of the Cumans, who took the side of the Tatars out of revenge. So, this led to a defeat at Muhi on 11th of April 1241 against Genghis Khan, who similarly to Attila considered himself, the Scourge of God. Fleeing from the battle, the King Béla's life was saved by a few self-sacrificing soldiers.

However, the wise king was thoroughly deceived: while the Tartars were devastating the country, Prince Frederick II of Austria was also plundering him badly, although he was the one who initially offered shelter for Béla IV. First, he took the king's valuables, then claimed Sopron, Bratislava and Moson counties as token. After this, the king managed to escape, to the castle of Trau on the Dalmatian coast through Zagreb, where the other members of the royal family also found refuge. Following this he turned for help to Pope Gregory IX and the French King St Louis IX, but he did not receive help from anywhere. Because Europe supposed that the Hungarian kingdom had been destroyed by the Tatar devastation. Meanwhile, Genghis Khan and his Tatar and Mongol armies caused apocalypse in Hungary and they were threatening Europe too. In some areas, more than 50% of the population died, whole villages disappeared from the face of the Earth.

After the retreat of the Tatars, the returning King saw the image of total destruction.

Béla IV was aware that he could no longer run away and he could not expect any help, thus he reorganised the empire and his life: he rebuilt the country. His experiences showed him aware of his earlier political flaws, therefore instead of confrontation, he sought agreement with the nobles of the country. In the depopulated areas he settled colonists from the neighbouring countries: Czechs, Moravians, Germans, Romanians. This is why he is referred to as the second founder of the state.

He did many things against new attacks: he built stone castles and he centred his policy around the issue of averting new attacks. He built modern stone fortresses, supported the idea of surrounding the cities with stonewalls. With his estate donations he also encouraged his subjects to do the same, he continued the policy of his father, Andrew II, under the condition that a fortress must be built on it. This way, an unprecedented number of castles were built. Thanks to this, by the time of the king's death, nearly 100 stone castles were standing across the country, in the meantime towns and villages were also rebuilt. The royal family itself set an example in castle-building: Queen Mary built Visegrád around 1250. The royal residence was transferred to Buda, where they also built a fortress. This part has been called the Buda Castle Hill until today. Finally, Béla IV settled accounts with his plunder, Prince Frederick II of Austria, from whom the

Hungarians fought back the three western counties. Prince Frederick himself was killed in the battle.

The central figure of the tarot card became Béla IV because from a 'fool', an individual searching his own path – he had to become a new man, a magician as a real ruler relying on his experiences in order to lead out his people from the crisis of trust and moral; set the country back on its feet again after the Tatar invasion and bequeath to his son a reconstructed, prosperous and stronger kingdom.

Nehemiah

Nehemiah worked as the cupbearer for the Persian king Artaxerxes in the castle of Susa. One day, Hanani visited him, who came from Judea. He informed Nehemiah about the miserable situation of the people living there, the destruction of the stonewall of Jerusalem and the burning down of its gates. Nehemiah was deeply saddened hearing this. The ruler certainly noticed the change and asked him what the matter was because he was not as calm and happy as before. Having explained everything to him, the king offered his support and allowed him to go home to help in the reconstruction. After arriving in Jerusalem, in 445 BC, he carefully organised the construction, apportioned the tasks. He did not take advantage of the privileges that came with his high position, he rather worked on the construction site with his own hands too. He set an example for others and not just by words but through deeds, he showed the correct path to follow.

I put him on the card because he was able to change, to start a new journey, while he was planning and calculating everything well. He also became a real magician and that is the message of the Tarot: beginning a journey into the unknown.

The mythological curiosity of the card:

The Fool can be associated with the Greek god Dionysus, who in his childhood was attacked by the Titans, that is by his wicked uncles. They played with him and after winning his trust, they torn him to pieces and devoured him. However, the child was reborn, so he would be the god of fertility, wine and joy.

Crowley associated The Fool card with Horus himself, who was portrayed sitting on his mother's lap with a solar disc on his head decorated with feathers. All this does not fall far from the depiction of Jesus in Christianity, considering that the Egyptians celebrated Horus' birth on 25th of December, which later became the day of Christ's birth.

Supplementary cards in the Major Arcana: Reason and Intuition

'If God is for us, who can be against us… ' (The Nádasdy family motto)

Reason and Intuition
Tamás Nádasdy (1498-1562) and Orsolya Kanizsai (1521 – 1571)

The explanation for the special cards

These two cards are unusual in tarot. We can use them to determine whether, in the current situation of our life, we should listen to our intuition or rather rely on our rational self. I rarely use them on their own, I interpret these cards more as part of the spread. However, more 'routinous', experienced fortune-tellers could try to determine the sex of the expected child with these two cards. If the pregnant woman picks the intuition card, a girl child can be expected, and if she picks Reason, the child is a male.

What is the difference between Reason and Intuition?

You cannot influence intuition, it comes from within, it is a completely individual and part of your Consciousness. This word has several interpretations depending on worldview and faith. Basically, it is about instinctive intuition built on experience. Many people however, see inspiration, spiritual and mystical things behind it. According to psychology, intuition is generally a faster and clearer realisation of the patterns of more correlations or events, chains, cause—effect. All this within the subconscious, at a certain level of development only as flashes. Everything contributes to what constitutes life and the creatures, events, cycles, dynamics it contains, because they constitute a system and always occur in repetitive patterns. Their visualisation and full understanding helps intuition and its faster, almost 'prophetic' application. This can also be developed. If you reach an already higher intuitive level, then you clearly understand the driving force and the structure of all things (human relationships, behaviours, emotions, groups, etc.) around you. This pure transparency only arises in the presence of high degree wisdom, when you no longer want to exploit anything out of it. Because you are in perfect balance with existence, with your emotions, death and the changing cycles in your life. You are perfectly at peace with yourself. Then you come to the moment, when you are in full possession of the necessary knowledge and ability of manipulating others, but at this spiritual level of development you will not use your intuition for this, no matter how many opportunities there are.

Rationality means reasonableness, that is, in the judgment of things, in decision-making, the individual listens especially to his mind, to rational arguments and rarely gets influenced by his own emotions. He is able to repress his intuitions and instincts. He finds it difficult to accept unrealistic or hasty ideas, and is a devotee of logical approach. In general, he is interested in the scientific approach of things. He is familiar with numbers, with the world of data. He grasps the meaning of things well, methodical, he is mostly precise and accurate.

According to Socrates, in order for people to understand the world around them, first they need to understand themselves through rational thinking. In his view, there are two parts of the soul: the irrational part that consists of emotions and desires and the rational part, which is our true self. He also thought that although the irrational part of the soul falls outside the sphere of conscious knowledge, it sometimes communicates with us through images, dreams and other ways.

The development of Intuition

You must have heard that piece of advice many times: listen to your intuition. It has certainly already occurred to you, that you remembered a long lost friend and the other day you ran into her/him; or thanks to some internal motivation you did not go to work on the usual route and subsequently found out that it was a good decision, because you had avoided a huge traffic jam or possibly an accident. This is not a mere coincidence, this is intuition which is worth to be developed a little further. Because if you create a balance between intellect and emotion, understanding and intuition, you can get even closer to yourself and also become more balanced. Now close your eyes and ponder when was the last time you had any kind of intuition? Did you follow or ignore it? What was the result?

The development of intuition has countless methods. However, until you really reach the stage where you can bravely dare to rely on it, you can use the O-ring test (e.g. in situations when you are uncertain in taking a decision). Later, if you practice hard enough, you may find that after a while you have no need for testing. The O-ring test is an exercise that can be learned by anyone. This test is nothing more than a diagnostic procedure that is used regularly by a high proportion of alternative medicine experts in the Far East, in disease, anomaly detection, setting up a proper diet and the selection of appropriate therapy. The method 'reads' the vibrations of the human consciousness. Its operating principle is the following: the electromagnetic radiation of living organisms changes due to disease and toxic substances. As the brain is connected to the whole body through the neural pathways, it perfectly detects the changes taking place in the energy field.

To proceed with the test, touch the tip of your thumb and index finger to form letter O. Tighten the rest of your fingers into a fist. Ask a friend to do the same with both hands and clasp his fingers into your O shaping fingers. It will look like three chains linked in each other. Now try how much force is needed to open your fingers. Once you have discovered how much force is required to open your fingers, you could try out what happens when something comes into contact with your energy field, that is if you take something in your hands or touch something. If it strengthens you, it will be difficult to terminate the grip, but if it weakens you, your fingers will almost open despite your will. This quick test helps you find out about everything and everyone, whether or not they are what you need, whether they strengthen or weaken you. The next level is when you already feel the intuitive signals somewhat closer. Think of something very positive, what you really love. How do you feel then? What does it make you do? Then compare this with feeling that a negative experience or thought would trigger in you. Something is very important: before you start, you have to believe that you are able to recognise your intuitions.

If you begin to listen to your perception constantly and take it into account, as well as understand it, it may even help you in taking important decisions. The key is to learn to trust your inner voice. This inner voice exists in each of us, it might be called sixth sense, divine inspiration or intuition also. The general stereotype suggests that women's intuition is better than men's: however, it is only about relating to this skill. Men tend to rely on rational arguments in their decisions, while women's 'spiritual receptors' are more sensitive to subconscious messages and therefore attribute much more importance to their intuitions as well. When you develop your intuition, you let the subconscious talk to you without any inner fear. If you improve this ability, later you can use it excellently together with common sense you can use it excellently. But do not forget: not everything is a sign!

Rationalism

(Briefly summarised, just in case you are a little interested in the philosophical background also)

In the time of the ancient Greek philosopher Socrates, thinkers did not trust their senses, so ancient philosophers declared that thinking illuminates things completely differently from what we perceived. Then came Descartes, whom we recognise as the first rationalist philosopher. He thought that the criterion of truth was the pure and definite discretion of reason. In his view, only eternal truths – the truths of mathematics, science epistemology and metaphysical foundations – can be obtained by way of learning; one can get acquainted with the physical world only empirically. According to Descartes, though dreams seem as real as the physical experiences, they do not increase people's knowledge. Today many argue with this, since dreams are also used by several therapeutic methods.

However, according to Descartes' method, nothing can be classified as knowledge that we cannot recognise with the help of the mind. Later however, Leibniz, who was the last great rationalist, rejected the dualism of Descartes and denied the existence of a material world. In his view, an infinite number of simple, indivisible substance aka monads exist, which are the basic units of reality, in relation to both living and non-living things. These units of reality represent the universe, but they are not under the effect of causality or the laws of space. Leibniz introduced the principle of pre-arranged harmony to explain the obvious causal relations in the real world.

The opposites formulated by Leibniz later became sharper in the philosophy of Immanuel Kant. First he was a rationalist and then in his work he published that the senses and the intellect are independent from each other. Each of them is a separate factor in shaping knowledge, but only the two together form real knowledge. Intellect gives the form of knowledge, and senses provide the matter of knowledge, the combined presence of both are needed in the creation of knowledge. After Kant, rationalism is revived again in the philosophy of the idealistic Fichte, Schelling and Hegel.

Rationalism experienced its heyday in the 18th century, this is when it was identified with the educated intellectuals' world perception and at defined the sciences, although its theoretical foundations had already been questioned. Contrary to the traditional forms of life Rationalism encourages reasonableness. (e.g. the French Revolution, the reasonable forming of national and social order also carries the stamp of rationalism). Additionally, rationalism aims at eliminating miracles from religion and thereby transforms religion into pure reason and morality.

Tamás Nádasdy and Orsolya Kanizsai

We owe the most beautiful love letters of Hungarian literature to Tamás Nádasdy and his wife, Orsolya Kanizsai. As the couple was often far away from each other, they could not talk about the events of their lives, so the function of information exchange was held by correspondence. However, we must not forget that the literacy of aristocracy in the 16th century was significantly different between the two genders: aristocratic men could write well almost without exception, but learning to write was still a serious problem for women. Although illiteracy was not typical among aristocratic women anymore, in some social circles the person not be able to write their name even had to make excuses.

Tamás Nádasdy was a humanist nobleman. His wife, Orsolya Kanizsai could write, their correspondence is among the finest aristocratic correspondences of the 16-17th century. Among the letters of Orsolya Kanizsai, many were written in her own handwriting, however, writing still meant hard work for her, thus every letter of Orsika was greatly cherished by her husband. He knew that writing was still a strenuous physical work for aristocratic women who are less accustomed to using pen.

During this period, correspondence was held in high esteem, every letter had its rank. Couriers rode with barons' writings, messengers raced with the letters of minor lords and the joy and mourning of simper people were delivered by occasional postmen. Reading the letters is a bit difficult because we have only part of the correspondence: sometimes only the question, sometimes only the answer. Regardless from this, we get a pretty clear picture about the quality of the couple's love relationship. The letters speak about the arduous work in the household as well as about Nádasdy's troubles living close to the king. Lady Orsolya reports how successfully she defended the castles in the area against the raiding Ottoman Turkish troops, in the absence of Nádasdy, – she also earned the salutation 'My enamoured lieutenant' from her husband and the aristocrat also gave a worried sign if he could not find the fabric for Orsika in the required colour for her new skirt.

Since they exchanged letters not only with each other, we gain a quite deep insight into the couple's everyday life (separately or together), we get to know them in various human roles: husband and wife, as a mother and a father, people coping with the difficulties of life, as Maecenas and as friends.

Briefly about their lives

Tamás Nádasdy was born in 1498, his family had an ancient history, but never was particularly wealthy or influential. He studied in Austria, then Rome and Bologna in Italy. He was an excellent humanist. As the secretary of Louis II after the disaster of Mohács, he took a position at the side of the Habsburg lords and the Queen. King Ferdinand appointed him the Castellan of Buda. After the double king election in 1529, he was forced to join János Szapolyai's party, but characteristic to his gallantry, first he requested the exemption from his loyalty oath to Ferdinand. His request was fulfilled. Afterwards Szapolyai appointed him deputy governor. Nádasdy belonged to those Hungarian politicians who tried to find a way out of the tragic situation of Hungary by rising above the strife of the two kings.

In 1531, he became engaged to Orsolya Kanizsai, who was the only heir of the former powerful and wealthy Kanizsai family. At this point, Orsolya was only ten years old, so there was a significant age difference between them. At first glance, it seems a rather odd marriage: a not very rich political careerist marries a girl 21 years younger than he, who 'by chance' is the heiress of a huge fortune. However, Orsolya Kanizsai did not inherit anything, because according to the laws of the 16th century in Hungary, female successors would inherit only under the special favour of the monarch. Her father however failed to 'masculinise' his daughter, thus after her father's death, the solution for Orsolya was to preserve her social status by a marriage. Thus Orsolya Kanizsai 'deigned' to accept Nádasdy's offered hand, although initially she showed not much willingness to establish a common family home with her husband. However, Tamás Nádasdy was serious about the marriage and got engaged in a clever operation to win Orsolya's heart as well, beside her hand. Probably as a result of this, the nobleman started to build the magnificent court of Sárvár, set up the printing house and the translation of János Sylvester Bible.

(The scriptures were printed and then translated into Hungarian mainly for women who hardly knew their way around in handwritten prayer books.) The gentle siege brought bright success, Orsolya fell in love with Nádasdy.

Later, their forced separation enriched the contemporary Hungarian literary remains: a collection of beautiful letters has been left to posterity. Beside the well-educated, widely travelled, polyglot Tamás, Orsolya became really cultured. In her beautiful writings, she urged her often-absent husband to return home as soon as possible, writing about the household affairs in bright lines that are far beyond the traditional turns of the age. The couple's letters written to each other in archaic Hungarian reveal everything, there is almost no need for comments. Thomas always started his letters with this line: *'This letter is to be given to my beloved Orsika!'*

Szerelmes orsikam, en meg azon napon
hog kübalmonn el valam te
nap vilagal beczbe iutotam ve
de az nap kival v fölseghevet
szembe nem iuthatek, mert
ersek vramnal addig noitok az
varzorat, hog el vstuekodgel

If we pay attention closely, it is nicely outlined to us that Nádasdy's key to success lay in the fact that he could make very good use of his social network, the most important points of which were the members of his family, particularly his wife, Orsolya Kanizsai. The marriage of convenience which was concluded in a big age and rank difference gradually changed into strong love, which became full of gentle feelings and sincere care for each other.

However, their happiness was clouded with only one condition: the delay of child blessing. They knew that if they did not show a male heir to the world, their life's work (the estate, and the court of Sárvár) would have got back either to some collateral relative, or *horribile dictu* to the king. Unfortunately, Orsolya Kanizsai was very sick: she had pleuritis, flu, feverish conditions several times during her life. Her eyesight was quite bad, therefore she used glasses. She had haemorrhoids, digestive disorders, liver and biliary problems as well. The biggest problem though was the delay of a male heir, which could have been a source of depression for her. We do not know the exact reason of her infertility, but we suspect that there could have been some tumour in the womb or inflammation of the epithelium or remaining infections from previous pregnancies might be the obstacle. Their doctor, Gáspár Kőrös treated the woman with medicines for years and by cleaning the uterus through enema, until their efforts were rewarded and in the end Ferenc Nádasdy was born. The mother and child's first months were documented and so they are rare treasures of healthcare and childhood history.

This long-awaited little heir, Ferenc Nádasdy, later became the legendary 'Black Bey', whom we recognise as one of the greatest military leaders in border garrison battles. As a result to his incursions, battles and castle conquests, he also acquired a dreaded name among the Ottoman Turks, just like his father. Ferenc became outstanding not only through military deeds, while being one of the richest aristocrats in the country, he grew into the leading figure of feudal opposition, and from his vast wealth, he was generously supporting culture also. Thanks to his father's care, in his childhood the Baron acquired not only military training, but also turned towards science and art with great interest thanks to his scientist educators. (Ferenc Nádasdy was the husband of Elizabeth Báthory, about whom you can read more on the Tower card.)

Tamás Nádasdy's personality already divided his contemporaries also, but his talent and diverse literacy rivalling with those of scientists, were recognised even by his enemies. His growing career from the gentry family until becoming a palatine, would not have been possible without his personality, his particular spirituality, a family providing a stable background and without his most loyal family members. Orsolya Kanizsai's figure is extremely important because without her, the life of her husband could not be fulfilled at this extent. They formed such a tight unit, that none of them can be discussed without the other. Orsolya's spiritual strength is also praised by the fact that after her husband's death in 1562, she did not slump, but ran the huge estate, took care of the education of their son and did not refer to herself as an 'orphan woman' unlike many widows of soldiers who were fighting with the Ottoman Turks. She spent the last days of her life working, among other things, she established a hospital for the poor.

In conclusion, that is why I have chosen to put Orsolya on the Intuition and her husband on the Reason card.

The Interpretation of Swords

Just as the Cups are the luckiest cards, the Swords are generally the most unfortunate ones. If Swords dominate in a spread, unfortunately it is not particularly a good presage in the love tarot either, because generally Swords symbolise war, bloodshed and death. For this reason, I am emphasising the positive aspects and giving you advice on how to improve yourself. At the same time in Love Tarot, they also symbolise struggle, intellect, intellectual and spiritual control and learning and it is connected with health issues as well. Swords belong to the Air element.

Ace of Swords: The card of Struggle and Triumph

This card symbolises the success achieved through difficulties and struggles, being an ace, it is also a kind of protection card. It promises great power, triumph and strength, which strengthens the currently evolving love, relationships and renews married life. The card also suggests fertility, so you may even expect to have children in the near future. At the same time, according to Golden Dawn, it is the card of the great power that serves good or evil, for example, the New Testament calls Satan the Great Prince of Air. Therefore, the card can also mean death, the old ones regarded it as the traditional death card. The following cards always show whether the Ace of Swords indicates physical death or just the drastic end of something.

In reversed position, it bears similar meanings as well, but unfortunately you may face even more negative effects. Upside down the Ace of Swords may represent violence, abuse of authority, injustice and denied love. It may also indicate infertility and barrenness or difficult childbirth the outcome of which will be positive.

Two of Swords: Harmony, peace and consensus

This period is about creating external and internal order and maintaining its balance, about inner strength, liberation of creative forces and about radical renewing and improving of emotions. You are balanced, so now you have to live with the already acquired knowledge, the power over your destiny and with your creative forces. The card's meaning is dual: if you are over hell (if you are over a terrible period) and chose the divine quality, now your life now can be about wonderful growth and material increase. However, if you have not built on true values, if you have not built from your own strength and innate talent, you may be very deep right now.

In the latter case, you need to move away from all the things you think your happiness may depend on and you need to understand that as long as you rely on other people and/or external things hoping for success and stability, you cannot use your creative power and are forced to get by on lower levels. You have hit rock bottom, so move toward the options that are more positive for you.

In reversed position the card indicates betrayal, mischief, false friends, lies and unfaithfulness. In general, it can also mean a trip abroad.

Three of Swords: The card of tears

This card means the breaking of relationships, the end of love affairs and the disintegration of marital ties. It is time to strip down all expectations, to let go the wrongly ingrained patterns and free yourself from what holds you back from fulfilment, from creation and from living in love. Now, it is time to stand on your own legs. Although your emotions strongly toss you toward despair, now it is more effective to take a self-examination: look in the mirror and observe what you hold against your own prosperity, happiness. What negative things do you believe in? What conditions do you claim to yourself or to your fellows? You have to learn that happiness does not depend on anything or anyone. Happiness is not outside, in external people or things. Be honest with yourself: whose hands should you let go and whom-what do you need to become independent from?

In reversed position the card refers to disturbed mental balance, but generally it could suggest war as well. Your task is difficult: you have to put down your fears and everything else that brings you down and holds you back from Completeness.

Four of Swords: Rest and Re-charging your batteries

The hitherto difficult period is going to follow by tranquillity and peace, nice and slowly everything is going to turn out for the better in your life. Fears are disappearing, stress and tension are decreasing. This is the time to rest and recharge your batteries. The card can also mean that you are recovering from a more serious illness. This is also the card of withdrawal and solitude. The card is related to burials, graves and coffins, although it does not mean death.

In reversed position the Four of Swords indicates an active, yet prudent and circumspect period. It points out that, although now it is important to economise, do not become greedy. It is the card of Testament too.

Five of Swords: The Lord of Defeat

This term derives from Golden Dawn, because it suggests failure and the enemies' conquest and their triumph. It indicates the fear of poverty and lack of courage as well. The biggest opportunity of this period is to recognise in yourself that low acting quality, which pulls you down and everything that does not push you forward on the road. You need to work consciously on their transformation. Now you are able to recognise how you are useful to yourself and to others;

distinguish what represents the light in you and what does not. However, this is only the first step. You are realising what you do wrong and where, in what circumstances you do not 'function' well. But if this recognition is not followed by inner work in order for you to change, you expect results in vain. Only you can raise your life to another level! The card also warns that in your entourage there is a malevolent, almost despicable troublemaker, whose sole purpose is to destroy you and others.

In reversed position too, the Five of Swords shows failure, but may also indicate more trouble and loss, mourning and funeral. Additional to the negative things, however, now a deeper inner gate is opening, through which you can see your destined tasks, commitments and missions more clearly. It appears again and again by recurring life situations, until it compels you to self-evaluation, highlighting the real values. Right now, if you really pay attention inward, despite these difficult times you will be able to surpass yourself and strengthen your bearing capacity, self-discipline.

Six of Swords: Success attained through hard work

You are managing to overcome difficulties, your living conditions have improved a lot. You have managed to leave problems and fears behind, along with your unnecessarily destructive remorse. You finally understand the eternal law: *'Do not judge, or you too will be judged'*. You have accepted that anything you judge becomes your business from then on. Whether it is a religion, a point of view, an idea, a situation, a state, human behaviour. From the moment you judge anything, it enters your karma for you to experience that thing and dissolve judging. A happier and more conscious period is awaiting you. The card may represent an unnecessarily taken risk, an extended journey and also the arrival of some news.

In reversed position, the Six of Swords promises a love confession, a surprise or a long-awaited announcement.

Seven of Swords: New plans and desires

Emotions, senses and moods are the most decisive in the next period. It is time to strengthen your self-esteem, vim and confidence. Now, the externals, beauty or physical pleasures may get a greater role, but the essence of teaching is precisely the fact that the real beauty is given by the interior content. It is time to distinguish between the packaging and the content, to accept challenges on emotional level, to make sacrifices if needed. This card may indicate your uncertainty, due to which now you are to give everything up in the last minute. Do not! Rather devote more attention to your soul's word, because the inner voice clearly knows, feels where your place is, what attracts and inspires you, in what circumstances you feel good.

The evening hours are also good for meditating on how you could be more productive and/or achieve financial security by doing what you love. For the moment, do not make compromises, it is time to stand up for yourself! The card also refers to an upcoming inland travel and also warns about possible sport accidents.

In reversed position, the card indicates disputes, quarrels, which can be resolved with wisdom. Now you may receive good advice from unexpected places. Home, family and motherhood are now receiving a more important role, however, the card's meaning also implies that it is time to find home in your soul as well, to return home and discover your inner 'temple'.

Eight of Swords: Crisis and crisis situations

This card means something bad. It could refer to bad news, unexpected negative criticisms, disease, isolation, hospitalisation or imprisonment. However, no matter how negative this card is, do not despair! This period launches you on the road of internal changes preparing the future, while you are becoming more and more aware that everything has two sides, because these two sides constitute a whole. If you are still capable to accept that you have induced this situation and finally you decide to make changes, after a few days of deep meditation you will be able to distinguish the ephemeral and the immortal, or timeless values, ideas, things and on this basis you can make conscious decisions (here too the word 'decision' means that enlightened state of mind, when you clearly see the right path, what this time is suitable for or where it is worth going). Be careful because you might get lost in the details! Get over your concerns and pay attention to clear information, right now life does not tolerate circumlocution, honesty is more emphasised than usual. Pay attention to the small print in legal documents and contracts!

Picked out in reversed position the card indicates an unforeseen, unexpected event, but can also refer to accidents. Be careful, because danger is lurking at you. The task of the next period is developing safety on spiritual and emotional levels and the realisation of spiritual stability. You can already discern the light from the dark, the constructive qualities of your life from the destructive ones. This can be perceived in your relationship, on emotional level and in your profession.

Do not forget that in order to enter a higher quality you have to bring sacrifices. By complaining and pouting you will never get better results, but only through awareness, acceptance and by voluntarily undertaken sacrifices. Of course, this resignation or sacrifice is only for a while, because the results, for which you have been waiting for a long time, are born precisely from these.

Nine of Swords: The card of severe misfortune

This card is very frightening. It could symbolise great misfortune, complete loneliness, misery, suffering, abortion, failure, discouragement, disappointment and sometimes could even bring death in some capacity. Still do not get sad. Think of the fact that your soul is infinite. Unlimited past is behind you, unforeseeable future is ahead of you and you always live the present according to what you are focusing on. If now you give up on yourself, on your life and take on the role of a martyr, this period will last for a long time. The fact is that pain has caught your attention and you just cannot ignore it. Not thinking about anything is possible only on a very high level of consciousness (only yoga masters and great teachers can do it), on the other hand anyone can think of something else. You cannot influence how you feel merely through will. Although everybody is telling you to think positively, no matter how much you want it is just not working… it is like when I say to my son in meditation not to think about the little white dog, of course in front of his mental eyes nothing else appears but the white puppy. Therefore, do not blame yourself for this. The only thing that can be made dependable on your will is your attention. This is not easy either, but it can be learned.

Therefore, in times of great woes you must learn to control your attention. Do not allow yourself to think of what your self-pity, weakness and inner child want you to. Because your mind can be controlled and diverted by attention. The secret of controlling your thoughts is not what you are thinking of, but what are you paying attention to. Because focusing on pain makes sense only until it enriches you.

You have the right to look over it, to step out of it, despite the magnitude of the tragedy that has befallen on you. Because this tragedy was nothing more than an initiation. It has taught you to release, taught you the art of survival. By this initiation you have gone through real Hell. If the initiation was successful, you have learned to live again, to hope and to trust yourself.

In reversed position, the card may indicate fear, bad feeling, mistrust and solitude. It can refer to a religious person, a priest.

Ten of swords: The card of Death and separation

This card is the worst among the Swords, even more ill-omened than the Nine. Something is ending, closing in your life, to which you have clung so hard, which meant the World for you. Your hopes and plans are crushing down, you feel that your life is crumbling down to ruins. You are squirming abandoned, clinging to the memories of the past, you are sharing your sorrow with the entire world. Since this is the Love Tarot, therefore the emphasis is on the loss of love. However, in the end separation is not bad, not negative and definitely not a coincidence.

Earth is a teaching planet, into which you have been born in order to experience and live. This includes the fact that sometimes you have to experience the loss of your loved ones. It is terrible to experience what it is like when you have to separate from your loved one, child or from your family members. Unfortunately, this cannot be avoided – the quality of human being inherently brings this along. In old times these were very traumatic, difficult experiences. Wars, epidemics, diseases claimed a lot of lives, even children lives. Families were broken up and spouses were replaced – in those days, primarily because of death. Today, however, the same thing can be experienced differently. With the progress of science and other changes, we can more and more overcome diseases and mortality.

Today, severe diseases cause less concern and one does not have to worry (in most cases) about the fact that your loved one is 'taken away' just like that, and not see him for years or perhaps not see him ever again. However, even today we cannot avoid those crucial experiences that are associated with the existence.

What does fate do if the possibility of change through death is eliminated? It searches for another solution. In the present age it has cleverly solved this issue by divorce. I think you are already aware of the fact that there are soul families, souls that belong to one another inherently. However, these belonging souls are usually not born into the same 'blood family'. Biological families are very diverse, they contain mixed souls, just think about that in some families there can be great personality differences between the members! It can be often perceived that some members of the family have totally different spirituality, they vibrate differently, as if they were the odd one out from the family.

Since it is imperative that the belonging souls find each other, it is not unusual that the firstly (or sometimes secondly) formed families break up, during which one experiences the loss of loved ones and subsequently comes the possibility when a new soul family would reunite. This is totally different than experiencing a deeper, more serious trauma! Of course, there are serious separations, yet, in most cases simpler, more conscious decisions dominate. Do not forget, deep down every self-conscious man knows very well, for WHAT (purpose) HE WAS BORN into this world, what he is undertaking. He knows exactly what awaits him in the earthly existence and had been ready for it long ago, he has brought everything he would need in this existence.

If the Ten of Swords is followed by the Ace or King, it explicitly means jail.

In reversed position the card indicates temporary gains and successes.

King of Swords

The card points to an experienced, prestigious man, who may be a lawyer, a doctor or a government official. He is disciplined, cautious, distrustful and suspicious. He is very intelligent, full of rational ideas and plans. Unfortunately, however, the implementation of all these does not occur according to the expectations.

In reversed position the card shows us an evil, selfish, stubborn, cold and cunning person, who has strong destructive intentions. He is not worthy of your trust. Picked out in reversed position it is the card of sadism and cruelty as well. In case of a lawsuit it suggests that you are not proceeding with the legal action.

Queen of Swords

This card illustrates primarily a widow or a sad woman, but also suggests a confident, sharp-witted, charming, very intelligent woman, who is a true diplomat, since she is able to manipulate others very well. It symbolises a person who once lived in well-being and happiness, but since the wheel of fortune turned, today she has got to know poverty as well. At the same time the Queen of Swords represents female unhappiness, infertility, poverty and grief. It can refer to the future loss of the spouse, in this case you should always check the adjacent cards.

In reversed position it indicates a very wicked woman, in whom hatred and malevolence are boiling. She is an experienced liar, a dangerous opponent. In general, the card can mean narrow-mindedness, vindictiveness, and narrowness, prudery.

Prince of Swords

This is the card of the hero and/or the brave soldier. The Prince of Swords is a smart, talented, energetic and courageous man, who is able to guide and inspire others. In general, the card may refer to heroic deeds, war and enemies. Beware! It becomes very unfortunate if it is surrounded by other ill-omened cards.

In reversed position it indicates a reckless, impatient, foolish man seeking to rule, whose personality is undecided, naive and bumptious. He lacks perseverance, does not listen to other people's opinions and does not accept advice from anyone. In general, the card may indicate a scam and damage caused by a woman or for women, it means a successful struggle fought with a rival.

Princess of Swords

This card represents an exceptional person who is a great negotiator, communication manager or an inter-mediator. She is not afraid to divulge hidden facts, she is insightful and very vigilant. She is versatile and can adapt to any circumstance or situation. This card may also refer to a boyishly behaving girl.

Picked out in reversed position this is the card of spy. In general, it may represent a serious illness, weakness, unexpected surprises and news. It could also refer to a false friend and an unveiled cheating.

The Interpretation of Wands

Wands usually give answers to work, business and business-related matters, but of course these pieces of advice, warnings and signs can be applied for love and relationship. While the Cups are linked to the element of Water and to the female emotional qualities, Wands represent the life force element of Fire and the quality of a creative man.

Ace of Wands: The card of prolific energy, ingenuity and resourcefulness

The Ace of Wands refers mainly to the beginning of a new business or new activity, but it may indicate the birth of a child as well. Here too the adjacent cards define the meaning, while your intuition also gives very strong signals, if you pay attention to it. It also indicates that now a big improvement (getting richer) can be expected in terms of financial matters and the card also promises social success. It can also refer to artistic successes as well. What is more, it could indicate an inheritance, gain or the beginning of a love adventure. If the Ace of Cups, symbolising the woman and the Ace of Wands, representing the man are next to each other in the spread, this suggests that your relationship is complete and your life settled. If they are not, but they are close to each other, this represents an increase of vitality and attractiveness and promises the realisation of your set goals.

In reversed position it refers to failure, helplessness and infertility. If you have been a proud person so far, the failures you are experiencing in the next period will teach you modesty. If the card has appeared in reversed position, it warns that now you should not start new businesses, because you may face serious problems right at the beginning, now every plan you are making is doomed to fail. Wait a while and make changes.

Two of Wands: The card of richness and good luck

This card represents two things. Firstly, you can achieve everything, you are capable of anything. Your power and influence are going to increase, you may have a great impact on others. The card therefore promises real radiance and glow. Secondly, it can represent an older, more mature man, with a dominant personality, who has established a huge company, businesses and with amazing results he is able to carry out everything successfully.

In reversed position the card warns that you must learn to be happy about your successes, rather than taking them for granted. Otherwise you will never be satisfied, and through your perfectionism you may induce serious diseases within yourself. In reversed position the card even indicates sadness, unexpected surprises and the questioning of faith, even loss of it. The change of your mood generates continuous conflicts: One day you are living under the spell of joy and admiration, the next day, however, in the trap, prison of your own fears and barriers. Strive for balance!

Three of Wands: Achieved Hopes

This card indicates excellent business acumen and successful negotiations. It is often linked to trading on water (shipping), navigation and the sea, perhaps also refers to expeditions. It also suggests that your partnerships are good, your business relations are becoming prominent, your plans both in the public and private sector are being accomplished.

In reversed position it indicates betrayal, so rather think twice before you accept the offered help from anyone. Your exaggerated confidence may seem as arrogance, be careful, as because of this your bigger goals may fail. If you are able to diminish your stubbornness a little, you will get through difficulties easier and you will wave goodbye to your troubles for a long time.

Four of Wands: Peace, tranquillity and well-being

This card shows the deserved gain of a well-done job. It is time to rest and re-charge your batteries. Your love life is fulfilled and your family life is becoming harmonious. The card promises happiness, abundance, success and joy.

In reversed position it refers to the contrary, that is the loss of tranquillity. Now you are perceiving everything to be uncertain, therefore slow down a bit and meditate on the particular situation. The card also indicates an unfulfilled love, but you are about to get over it soon.

Five of Wands: Disputes and hardships

The Five of Wands draws your attention upon the difficulties of the struggle you are bearing to achieve success. At the moment nothing is coming easy, you have to work for everything with double effort. Your love life is unbalanced as well, the relationship is lacking understanding and acceptance during this period. This card urges you to have great patience. Do not rush. Do not plan. Do not look ahead. Do not act for the future yet.

In reversed position the card indicates legal proceedings, prosecution and various legal affairs. Now you need to become extra cautious, but do not get upset, because this period, no matter how incredible it sounds, later will turn to your advantage.

Six of Wands: The deserved success

Your perseverance and hard work are now bearing fruits. You are finding yourself. You are becoming complete, what is more with faith, hope and confidence. Your personal charm is also increasing, now the time of the Great Conquest has arrived.

In reversed position the card draws the attention to bad presentiment, fears or infidelity. Your rivals are strong, so take a deep breath and dissolve the conflicts you nurture towards them and also dissolve the fears taking place within you. Be careful about deadlines, now you are tending to miss them and this can have serious consequences. It is time to let your fears go, step out from your imagination into reality, from the future into now, from fantasising into the efficient and persistent world.

Seven of Wands: The card of challenges

The Seven of Wands promises challenges which, with perseverance and courage can be converted into excellent opportunities. Start implementing the things you have been planning for long and take action boldly. During this period, you are going to receive the right prospects for your energy, the strength for your thoughts and the possibility of implementing them physically. Remember: now you can count only on yourself, you have to solve everything by yourself. Now, invisible dangers may threaten your work and position, thus you may feel unmotivated, puzzled, and sleepy, in serious cases, hopeless or even depressed. Rise above these feelings, trust yourself even more, because now you are able to turn the unfavourable situations to your advantage.

In reversed position the Seven of Wands is the card of indecisiveness itself. The Healing-Helping effects that are reaching you are confusing you, although their sole job is to wipe off the injuries of your previous lives, childhood and the past two years. All this is important for you to be really able to live your life in a balanced way and to repair your relationships. And if you still have not found the right One, then now it is time to make place for Him/Her. The most important is not to procrastinate and to step out carefully from difficult and perplexing situations.

Eight of Wands: The card of speed

Everything is happening too fast: you are deciding too fast, you are progressing too quickly. This hurry-scurry, rush and haste are leading to hasty steps, which are bringing back defeatism and paranoia of the last months. Slow down, this period is very good for self-reflection and to observe your motivations and habits. If you are clever, now you can put down your old habits and new events can flow into your life energetically. The card also warns that your developing new romantic relationships are going to end quickly, while those living in a relationship can expect fierce quarrels, the purpose of which is to raise the relationship to a whole new level or to end it.

In reversed position the card indicates bad luck, disputes, conflicts, jealousy and remorse. However, in this period, you can sum up the path taken so far, your experiences and you can complete a fate circle, preparing yourself already for a new beginning. Therefore, instead of disputes, it is time for clarifying discussions.

Nine of Wands: The card of difficult changes and transformations

You are over-exhausting yourself, you are overloaded, and you are carrying a heavy burden on your shoulder. If you are able to put down the unnecessary tasks gradually, you will progress in small steps but effectively. The card refers to changes and transformations of the patterns that you have brought or created about human relations. Embrace your feelings, stand up for yourself and your problems are soon going to be resolved. At the same time the Nine of Wands means clarification of the past, putting down the burdens you have been carrying from the past. The next interval will be ruled by inspirations and thoughts woven about the future, before that however, in terms of emotions a quieter period can be expected. The card may indicate the end of an illness as well.

In reversed position it has an ominous meaning, it refers to the difficulties and losses of the next period. It can also suggest the appearance of a cheater, a traitor, and on lower levels it refers to intrigues, poor health, disasters and misfortune.

Ten of Wands: This is the card of vengeance

It indicates that there is too much pressure on you. At this stage of your life selfish, financial goals are coming to the fore, because you forgot how to meditate in the spiritual sense and get acquainted with the soul's hidden, less conspicuous functions. It does not hurt if you remind yourself again about the fact that spirituality has nothing to do with the 'divinations' and pink illusions widespread in public consciousness. Spirituality is a rock-solid self-knowledge. To all questions you will find the answer within yourself, as the picked-out cards reflect only you. You must deal with what the outside mirror points at. You have to look within yourself, because you have something to be repaired, of what you have received signs. There is a reason why this 'something' has just emerged out of you. Notice it and deal with it. Instead of selfishness, revenge and disappointments, choose self-knowledge! Through tough self-confrontation, clarify with yourself that you do not wish to squirm in the trap of selfishness and dependencies!

In reversed position also, the card indicates deceit, loss and disputes. In any case, it intends to draw your attention to the fact that you are too stuck in the material, it is time to quit this trap loaded with low-energy. Now you should think through what kind of common view, ideals and entrenched opinions to break out from in spiritual sense, with regard to what Fate wants you to see the functioning of things totally different. Meditate on the idea you have been clinging to so far, but life has disproved of its functioning, its correctness.

King of Wands

This card indicates a sincere, generous, honest and conscientious man, who stands out from the crowd by his erudition, maturity and wisdom. If the situation calls for it, he is capable of great passions, but romance is also close to his personality. His family life is in order, he is faithful to his wife, towards his children he is understanding, sympathetic, friendly and dedicated. He tends to behave fatherly with others as well. He is a real old-fashioned gentleman, who likes to work and has a great sense of humour. The card may also refer to a good marriage or inheritance as well.

In reversed position the card shows us a rigid, strict, moral man, who is intolerant, does not tolerate contradiction. He is proud and shrewd. More generally, the card can mean good advice as well.

Queen of Wands

The card indicates a charming, warm, loving woman, who is practical and surprisingly calm at the same time. Her whole being emanates that she is the Mistress of the House. Her charm, fineness, elegance and sincere interest sweep everyone off their feet. She is an excellent housewife, hospitable. In terms of financial matters however, she is selfish and greedy. The card in general indicates business success or even a good harvest as well.

In reversed position the card indicates a very virtuous woman, who is stubborn, arrogant and unpredictable at the same time. Although she is a good leader, she is prone to mood swings and outbreaks of temper. Because of the alleged grievances, she tends to turn against her friends without any explanation.

Generally, the card may refer to insecurity in yourself, unreasonable jealousy or envy and infidelity as well.

Prince of Wands

The card shows an unpredictable, quick-witted man. Although he is active and energetic, he lacks perseverance. He is generous and friendly, but sometimes can be frighteningly stubborn. If the card does not refer to a person, it can mean moving, change of residence, divorce, sudden separation and even escape as well.

In reversed position it points at a cruel, narrow-minded person. In general, it refers to conflicts, feud, quarrels, break ups and the disintegration of any personal relationship.

Princess of Wands

The card illustrates a very attractive, very appealing, bold and energetic woman, who is faithful both in love and friendship. She is a reliable emissary, messenger and a reliable ally. Be careful! If the card is followed by the Princess of Cups, then the Princess of Wands symbolises a dangerous rival!

If picked out in reversed position, the card indicates an indecisive, superficial and impressionable woman, who is impossible to be entrusted with secrets. Since being terribly gossipy, tell her only the news you want others to know as well. Anyhow, this person can cause serious problems. In general, it represents bad news, incapability of making decisions and malicious rumours.

The Interpretation of Cups

The Cups are the luckiest cards in the Minor Arcana. You are extremely lucky, if you pick mainly these cards. The Cups are connected primarily to the element of Water, female quality and through this to Love. Thus these cards answer best to questions related to emotional life. We can claim that the Cups really show us the characteristics of human relations, relationships and marriages.

Ace of Cups: Happiness and fulfilment

This card is very lucky. It symbolises happiness and fulfilment, at the same time it is the card of fertility, motherhood and abundance also. It implies a happy marriage or relationship. It may also indicate the arrival of a love letter as well. If you pick this card, it means that in this period, you feel that life is perfect, you are surrounded by love, beauty and pleasure. Whatever you desire, now you can accomplish it easily.

In reversed position it suggests changes, it draws your attention to the need for changes. You have to do something in order to survive this difficult, sustained period, because if you collapse and escape to self-pity, you will have to experience absolute depth. The card indicates also unrequited love and may refer to infidelity, infertility as well.

Two of Cups: The lord of love, the garden of love

The card received its name – Lord of Love or the Garden of Love – from ancient wise men, because this card represents the deepest tenderness, fulfilment and union found in love and in other emotions. During this period, you live your life in peaceful harmony, new relationships are formed and you are surrounded by true friends. Now even an old friendship can be renewed. Your every action is permeated with passion, joy and play. This card may also refer to engagement and/or marriage.

In reversed position it draws your attention to separation, divorce, failed dreams and false friendships. It also suggests, that the stormy relationship in which you live, does not lead anywhere in the long run. Now you should focus the most on your own needs and desires. Do not jest serious issues by fooling around, pull yourself together instead, even if you feel that you are already fallen apart inside. Now your clear judgment and strength is needed the most, otherwise the misunderstandings will lead irreversibly to fatal quarrels and the break-up of the relationship. Be careful, do not start to spend money and squander now.

Three of Cups: The card of realisation

Abundance and good fortune are accompanying you on your way, now all your wishes can come true, because the Three of Cups is indeed the card of realisation. The achievements are going to fall into your lap effortlessly, you do not have to do almost anything in order to achieve them. Right now in your life, sensuality, joy and dancing are receiving main priority. Buy new clothes, socialise boldly, go visit someone, maybe you may invite someone else over and do not skip any social events, because you may build up beneficial relationships.

The card may also suggest promotion, solution for problems, recovery, a new love relationship, marriage and birth as well.

In reversed position it suggests that you are exaggerating in everything, be a little more restrained. It marks the end of old work, represents the lack of well-deserved recognition, prestige loss and also draws your attention to delays. At the same time, it may indicate the beginning of a relationship, in which overwhelming passion takes a prominent position.

Four of Cups: The card of home

This card suggests stability, at the same time it also indicates that although everything is harmonious, you yourself are becoming 'surging'. Sometimes satisfaction lifts you, and sometimes dissatisfaction tosses you into the deep. Therefore, you are risking this peaceful, happy period by feeling bored and perpetually looking for fault in others. You should rest, because you are tired and if you are not careful, as a result of your scattered feelings, this period will be fed-up, the happy marriage and family life will either continue or end. If you feel unhappy in your current relationship, this is the best time to step out nicely.

In reversed position, it brings new relationships, new opportunities into your life. However, do not be so glad, these will not be good in the long run. Still they are good for making you see your old problems differently and thereby start advantageous changes.

Five of Cups: The card of disappointment

In the Minor Arcana none of the fives bears positive meaning, as the fifth card of the Major Arcana is not clearly a positive card either. The Five of Cups indicates disappointment both in love and friendship. It can refer to a broken engagement, fraud, betrayal, and even a marriage without love too. It may indicate a partial loss written in a testament, or a delayed inheritance. Characteristic feelings for this period: sadness, regret, self-pity and frustration.

In reversed position, it shows the return of an old friend, in terms of relationship it indicates reunion, unexpected return and starting again. You may find new allies, build new relationships. However, do not plan ahead for a lifetime now, because your plains may fail. You may feel free to plan three months later.

Six of Cups: Surprise, unexpected arrival or return

This card has an ambiguous meaning. On the one hand it may indicate dear, embellished memories of the past, the happy childhood and the nostalgic longing after these. On the other hand, it may also indicate that one of your wishes is becoming a reality. Now you feel brilliantly comfortable with yourself in every new situation, you may do the first steps on the path leading to the desired happy goal. At the same time, be careful, do not be overconfident, rather be thankful for every little thing. Do not despair if minor failures come to your way in this period, they just show you that a replanning is needed.

In reversed position it indicates the future itself, the card along with the adjacent cards indicate the options available in front of you. If you read well from the cards, you realise, what are the plans that can be implemented immediately and which ones are doomed to fail. Give up the latter ones and find new purposes in meditation.

Seven of Cups: Sin, guilt, prodigality, violence

This card bears one of the strongest meanings in the entire Minor Arcana. On the one hand it refers to violence and dissolute lifestyle, on the other hand, it draws the attention to the fact that you live in the world of illusions, you are imagining things and therefore you are capable to lie to the extremes, deceive others. You are making one mistake after the other. You are making plans, the implementation of which may seem good now, but in the future, they may have horrible and unpredictable consequences. 'Triumph' will be rather bitter than sweet.

In reversed position, it indicates smart decisions, good plans and wishes that can be accomplished. If it is followed by Three of Cups then success is guaranteed and soon you are going to reach your goal. It also refers to good choices, strong will and good recognition of situations.

Eight of Cups: Loss of interest, laziness

You are dissatisfied with the things you have achieved so far, therefore you are not concentrating enough on your desires and are not paying attention to implement your plans. You feel that there is no point to continue, so you want to give everything up. Do not! The situation is not as hopeless as you perceive it to be. If you start over after a short relaxation, you can do amazing discoveries:

what you have considered valuable so far, it is no longer so valuable. Actually, what you have so far considered worthless, suddenly becomes interesting. This way you can re-plan your life.

In reversed position, it indicates that you should carry on, do not give up, even if your faith has shaken a little. Success is very near, soon you are going to be celebrating. The card promises happiness, joy and merriment.

Nine of Cups: Good fortune, material happiness, total success, certain future

This is the card of outstanding successes and triumph. Your wishes are coming true, you can continue to plan your future safely. Now you can wish for anything: your love life is full of delight, your financial situation is brilliant and you are enjoying fantastic health. This card is the luckiest for soldiers.

In reversed position it suggests material losses, failures and lack of success. Choose your words, because now in the wrong places spoken words can cause even more damage than ever before. The card also indicates disputes and serious fights.

Ten of Cups: Constant success, good financial situation, spiritual wealth and achieved goals

This is a very good card. It indicates that in all areas of your life, you may consider yourself lucky. You have settled down together with your loved one, your family is beautiful, your home is harmonious. You have finally done it. Your reputation is outstanding, others talk about you with great respect and you are surrounded by true friends. However, this was not always so. You had to do a great deal in order to achieve all this, but now you see that it was definitely worth it. Happiness and joy, pleasure and satisfaction surround you. This card may symbolise home and the homeland.

In reversed position, this card refers to opposites, violence, ugly disputes and separations. Family quarrels are inevitable, but be careful what you say and when, because now can lose everything: love, happiness, family and also about a few friendships may turn out that they do not stand the test of this period.

King of Cups

This card represents a generous, intelligent, mighty, responsible and aspiring man. He may well be a lawyer, a businessman, a priest or a scientist. He is prudent and reliable. He enjoys great respect from others. Nevertheless, he can be a good or bad person, because if the situation calls for it, he is capable of anything. He is passionate. He always walks in his own way. (This card depicts my husband's face.)

In reversed position, the card indicates an evil and untrustworthy man, who can double-cross everyone. He is immoral and sly. The King of Cups may refer also to losses, scandals and injustice as well.

Queen of Cups

This card represents a warm-hearted, kind woman, who is a good wife and mother. She loves and is being loved in return. She adores literature and arts, also she loves to read. She has a huge imagination, she is a big dreamer. She loves to flirt, however she is faithful and prescient.

In reversed position the card indicates a gossipy, untrustworthy woman, who does not stand up for anybody ever, she changes her opinion, as it fits her best. She is prone to depravity and immorality. She is not always able to endure the hardships of life with her head held high, therefore she may become a debauchee quite early. Her slyness and malice knows no boundaries.

Prince of Cups

The card indicates a sensitive, romantic and lovable man, who, however, can make very serious, unexpected decisions, though according to some people he is superficial and sluggish. However, this is only the illusory appearance, which he is very quickly able to turn into his advantage. The card also means the arrival of messages, tasks or invitations. Or it reinforces the event indicated by the following card.

In reversed position the card indicates a born adventurer. He is sensual and lazy, a masterful liar. He may be a drug addict or an alcoholic, possibly even a schizophrenic. The card also suggests a swindler, scam, fraud, cunning, deception and deceit.

Princess of Cups

The card represents a pretty, hardworking and ambitious woman, whose beauty and sensitivity are rivalled only by her elegance. She loves to dream, to desire and to daydream. She is intelligent and a great thinker. She is someone who can be counted on, because she is honest and faithful, for the matters she considers to be good she is able to fight to the bitter end. She comforts those who have suffered disappointment in love and provides support for the weak. The card also suggests weird thoughts, meditation and news. (This card depicts my daughter's face.)

In reversed position, the card represents a selfish person, who, by blandishment, is able to enchant and fool everyone. Her main weapon is seduction, thanks to her duplicity she is capable of anything. She is a good spy and informer. The card also represents temptation, seduction and deceit or cheating.

The Interpretation of Coins

The Coins are linked primarily to the element Earth, thus the cards mainly refer to money, status, livelihood, worldly influence and material safety. At the same time, of course, we may receive answers regarding our love life as well.

Ace of Coins: a lucky card. We have good prospects regarding the financial area, money is just flowing toward us. It promises a secure position and a stable situation. All your plans are coming true, now you are carrying out everything you have planned. Your emotional life is wonderful, almost perfect. With your loved one, you can experience great pleasures, your relationship has matured, it may even get legally formalised (marriage). The card refers also to the harmony of material and spiritual development. You live the way you want. You are surrounded by people, whom you have chosen. You are surrounded by happiness, wealth and comfort. The card may also indicate valuable works of art.

In reversed position, this card also symbolises welfare, however, it does not bring happiness. People do not love you for yourself, but for your position and money. You are using your wealth for the wrong purposes, you are choosing your relationships and counsellors badly. You are stingy, greedy and voracious. You should re-evaluate your life, so you would get back in line with yourself.

Two of Coins: This card refers to the alternation of good luck and misfortune. Ups and downs follow one another in our lives, profit and loss are both present in this period. Now, it is more difficult to accomplish your plans, but this does not mean that it is impossible. You have to become more consistent and it is time to set smaller objectives in order to build up the 'big dream'. You are experiencing the difficulties on a deeper level, thus it is important that instead of self-pity you rather raise your head high and start to implement your plans. The card may indicate smaller, eventful journeys, business trips or social events. There are a lot of lies in your relationships, you may receive a lot of rejections now if you do not clarify your feelings. Your love affairs are entangled, if you do not straighten things out, it could cause a very painful break-up.

Picked out in a reversed position, the card indicates writing talent. At the same time, it may also refer to drunkenness, simulation, now you should discard false pleasures. An unexpected message or letter may arrive.

Three of Coins: This is a very favourable card, it supports the implementation of any plan or idea. It indicates profit, the construction of something, as well as a promotion at the workplace. Now you may become more and more popular, your reputation may grow. Your family life is in order and balanced. Many people are turning to you for advice, because they consider you to be the holder of masterly knowledge and because they trust you. This card also helps your love life, your emotional life is now really fulfilled. Your relationship is harmonious and sincere. Your friends also are very attached to you, they would like to spend more and more time in your company.

Picked out in a reversed position, it symbolises mediocrity, average performance, which can be changed if you are able to reinforce your confidence and concentrate on your plans. Your financial problems can make you superficial, your trivial thoughts can drive you away more and more from your friends and family.

Four of Coins: the card indicates great financial success, strong power, status and prestige. In all areas, huge success can be expected, so now is the time to place your businesses on solid foundation. Your relationship is solid, but be aware that you do not become a miser. Lavish every good thing on your family, learn to give from your heart again. Although now your financial prospects are good in all areas, do not risk much in this period, because even if you may expect profit from gambling, do not give your future solely into the hands of Fortuna. Stick to what you have. For an independent person, this card brings good news from a desired person.

In a reversed position, it symbolises uncertainty, quarrels, contradictions and delays. Obstacles are making your life difficult, people consider you a miser, a cheapskate, even your family may turn away from you.

Five of Coins: this card indicates your fears. Your financial situation is not turning out well, your revenue is going to be less than expected, so you are slowly becoming poor. It is a difficult period, because both your relationship and your job are in jeopardy, your situation has become uncertain in all areas. You have become distant from your darling, you are in the middle of a divorce risk. Now it is highly important to pay attention to your thoughts and actions! Live more sparingly! This card refers to a very difficult period, but do not despair, it is only temporary, as long as you can see your situation clearly and act from a new perspective. It is important that, instead of worrying and having a nervous breakdown, now search for new opportunities more assiduously.

In a reversed position, it means that although you suffered serious financial losses, you will be able to reverse the situation. Be much more prudent, reconsider every possible change thoroughly. Your marriage and love life are being fixed, together you are able to solve the problem by yourselves and raise the relationship to another level.

Six of Coins: This is the card of abundance and generosity. Now you can count on helpful, well-intended people, protectors, rewards and gifts. Thanks to your philanthropic character, you yourself are doing charity, and also you are nice to others. This stage of your life is being permeated by charity and gratitude. Your relationship, your love life is balanced and happy.

Picked out in a reversed position, it suggests envy, greed and avarice. You are not yourself and others are noticing this. The card indicates unpaid loans, which can be very difficult to settle. Your bad habits do not lead to any good, start to change your lifestyle, pull your life together!

Seven of Coins: Whether we pick out this card in normal or reversed position, in any way it indicates something bad. The expected successes or profits fall short. Losses and disappointments can be expected. The work invested is not bringing fruit. You have to separate from someone you love.

In a reversed position, it indicates that this period is burdened with fears and it is very difficult. You are impatient and this might make you do stupid things.

Be careful, pay attention to your words and actions. If now someone is asking for a loan from you, do give, but only if you accept that he or she will be able to give it back very difficultly, maybe you will not get your money back at all.

Eight of Coins: This is the card of learning and finding love. Now you have to figure out how you should behave in society, in order to achieve more professional success. Your extraordinary professional knowledge, honesty, modesty and efforts are helping you in this. At the same time be careful, in reversed position the card indicates that you are paying attention to minor things instead of the important tasks. You are lacking real ambition, enthusiasm and momentum. You are beginning to give up your real dreams. Your wangling is leading you to a small amount of money, but this does not solve your situation.

In reversed position, it may also indicate dishonesty or illegal business. Pay more attention to contracts, agreements, because you are surrounded by unreliable and false people. This card could also mean intrigue and money loan or usury.

Nine of Coins: This is the card of fulfilment. Your finances are turning for the best, your financial situation is improving. You may count on an inheritance, gain or reward. Now in anything you are starting doing, in anything you are getting into, you can count on your discernment and intuition. With their help you can see what you should focus your energy on momentarily in advance. This stage of life is promising convenience, material welfare and safety.

In reversed position, it indicates two-facedness, slyness and envy. Your safety is in danger, at the moment you may lose something very precious: an asset or an old friendship.

Ten of Coins: This is the card of a great fortune, it indicates enormous riches in all areas. Your financial situation is brilliant, the family fortune is secured and you may even expect an inheritance. Your family life is intimate and safe. The card also indicates the place of residence or it may also refer to kinship. Here too, as in all the cards, pay attention to your intuition and the adjacent cards.

In reversed position, it warns that you might get mugged, in gambling you can lose high sums or you may even have to pay higher taxes. It may also indicate a disputed/lost inheritance.

King of Coins

This card illustrates a simple, reliable and practical man. He is an experienced and successful leader. He is working in a serious position, business life was invented for him (or possibly he is a teacher). He is intelligent and very successful. He is a loyal friend, but does not show mercy to his enemies. He always finds a way to get out of any situation as a winner. He is a great husband, devoted and reliable. If the spread indicates such a person (even a friend, mentor, or a man in love), you can be sure that this person has a positive effect on almost every aspect of your life.

In reversed position, it means an aggressive and corrupt man, who does not have the backbone, because he does not have any principles. It can refer to bribery, greed and use of any means to achieve the desired goal. It can symbolise infidelity, prodigality and danger, also may indicate an old, evil man around you as well. Always observe the adjacent cards and listen to your intuition. This card can represent not only a person, in the spread it can appoint the bank as well.

Queen of Coins

The card represents a kind, sensitive, generous, noble, captivating and charming woman, who provides a comfortable home for her family. Although sometimes she is unpredictable and capricious, you can always count on her, because she is generous, honest and extremely intelligent. The card promises security, wealth, welfare, abundance and luxury and indicates a happy marriage.

In reversed position it means a stupid and unreliable woman, beside her fear and uncertainty awaits everyone. The card may also indicate a serious illness, if it stands next to a negative major Arcana card. As an alternative, it refers to your neglected duties and warns of an evil person around you.

Prince of Coins

The card symbolises a mature, reliable, responsible person. His patience and perseverance are unmatched in the world, therefore he is able to carry out every task. He is a very organised and hardworking man, who finds solution for every conflicting situation. The card indicates that you are getting in touch with an important person, who will facilitate your professional life.

In reversed position, the card refers to a long-standing difficult situation, in which you have been helpless for a long time. You are lacking the goals and your perseverance is not sufficient either to break the deadlock. Laziness does not lead to results, pull yourself together, formulate your goals and do something in order to achieve them!

Princess of Coins

The card presents a serious, hard-working person, maybe she is dealing with administration or economy. She is responsible, conscientious and extremely prepared. She respects Knowledge, loves to learn. She always wants to do good, but does not always succeed. She thinks information is power, she is always well-informed, therefore she can even manage to be a messenger as well. Unfortunately, she does not always transmit positive news only, with great fervour.

In reversed position, it means a prodigal child and a rebellious person living a lavish lifestyle. The card indicates either a young man or woman, who lives in a dream world, being prisoner of his/her own illusions. On the other hand, it may also indicate that bad news is coming to your way and there are going to be losses, because you are incapable of clearly formulating your ideas. Now you cannot even realise your goals, because you are thinking illogically.